THE NEW
PERIOD SHIP
HANDBOOK

THE NEW
PERIOD SHIP
HANDBOOK

Keith Julier

SPECIAL INTEREST MODEL BOOKS

Special Interest Model Books Ltd.
P.O. Box 327
Poole
Dorset
BH15 2RG
England

First published by S.I.Model Books Ltd. 2004

ISBN 1-85486-233-2

Contents

List of Colour Plates

On pages 113 - 116

Introduction

Building model boats is all about enjoyment and the construction of a period ship model is, in particular, a source of great pleasure and relaxation. It affords the model maker the opportunity to be creative, to demonstrate his craftsmanship and, perhaps to acquire new skills.

Many would-be modellers are hesitant, I am sure, because that they feel that they either do not have the ability or possess an adequate workshop. For these people the kit is often the solution to the problem and it is to them that this book is largely addressed. Over the last few years, kit design has progressed in leaps and bounds with the advent of computerised manufacturing techniques that permit many parts to be pre-cut either by laser or router to high degrees of accuracy. The use of etched brass parts also helps to bring the possibility of producing top class models to those with less experience and smaller tool kits.

One of my aims has been to encourage the hesitant and to enthuse the beginner to take on more ambitious projects. There is always a new challenge to be met and always something new to learn; in fact, you can spend a lifetime in the hobby and still come up against a new experience or a new technique to master.

The book is not intended to be a contribution to the age-old, kit-built versus scratch-built discussion, but an attempt to show that a high-class model *can* be built from a kit. My efforts have come together by looking at a series of kits for models of varying degrees of difficulty and type. They have been selected to provide the widest possible range of features the model-maker may come across; they are not in order of degree of difficulty. This book will be of use to any person building a model of a period ship, whether from a kit or from scratch.

Many of the techniques described are fairly standard procedures used by many model-makers, while others are perhaps more unique to my own way of working. Nothing is mandatory, and the best way is usually the way that suits *you*. It is better defined as the way that gives you the best results in the easiest possible manner. Always be prepared to listen to, and try suggestions, new ideas and methods but, at the same time, develop your own skills and ingenuity. I trust that you, the reader, will find things of interest, encouragement and pleasure in this book, in which case I will be well satisfied.

A project of this nature does not come to fruition without the help and support of a number of people and it would be remiss of me not to acknowledge their services.

Nothing could have been made or written without the kits from Amati, Artesania Latina, Billing, JoTiKa and Panart. I am particularly indebted to Andrew Horne and his staff at Euro Models of Twickenham, John Wright and his staff at JoTiKa and to Christopher Watton of Victory Models, whose model making skills set a standard to be envied by us all.

The help of John Cundell at Model Boats magazine continues to be invaluable, as does the preparatory work contributed by Bill Burkinshaw at Special Interest Model Books Ltd.

My wife, Edna, continues to be a source of encouragement to my entire model making activities. No longer able to contribute in a practical sense, her critical eye provides a quality control second to none.

Keith Julier

CHAPTER 1

The Tool Box

Obviously, the more you have in the way of tools and equipment, the easier everything becomes, but it certainly is not the case that the potential builder has to acquire an all singing and dancing workshop before he can begin.

Thus initially, it is really a matter of deciding *needs* rather than *wants* and, for kit building, the needs are relatively small. However, please be warned that this is an extremely personal choice you have to make and one that depends entirely on your own skills, innovative talent and, of course, the depth of your pocket. Your own feelings on this subject will undoubtedly change as you progress further down the path of model making. What was at the beginning a luxury item, rapidly becomes a tool you wonder how you coped without. I have tried to make my suggested list of tools as realistic as possible and can only call on my own experience and memories as to how I started.

Basic tools

A modelling knife, preferably with a selection of differently shaped blades, a razor saw, fine-nosed pliers and side cutters together with a light hammer are, in my opinion, absolute essentials. A range of twist drills up to about 2mm diameter and a pin chuck with which to turn them will cover most drilling needs. A small David plane will always be a most useful tool to have.

Clothes pegs make very useful holding devices, particularly the wooden ones, which lend themselves to a bit of customising at the business end. However, I have to say that a few electricians' "crocodile" clips are vastly superior in terms of size/grip ratio.

As I recall, the next major addition to my kit was a 12-volt electric drill and transformer. I was fortunate enough to receive some good advice at that time and, as a result, spent perhaps a little more than I had originally intended and bought a high output transformer with several outlets. This was a purchase really appreciated later on when I added further electric tools to my collection.

For many years, I worked without a cutting mat, but now would not be without one. These self-healing pads come in several sizes although I find the A4 completely adequate.

There aren't many kits that couldn't be built with the basic kit of tools so far listed until you get towards some of the "biggies" and, even then, it will often be more a matter of ease and convenience rather than absolute necessity to have something more sophisticated. Not that I am against sophistication, and I certainly do not subscribe to the argument that a model has an extra quality for having been built on the dining room table with only the use of a razor blade and a piece of sandpaper. On the subject of simplicity, it is a fact that today, some kit manufacturers strive to produce as many pre-cut parts as possible in an attempt to de-skill the construction process.

Extending the tool box

So, just what are we talking about when we consider more sophisticated tools? I suppose the first things that come to mind are further pieces of 12-volt equipment, a sander, flexible drive, pedestal drill, the list goes on and on. Now you begin to appreciate the better quality transformer.

Over the years I have tried all sorts of dodges for bending planks and there are some very costly pieces of equipment around. I have to say the tools that get most use during my planking sessions are the Amati plank nipper and a tall vase to hold some hot water.

Gadgets for clamping long strips for tapering and universally adjustable cradles for holding the model under construction are available. Most of the specialist shops will provide a list of these items and you can add to your tools in the way that best suits *your* way of working. Of course there are many more tools that I haven't mentioned - the list is endless and I have no doubt that my critics will express their absolute amazement that I didn't list a "balzover pad" with a built-in "gotcha pin"! Never mind.

Finally, be wary of the "fast answer" gadgets, they invariably aren't. The old adage applies; if it looks too good to be true, it usually is!

Having dealt with the "capital" equipment, now let

us have a look at what is required in the way of consumables. These fall mainly into two categories, fixing and finishing. We are therefore talking about adhesives followed by abrasive papers, paints and varnishes.

Adhesives

Adhesive technology has advanced so much over the years that it is just about possible to stick anything to everything. However, for optimum convenience when building model boats, I manage to find a use for four different types and, while they may not be needed for all kits, I always like to make sure that I have an adequate supply on hand before starting a project.

White PVA is an absolute must - it has a reasonably fast grab capacity permitting work to continue after about 20 to 30 minutes, always remembering though that total cure can take up to 24 hours. It does not have an unpleasant smell and dries transparent. However, it is important to remove any excess particularly if the wood is to be later stained and/or varnished.

There is a whole range of contact adhesives from which to select, my own favourite being Dunlop's Thixofix. I choose this mainly because of its viscosity, being what is best described as a gel that doesn't string, making for easier application and cleaner working.

An equally wide choice is available in the field of cyanoacrylate, or super-glues; those liquid and gel adhesives that exhibit a virtually instant stick capacity. A little goes a long way and thus, with practice in their application, they don't turn out to be as expensive as you might at first think. They come in very handy when constructing small deck fittings and other tiny assemblies; just make sure that you assemble the parts correctly first time! They should not be used for sealing knots on rigging thread unless you are very familiar with the quality of thread in use. The adhesive will soak through some of the thinner threads with the result that the thread can become brittle and break. The golden rule when rigging is, if in doubt, don't use cyanoacrylate, use dilute PVA instead.

Finally, for those occasions when metal has to be stuck to wood or other pieces of metal, two-part epoxy adhesive is a lifesaver. However, its success is very much dependent on adequate joint preparation, cleanliness and correct mixing of the two constituents.

Adhesives are not the only means of fixing that are used. Brass or steel pins are frequently used to supplement a glued joint. For the most part, these are provided in the kit so that you do not have to make a choice of length or material. If you do have to buy, you will find that 10mm and 14mm long brass pins will suit most purposes. There are two types of head styles normally available, lost head and round head. The former style is used where the head is hidden and the round head where the pin is decorative or the fixing temporary and the pin has to be removed. Quality is important; take particular care that the points are sharp not spade ended and that the heads are well-formed. Although you are probably going to extract them

and throw them out after use, trying to push just a few spade ended pins into pre-drilled holes soon plays havoc with your fingers. Pulling them out is also much easier if the heads are well formed and don't pull off.

Abrasive Papers

We are all familiar with what we commonly call sandpaper. In fact, this is a general name for abrasive papers that may be coated with any of a wide selection of materials. Just take a look along the shelves of your local DIY store and you will see that there are several grades of glass-paper, garnet-paper and sheets coated with silicon carbide, the latter being better known as "wet-and-dry".

For general use, glass-paper is quite adequate although you should find that garnet-paper provides a much cleaner cut and retains its "bite" for a longer period of time.

Provided that the model can withstand a degree of dampness, wet-and-dry papers can be used particularly on filled surfaces, but do remember that damp wood will not take a final finish with any type or grade of abrasive paper.

Don't go mad with the coarse grades - they may get rid of a lot of material at a fairly fast rate, but the scratches they leave can be very difficult to remove. Work down through the grades until the required finish is attained. Worn coarse paper does *not* equate to a finer grade.

A cork sanding block is most beneficial to getting a nice even finish on a planked hull and the shaped Draper Sanding Sponges are ideal for finishing the compound curves of a hull. Large areas may sometimes be better dealt with by use of a cabinet scraper or even a single edged razor blade. It is always worth spending a little time to make the right selection.

If your selected model involves a general paint job, it could be that the use of fine grade wire wool will be beneficial, or even some of the very fine abrasive finishing papers.

Finishes

Stains and varnishes form the basis for most finishing operations, there being only a minimal requirement for large painted areas. Colron stains are ideal for colour whilst Cuprinol acrylic matt varnish serves as both finish and rigging sealer with the bonus that brushes can be cleaned with water.

If paint is called for, then the vast range of Humbrol paints will usually fit the bill. For larger areas like the white stuff or brown coating (or anti-fouling) on the undersides of some vessels, consider small 50ml tester pots that many of the major paint manufacturers produce.

I would like to stress that where reference to specific products and trade names are made, this is done because I have particular experience of them.

There are undoubtedly other equally good alternatives and, like many things in model boat building, it comes down to personal choice; what suits you and what helps produce the best result.

Many kits now contain etched brass parts. Most modellers recognise the fact that such parts need cleaning before the application of paint and wash the pieces with dilute washing-up liquid. This may be acceptable if you are going to paint directly with the required colour, but if you wish to guard against paint flaking or being chipped, this is not really adequate. For best results the parts should be cleaned with a solvent such as cellulose thinners, then coated with an etching primer before painting. For this process, washing-up liquid should not be used as it may chemically react with the primer. The other essential in this process is the wearing of a suitable mask or respirator.

I like shellac based sanding sealer. While it obviously serves well for its intended use, it can also be used as a finish for the model left in natural wood. When rubbed down with really fine abrasive paper, it produces a truly flat and hard surface. This should not be confused with the cellulose based sanding sealer which, although ideal as a sealer, does not have the same finishing qualities as the shellac based product.

Tool Condition

Tools need to be maintained in tip-top condition if they, and you, are going to function safely and produce the best results. Blunt tools are not only useless for working with, they are downright dangerous. An oilstone to keep cutting edges keen at all times is, therefore, a sound investment.

If you use scalpels with replaceable blades do change them as soon as the edge goes off. The temptation to do one last cut has resulted in many an accident.

Safety

Some of the operations involved in the building of model boats are potentially hazardous and a couple of common sense precautions are advisable. The rubbing down of hull surfaces produces a lot of dust, so do wear a mask to avoid breathing it in. A suitable mask should also be worn when involved in long sessions using solvents or cyanoacrylate. Exposure to the latter can cause quite serious breathing difficulties or make you feel quite unwell. Also, with solvent vapour risks in mind, I have always kept a small domestic fire extinguisher in my workroom, just in case.

If you are fortunate enough to have your workroom inside the house, then personal experience tells me to recommend that you keep a vacuum cleaner handy *and use it fairly frequently*, not only for personal comfort but out of consideration for other members of the household.

I have not mentioned lighting in the workplace and I suppose that, indirectly, it could be classed as a safety item. Good lighting can certainly reduce any strain on the eyes and, of course, contribute to better and more accurate work. Two sources of fluorescent light as a minimum are required for a satisfactory degree of shadow-less illumination. Of course, if you can run to an adjustable lamp for optimum working, so much the better. This should, I hasten to add, be an additional not an alternative source.

The matter of First Aid should also be considered. I guess that most of us have cut fingers at some time or another and have had to reach for the plasters, a supply of which I always keep in my workroom together with a bottle of TCP. However, I would make what many would describe as a typical model maker's comment. If you do cut yourself, try not to get blood on your treasured woodwork, it's the devil's own job to get rid of!

CHAPTER 2

Choosing The Kit

Kits come in various degrees of difficulty and some are definitely not for the beginner. I should also add that the cheapest kits are not always the easiest to construct. Many kits featured in this book provide the means for producing a fine museum standard model, albeit that a little bit of extra work and research may be necessary to attain such a standard. Some of the kits have been reviewed by *Model Boats* magazine. These articles provide an excellent insight into their contents, the standard of craftsmanship required, the tools needed and whether you are getting reasonable value for your money. Further information is also available on the Internet, many distributors and modelling retailers having their own web-sites. If your choice of subject is a well-known vessel, then your local library may well have some useful information about the actual ship and its history or, there again, a browse on the Internet may prove useful.

It may seem unimportant at this stage, but it really does help to establish in your own mind your aims in building the model. Are you going to build a representative model that is more for decorative purposes in your office or den or one that also achieves historical accuracy? Do you want to rig your model with, or without, sails? It is always wise to have a target, but not be over ambitious. A finished job that fulfils your aims gives wonderful self-satisfaction - next time you can always aim a little higher. Besides which, the answers to all of these questions are all things that can influence the choice of kit.

Consider too, where you are going to build the model. It has to be said that they are not normally dining room table projects and, ideally, you need a place where partially completed work can be left undisturbed until your next modelling session. When considering the space required, remember that it is not only the size of the finished model that has to be catered for, you also need space to work on sub-assemblies that have to be completed away from the main structure. There are no extra prizes for the model made entirely on the dining room table using only a razor blade and a piece of sandpaper. Such attainments are usually obvious. A major

consideration is manoeuvrability when rigging. You have to constantly change from working on the port side to the starboard side and, if you don't have an "island" bench, the model either has to be picked up and turned, or you have to have enough room to swing it on some sort of turntable device. Size will also matter when considering where the model is to be displayed.

Scale undoubtedly has an effect on the amount of detail built into a model. This is a little more complex than you might at first think. In general terms, the larger the scale, the greater the detail which, in turn often demands a greater degree of craftsmanship. Too small a scale and you may finish up with a rather sparse looking ship and some clever person pointing out that you haven't got a ships' binnacle. On the other hand, one should not equate scale to difficulty in construction. In many instances the larger model is easier to make, there is just a lot more of it, requiring greater attention to detail. The bigger model provides more space for getting your hands and fingers around the rigging, particularly if you have chosen to rig sails.

The kit usually contains all the required materials and drawings, the research has already been done and, due to the pre-cut and pre-shaped parts normally featured in today's product, the model makers' tool kit needs only to be fairly basic. In spite of this preparatory work, do not run away with the idea that the construction is merely an assembly job - it isn't. In fact, the innovative skills sometimes required when building from a kit surpass those of the fortunate amongst us who possess a sophisticated workshop, where switching on and turning a couple of handles does the job in a fraction of the time.

Making all the right decisions when choosing a kit is absolutely vital to get the most out of this fascinating hobby. If you are a complete beginner, do not be over-ambitious in your selection of subject. A good guide can often be given by looking at the general shape of the hull. Tightly rounded curves are always going to be a problem, particularly if you don't have some sort of plank bending aid. The old Coast-guard cutters and Baltimore Clippers offer a reasonably trouble-free shape where the planking lines at bow and stern are not too severe. It pays to look at the box carefully too; sometimes the manufacturer will indicate the standard of expertise required.

Don't be put off by what appears to be an absolute mass of unintelligible rigging. It has more to do with quantity than difficulty and it just takes more time to rig three masts than two. Comprehensive rigging details are normally provided in the kit.

The quality of today's products far exceeds that provided only just a few years ago and the listings in hobby journals, notably *Model Boats* magazine, advertise kits that can be relied upon to give the potential model builder good value for money. The market place will not sustain rubbish and poor quality. Many retailers are enthusiasts themselves and will willingly give advice and answer any specific questions that you may have. It may be possible to look inside the box in the shop, but please ask first. Many boxes are packed in a particular sequence and, if things don't go back in the right order, you just can't get the lid back on!

So, having got the lid off, what do you look for? Be suspicious of the big box that is only half full. It is an old dodge to make you feel that you are buying more than you actually are. However, on the other hand, boxes tend to be made in standard sizes and a special size can be expensive adding to the overall price of the kit. So, if the contents are just too much for the next size down, inevitably there will be some spare space in the box. However, you can usually judge if that space is excessive.

Don't be put off by foreign kits, the manuals are usually multi-lingual or, at least, have the main part of the instructions translated into English. This is perhaps more important for the beginner, whereas, for the experienced, a good set of descriptive drawings and sketches will often be adequate without the written word.

These comments assume that there is a manual or set of instructions to look at in the first place. If what comes to light amounts to only a couple of typewritten sheets, then either the kit is directed towards the more experienced or, it is of fairly poor quality. A good instruction manual, backed up by well-detailed drawings is an absolute must, particularly for the novice. It will usually tell you not only what to do, but *when* to do it. It is always helpful to see a parts list included, either as part of the drawings or the manual. Numbered parts cross-referenced to the drawings, and properly identified, are encouraging signs that someone has given the production of the kit some constructive thought. A ready indication as to the material from which they are to be fabricated is also helpful.

It won't usually be possible to examine all the fittings because of the way that they are normally packed, but these are not generally too much of a problem. The main difficulty encountered with them is that sometimes kits are made up using standard items from the manufacturer's fittings catalogue. Thus, there are occasions when items like winches, capstans, pumps and anchors are not quite

the right size or style for the vessel in question. This is not usually disastrous of course, but don't look upon standard fittings as items that can always be taken straight from the pack and assembled onto the model. However, it has to be said that the modern day modeller is more demanding in his desire for historical accuracy and, as a result, many kit manufacturers provide fittings whose design are specific to the subject kit.

Pre-cut parts from sheet material can be expected to be either laser or router cut, both of which will have been computer-controlled to attain the high degree of accuracy found in modern kits. Both have advantages and disadvantages; the laser cut sheet has a fine and narrow cut, free of all burrs but requires more intense cleaning to remove "charred" edges. Routed parts, by the very nature of the process have wider cut lines, frequently impacted with swarf which can be messy, but have clean edges which is helpful particularly when tidying up small parts. The big advantage with routed parts is the facility for multi-depth cutting which permits the pre-production of joints and ornamental scrollwork.

Should you encounter any large blocks of hardwood, even though roughly pre-shaped, think about whether you have the facilities to carve or finish shape such material. In fact, you come to realise after a while, that some pre-shaping is not as advantageous as first thought, making the initial holding of the piece somewhat awkward. The lamination of several parts cut from the sheet is frequently the best bet.

The quality of the timber is usually fairly easy to assess and bundles of straight and fine-grained strips, bodes well. These checks should equally apply to dowel rods that are provided where any warps or twists are totally unacceptable. A point often overlooked, however, is consistency of colour. This can be particularly important if the model is to have a natural wood finish, a feature often preferred by period ship modellers. So, it is worth having a special look at the timbers provided for finished surfaces to ensure that they are all of the same basic shade.

Many kits today include photo-etched brass parts. Some modellers like them and some don't. However, they are a fact of life and, if included in the kit of your choice, should be presented flat in a well-protected pack to avoid damage.

A feature that I always look for is a stand for the finished model. To buy a finished board and pedestals can add somewhat to the cost of the project. Fortunately, these days most kits contain something on which to stand the model, even if it is only a simple cradle, which with a bit of thought, can often be enhanced and made quite presentable. It is certainly better than leaning the model against a bowl of fruit on the sideboard!

Kits can normally be expected to provide several sizes of cordage for the rigging. Look for two colours, black or dark brown for the standing rigging and tan or

A new kit from U.S. manufacturer Midwest for the sloop "John Alden".

natural thread for the running rigging. White is not really suitable and looks very artificial. To see it in a kit today gives the impression of cheapness and cost cutting.

A similar thing can be said about sail material. White, for most period ship models, is going to look too artificial and can spoil the effect of an otherwise excellent construction. Strangely, most modellers will accept the dyeing process for sails whereas it is felt that the cordage is more the responsibility of the kit manufacturer to get right. Apart from the colour of the sail material, the texture is also important. However, at the stage when you are buying the kit, it is difficult to make the assessment as to whether it is going to hang right when converted into a sail. Some kits do not provide any material at all, perhaps on the basis that sails cover up all that beautiful work you have put into the building and rigging. This is a valid point and many modellers refrain from rigging sails because of it. Also, you might listen to the argument that

a material has not yet been found to properly simulate a wind filled course, but more of that later in the book.

All that I have written so far about kit selection has presupposed that the purchaser has the opportunity to visit a model shop with a wide-ranging and adequate stock. So what do you do if you have no other option than to use mail order? As I said earlier, the people who distribute and retail kits are often both specialists and enthusiasts and most willing to offer advice and assistance. However, if you want their help, might I suggest that you confine your telephone call to a mid-week afternoon and not expect their best response at times when they are likely to have a shop full of people.

One of the purposes of this book, of course, is to offer as much valid information as possible on the kits used for building the various models as well as the construction techniques involved and you can refer to the Appendix for further sources of help and information.

The sloop "John Alden".

CHAPTER 3

Making a Start

Do not be too anxious to start cutting and sticking pieces together. A thorough study of the drawings and instructions will pay dividends as you proceed through the building of the model. I don't know what it is about some modelmakers, but reading the instructions seems to be an area of some reluctance except when things have gone wrong. Don't fall into the trap of considering that the instructions for the next project will be superfluous once you have made your first model. Remember that instruction manuals are as much about *when to* as, *how to*, and it is easy to find yourself in a situation where, because you have done things out of sequence, you have denied yourself access for the next stage of construction.

Some manufacturers even go as far as to provide a cutting list that defines from which piece of stock material each item is cut. This, of course, helps to ensure that there is enough material in the kit, but not too much! It also means that you deviate from the list at your peril since you could finish up needing a 200mm length of strip with only a length of 180mm left in the box. So beware.

It is often identifying particular features of a model and treating them as individual mini-projects within the overall construction. Winches, anchors, capstans, etc. all lend themselves to this approach and there is a psychological aspect to this way of working that frequently makes for better results.

If you have decided that the kit is to be the basis for a more enhanced model, in conjunction with the necessary investigation and research, identify the areas that will benefit from additional detailing or modification. It is important to make these observations at this stage since your decisions could well influence the sequence and procedures laid down in the kit instructions. It might be sensible to make a note of these points just to jog your memory when the particular stage of working is reached. Note should also be made of additional materials needed and these bought well before they are needed.

Some of the kits, especially those produced for the more experienced modeller, may be found to have instructions so sparse as to make the formulating of your own procedures the first task. The usual problem here is the aforementioned sequence of working and careful study of the drawings is required to ensure that the required access for later stages of construction are not shut off.

As to the actual construction techniques, the following pages look at a range of models of different shapes and sizes which provide the opportunity to examine most of the procedures that you have to contend with when constructing a model ship or boat. While much of what I have written describes ways and means around those problems arising when building from a kit, there is also much that will be helpful when building from scratch. There is absolutely nothing mandatory about these procedures and they are not claimed to be the only, or the best way to tackle particular facets of construction. They are ways that I have found successful over a period of some sixty years of modelmaking.

Make sure that your tools are in good shape and that you have everything needed to finish the job to hand. Spare blades for your craft knife, paints and adhesives come to mind as the items to be looked at first. There is nothing worse than finding that you have run out of adhesive, for instance, just five minutes after the shops have closed.

Finally, leave pre-cut parts in their sheets and fittings in their packs until actually required. Most manufacturers or distributors will assist in the replacement of lost parts, but this is very inconvenient when you are in the mood to get on with your model. I repeat, do read the instructions and study the drawings; someone, somewhere has spent a lot of time putting them together for your benefit.

CHAPTER 4

H.M.S. "Victory"

In using the title, H.M.S. "Victory", I realise that this really needs qualification by adding something that tells the reader at what stage in its history the model is supposed to represent. Herein lies the great problem, because the ship that can now be seen at The Historical Dockyard at Portsmouth is somewhat different to what it was at the time of Nelson's epic victory at Trafalgar in 1805, which, in turn was not as built and launched in 1765. However, the matter does not even rest there because it appears that right up to recent times, during the restoration programme, documentation and other evidence has come to light that changes some hitherto accepted data.

In preparing their kit for this famous vessel, JoTiKa Ltd. worked closely with the people on the restoration project in order to attain the highest possible historical accuracy. I make absolutely no claim to be an expert on "Victory", so on matters that concern historical accuracy and the kit, all I will say is that I know that every possible endeavour has been made to achieve authenticity. In fact, I understand that the start of kit production was delayed in order to accommodate the very latest information that had been discovered.

"Victory", a first rate of 100 guns, was designed by Sir Thomas Slade. Built at Chatham, first under the supervision of Master Shipwright, John Lock then, after his death in 1762, completed by Edward Allin. Launched in May 1765, the ship was laid up after sea trials and was not commissioned until 1778.

As built, "Victory" was quite different in appearance to the vessel to be seen today, having open galleries and a very ornate stern. Her figurehead and trail-boards were also far more elaborate. The bottom was coated to the waterline with a white finish and not replaced with copper sheathing until 1780. The now familiar yellow ochre bands on the line of the gun-ports first appeared in 1783 although the outer surfaces of the gun-ports were not painted black until just prior to Trafalgar.

The major repairs that took place during 1801 to 1803 saw the removal of the stern galleries and the closing in of the stern with far less decoration than hitherto. The Prince of Wales feathers that adorn the stern today did not appear on the taffrail until 1837 and were salvaged from H.M.S. "Prince" before it was taken to the breakers.

What decoration was there at the time of Trafalgar is still the subject of ongoing research at the time of writing this review.

Battle honours included Ushant and St. Vincent, but most memorably Trafalgar, where Horatio Nelson met his tragic end in the hour of victory.

"Victory" has been in harbour service at Portsmouth since 1824 and in dry dock since 1922 and is now coming to the end of her second phase of restoration.

The kit

This was a most impressive box of parts and straight away it became very apparent, that the claim by the manufacturer, that as many parts as possible had been pre-cut was borne out by the number of sheets containing a myriad of parts, large and small. Because of the third axis facility available on the CAD/CAM system used, many parts had been shaped as well as profiled, thus avoiding even more detailed carpentry work by the model maker.

There were bundles of strip material and dowel which, at first sight, appeared to be of high quality timber. Bearing in mind that most of these ply sheets and strips were cut and sized in-house, accuracy of a high order was anticipated.

To recognise the complexity of construction of the model, three manuals were provided, each covering a particular facet of the build and supplemented 18 sheets of highly detailed, true scale drawings. One of these manuals was essentially a comprehensive parts list and absolutely vital to the recognition and correct identification of the hundreds of smaller items contained within the kit.

Extreme care was exercised in the handling of the several sheets of etched brass parts and in fact these were immediately removed from the box and put safely to one side until required.

Castings and turned parts were boxed separately; the castings were clean and would require minimum attention before use. These parts were not from a "near enough" standard range, but cast or turned accurately for the model in hand.

As a portent of the rigging job to be done, over a kilometre of rigging thread, black and natural, of various sizes was provided.

The model is to a scale of 1:72 and thus has an overall length of 1385mm, a height of 940mm and a width across the main yard of 525mm. This requires a rather large "turning circle" during the rigging process if you don't have an island bench whereby you can walk around the model without moving it.

Tools required

The recommended list of tools shown in the manual is as follows.

Craft knife
A selection of needle files
Razor saw
Small wood plane
Pin vice or small electric drill (recommended)
Selection of drill bits (0,5 to 3,0mm diameter)
Selection of abrasive papers and sanding block
Selection of good quality paint brushes
Pliers/wire cutters
Tweezers
Dividers or compass
300mm Steel rule
Clothes pegs or crocodile clips
Tee square
Pencil or Edding pen
Masking tape

This list should be treated as a minimum requirement and that most model makers will have their favourite additions or alternatives to the listed items.

Craft knives, for instance, come in a variety of shapes and sizes and I would suggest that the more delicate blade, for removing parts from the thinner of the ply sheets, would be inadequate for taking out the 6mm bulkhead parts.

One electric tool that I find most useful in addition to the drill is the 12V disc sander which has so many practical uses. I would also recommend the use of a cutting mat, which can make a considerable difference to the quality of any cut.

Perma Grit abrasive tools are excellent for rapid removal of excess wood in general and for the bevelling of bulkhead edges in particular; a variety of shapes are available.

Most cutting and sanding processes result in the creation of dust and wearing a mask is most advisable. If you wear glasses the problem of lenses misting up the can be overcome by using a mask with a built-in valve.

Consumable Items required

Paints and adhesives always prove to be quite an additional expense particularly when, as in this case, the model is very large. Quantities to buy are difficult to assess in the context of a review and much will depend on the standard

of finish attained on the relevant surfaces prior to painting. What is certain is that quite a large amount of cyanoacrylate will be required when applying the copper plates to the underside of the hull. The following list is as recommended in the manual:

White PVA wood glue
Walnut wood dye
Cyanoacrylate, thick and thin grades
Walnut wood filler
White spirit
Matt polyurethane varnish
Black paint (Humbrol 85)
White paint (Humbrol 34)
Blue paint (Humbrol 25)
Yellow Paint - Linen (Humbrol 74)
Red paints (3 parts Humbrol 60 mixed with 1 part Humbrol 70)
Copper paint (Humbrol 12)
Gold paint (Humbrol 16)
Brown/leather paint (Humbrol 62)
Olive green paint (Humbrol 155)

The Humbrol black paint 85 is actually coal black and is from the Humbrol satin range. Some modellers prefer the slight sheen, but I always prefer to use matt black 33 for wooden surfaces which usually looks totally black under most exhibiting conditions. It also retains its colour during photography. The satin black 85, I use for metal parts, gun barrels, hammock cranes, buckets, chain plates etc.

In addition to these items there are one or two other materials that, while not essential, can make life a little easier.

Poor quality masking tape can be a nightmare particularly if, on removal it also takes half of your paint job with it. If you don't already have a tried and trusted favourite, try Tamiya, a little more expensive but well worth it for the reliability it affords.

There are a number of castings and etched brass parts in the kit that will need painting and the use of an etching primer makes for a much better job. If you go down this path, parts will need to be cleansed with cellulose thinners prior to priming and brushes or other equipment will have to be cleaned up with dedicated thinners.

Sanding sealers provide a fair surface for painting and should not be overlooked if you are seeking a really nice finish. A shellac-based sealer is a good choice.

Health and safety precautions again come to the fore and a suitable respirator is essential if the worst effects of inhaling fumes from cyanoacrylate, etching primers and cellulose thinners are to be avoided.

Preliminaries

The first important thing to be done was to register the kit with the manufacturer. JoTiKa have an excellent replacement parts service for all their kits but in this case there is an additional advantage to be gained by registration. Research and restoration is still ongoing

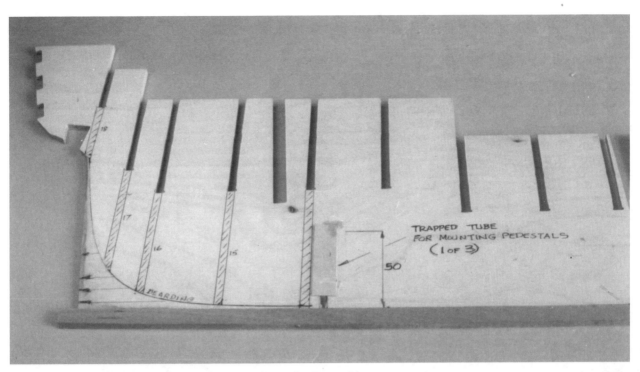

Fig.4.1   Establishing the bearding line and stand tube position.

on "Victory" at Portsmouth particularly with regard to the taffrail decoration at the time of Trafalgar. The kit includes the trophy of arms and the Prince of Wales feathers as can be seen today, but JoTiKa will provide, free of charge, all registered kits with whatever research decides was in place at the time of Trafalgar as soon as such information is defined.

The three manuals were studied in conjunction with the drawings to get an overall picture of the building process and to become familiar with the finer detail of the model. A worthwhile aid to this is to thoroughly check the kit contents against the parts lists provided by Manual No.3. The primary identification of the pre-cut parts is the sheet thickness and I found it most helpful to first take each sheet, put it into its correct orientation as outlined in the manual and clearly mark it with the relevant thickness. The parts were sequentially numbered according to sheet thickness and listed as such in the manual, thus rapid identification of sheet and part was possible.

This task is not one for the dining room table however, since one of the penalties to be paid for clean cut routed parts is the accumulation of dust and swarf in the gaps between part and surrounding sheet. Keep the vacuum cleaner handy!

The manual also contained helpful tips on safety, a subject most model makers seem to overlook. Fumes from adhesives are quite noxious and a suitable mask or respirator is essential when sticking 2500 copper plates in position with cyanoacrylate. Be warned that prolonged exposure can make you feel quite ill for several days in addition to any long-term effects on the respiratory system.

The construction manual suggests that this project

will take between 2400 and 3000 hours but, obviously, much will depend on personal skills and craftsmanship and the standard of tool kit available. All I can say at this juncture is that the kit content is quite awesome and construction will not take just a few weeks!

Another point that should be emphasised is that the sequence of construction in the manuals is important. While some model makers, myself included, will perhaps leap ahead to make things like deck fittings as a change from monotonous tasks such as planking or gun-port lining, the permanent and basic assembly sequence should be adhered to. The manuals were written as part of the on-going process of building the prototype and, as such, help the builder avoid many unforeseeable problems.

Building the basic carcase

Like most kits today, the structure conformed to the practice of slotting bulkheads onto a false keel. However, unlike most kits, the parts supplied in this package went together without any preliminary work on the slots. What was absolutely imperative was to mark all the parts with their relevant numbers before removing them from their respective sheets. With 18 bulkheads and various cross beams, the last thing needed was to get items in the wrong place.

All bulkheads were assembled dry onto the false keel before attaching the walnut prow and keel parts so that if any slot adjustment had been needed, it could be done first. The accuracy of the pre-cut routing was such that, not only did the eighteen bulkheads fit neatly into place (and at the correct height), but the middle gun deck also dropped into position without any adjustment to firmly lock everything up, **(Fig.4.1).**

While I had the bulkheads in place, I marked the

Fig.4.2   *The false keel, prow and keel parts assembly.*

Fig.4.3   *The bulkhead assembly.*

Fig.4.4   *The dummy gun barrel mounting strips in place.*

bottom position of No.'s 14 to 18 onto the false keel in order to establish the bearding line.

Having taken the dry assembly apart, I considered what needed to be done to mount the finished model. My own favourite method is to fix three brass tubes into the false keel to accept rods attached vertically to the base-board and which pass through intermediate pedestals. These were duly put in place ensuring squareness and in positions that would not weaken the false keel.

I then tapered the rear surfaces of the false keel from the bearding line to the seating edge of the sternpost, ensuring that the varying taper was always being produced in a horizontal direction. The degree of taper was such as to leave a 2mm width at the sternpost seating. This ensures that when sanding down the two layers of planking, their thickness will be reduced by only about 12mm in order to match the thickness of the walnut sternpost. To make a neat and tidy job, I normally do not assemble the actual sternpost until after the second planking has been put in place when both post and planking can be rubbed down together.

The bulkheads were then re-assembled dry in order to assess which of them needed to be chamfered on their edges; this was done by using a planking strip at various levels to see the amount of chamfer required. The bulkheads were removed and the chamfers *roughly* produced on the bench.

The prow was temporarily screwed into place at the front end of the false keel, followed by the gluing and pinning of the two walnut keel parts, **(Fig.4.2)**. I chose not to permanently fix the prow at this stage because it's side faces are somewhat vulnerable during the edge shaping and finishing of the bulkheads and plank termination pieces and thus, it could be removed during that process to avoid damage. This would be particularly important to those model makers who prefer their model to have a natural wood finish rather than plated and painted.

All bulkheads, apart from No.1, were then glued onto the false keel and the middle gun deck dropped into place to lock everything up. The assembly was left clamped onto my building board overnight to thoroughly cure. **(Fig.4.3)**.

The four dummy gun barrel mounting strips were then assembled. Having checked the lengths, I found that the amount protruding beyond the rear face of bulkhead No.17 was sufficient to permit one end of each strip to have a 10mm x 20Ú chamfer on all four faces. This prepared end was fed into the relevant slot of No.2 bulkhead and gently tapped through the length of the hull with a light mallet, the chamfers providing a suitable lead-in to each bulkhead. No soaking or application of heat was required. The position of each strip was adjusted to match the rear face of No.1 bulkhead and the residue beyond the rear face of No.17 was then cut off. The strips were glued and left to set before cutting away that portion of the upper strips between bulkheads

Fig.4.5   The gun-port patterns relate to deck levels.

No.9 and 10 to recognise the position of the side entry ports. The finished result is shown in **Fig.4.4**.

The chamfering of the bulkhead edges was then finished, again using a planking strip to check that the planks would seat right across each bulkhead thickness.

Before proceeding further, it was important to read the manual and become familiar with the procedure for positioning and fixing the ply gun-port patterns. The position of the top gun-port pattern was critical since it establishes the position of the other patterns and thence the alignment of gun-port apertures on the inner bulwarks, **(Fig.4.5)**. Major reference points were given in the manual and were used to correctly put everything in place. The front end of the major patterns each side needed to be thoroughly soaked in order to coax them round the bows, **(Fig.4.6)**. Even so, particular attention was given to that area below the front of the forecastle deck, where the bends commence adjacent to the first gun-ports in the row. There were compound curves to contend with and, of course, the patterns had a reduced cross-section at the gun-ports and so bent more freely at those points. I soaked the ply pieces for a long time so that the material could almost be moulded to the hull before pinning and gluing. The arrangement at the back end is shown in **Fig.4.7** and the hull ready to start planking in **Fig.4.8**.

The first planking

The secret to the success of the planking was to ensure that the edges of the bulkheads had been properly chamfered and a final run-over with a planking strip was done to check the lines.

The planking operation was straightforward and started from the lower edge of the bottom gun-port pattern. I found that soaking the plank ends was beneficial and, having done so, a plank nipper was all that was required to induce the curves fore and aft. I kept a tall vase specifically for soaking the ends of planks, which, obviously, meant that only one end of the plank could be treated. However, to get around the problem of planks that required serious bending at both ends, I laid these in two pieces making a butt joint at a convenient bulkhead amidships.

All planks were both pinned and glued with PVA at each bulkhead. Holes 0,5mm diameter were drilled for the pins, this being just the right size for a tight fit so that they could be left proud for easier removal later on.

Apart from the first few planks each side, most required some degree of tapering, which could be done with either a craft knife as described in the manual or, if you have a plank clamp, by use of a David plane.

It had to be remembered at all times that the best planking job is always that where each plank conforms to its natural run. Twisting or distorting the plank in any way would create problems when later rubbing down. Thus, there were areas at the stern particularly, where triangular gaps were left that required the fitting of stealers. All planks were left overhung at the rear of the false keel (the seating for the stern post) and to the

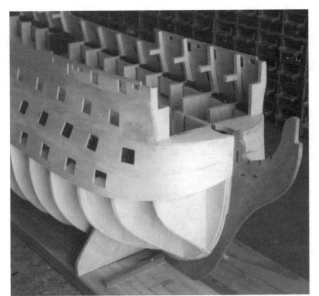

Fig.4.6   *The gun-port patterns at the bows.*

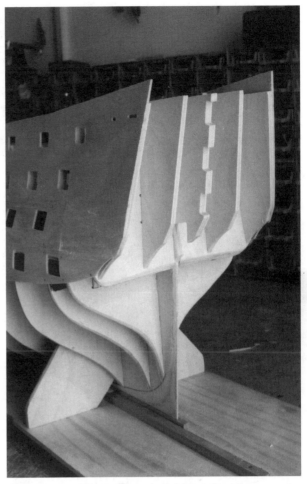

rear of bulkhead No.18 for later trimming. After the hull had been completely covered with the first planking, it was set aside overnight for the adhesive to thoroughly cure.

An initial rubbing down with course abrasive paper was done prior to filling any odd gaps. Shaped sanding blocks were most helpful when working on those areas around the stern, as indeed were some of the Perma Grit files from my tool kit. Finer grades of abrasive paper were used to finish the task. This was a dusty job and the wearing of a dust mask absolutely essential. It was also a long job, due to the large area involved, even if the planking was well done.

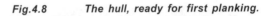

Fig.4.7   *The gun-port patterns at the stern.*

Fig.4.8   *The hull, ready for first planking.*

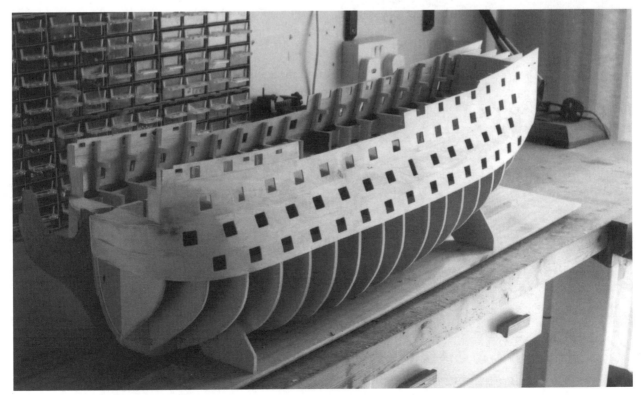

Fig.4.9 *The first planking complete.*

Having established a sound surface for the second planking, the overhung ends of the planks were carefully trimmed. The hull with first planking complete can be seen in **Fig. 4.9**.

The kit provided parts for a building cradle, which

Fig.4.10 *Quarter gallery patterns.*

was made up and secured to my building board. This helps enormously in keeping the model stable while proceeding with further construction as well as being a convenient parking place while making up deck fittings etc.

The quarter galleries

Together with the head rails, this part of the construction would normally cause the greatest headache to the period ship model maker. In this case, the kit provided pre-cut parts and a sequence of instructions that were certainly better than anything I had hitherto found in a kit. Even so, it was not merely a case of clicking bits together to get a successful job. A lot of patience, time and cold fitting was required to achieve that end. I found that provided the instructions were followed implicitly, the results were very good.

The inner stern fascia was first pinned into place, ensuring that it was absolutely central before *and* after pinning and using the lower edges of the stern extensions as a guide to height. This was followed by the upper stern counter pattern.

The main quarter gallery inside pattern (373) was then dry assembled with the smallest top quarter gallery pattern (215) and located into the pre-cut slots in the side of the hull gun-port pattern. This procedure was adopted on both sides of the hull to ensure that everything was symmetrical and correct before gluing the main gallery patterns (373) in place.

The quarter gallery patterns were now dry fitted to assess the treatment required to their edges to facilitate the snug fitting of the gallery skins with windows. On balance, I think that this was better done before permanently fixing the patterns in place, but this is really a matter of personal choice. In fact I started at the top and worked my way down, first dry fitting then, having established edge angles and positions, permanently gluing bits in place, **(Fig.4.10)**.

I would offer one piece of additional advice not contained within the manual about the glazing of the skins, which has to be done before assembly. If you want to use PVA, then the skins *must* be bent into their correct shape *before* sticking the glazing material in place. It is also recommended that the area on the glazing strips that takes the adhesive be scratched up with the point of a scalpel to make a key. If the skins are not bent before putting the glazing strips in place, the act of bending will ping them off! The scratching of the glued area is a belt and braces operation, but if the glazing became detached after assembly, it would not be possible to get at them for replacement.

As pointed out in the manual, cyanoacrylate was not an option due to the clouding of the glazing material by fumes from the adhesive. I found that an excellent result was attained using polyurethane gloss varnish. The varnish was painted onto the inside of the skins, *not* applied in blobs that would spread to the visible areas of the clear material, **(Fig.4.11)**.

The lower stern counter pattern was then put in place, **(Fig.4.12)**. Centring was again the keyword, but it was equally important to attain the right match with the first planking along its lower edge. I left the pattern sufficiently proud to provide a butt for the ends of the second planking.

Fig.4.12　　**The lower stern counter pattern.**

The middle gun deck planking

An appreciable area of this deck will be seen through companion ways of the deck above and thus it was necessary to plank between bulkheads 4 and 12 out as far as the bulkhead risers, **(Fig.4.13)**. The space behind the entry ports and between the adjacent bulkheads also needed to be planked, sealed with a couple of coats of matt varnish and sanded smooth. PVA adhesive was used throughout for this operation, applying a thin bead of glue to the deck and stroking the planks into position with a damp cloth. This squeezed the glue up between the planks and removed any surplus from the deck surface.

The mast sleeves were glued together before tidying up the inside and outside diameters. Care was taken to ensure that they were properly concentric and left to dry overnight before taking a file to them. The outside was cleaned up first then, using the 12mm dowel provided; an easy slide fit was attained on the inside diameter. The assembled ring was then glued in place on the deck, making sure that it was central over the mast hole. Only when the glue had completely cured was any attempt made to gently file through the hole to set the rake angle for the mast.

The entry ports were lined to finish up with a width of 10mm between the sidewalls.

The outer faces of the dummy barrel strips and other adjacent areas that may be seen through the gun-port apertures were painted as instructed.

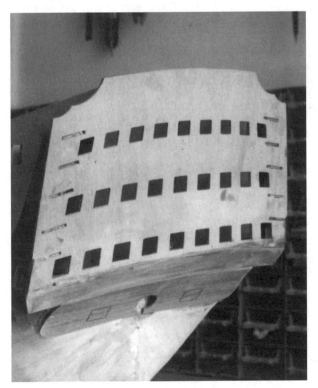

Fig.4.11　　*Pre-glazed quarter gallery skins in place.*

25

Fig.4.13   *Middle gun deck planking.*

The second planking

There are one or two dodges that I have learned over the years that frequently make for an easier and less time consuming job. These did not in any way conflict with the instruction manual, but rather enhanced the guidance given.

The second planking was done following the same basic procedure as for the first, the main difference being in the type of adhesive used. It was intended to use cyanoacrylate as the prime adhesive to avoid pinholes. However, it was seen that with the size of the model in question this could be quite an expensive choice, so I opted to use both cyanoacrylate and PVA to reduce the cost. Basically, cyanoacrylate was used where

Fig.4.14   *Second hull planking butt joints at fender positions.*

Fig.4.15   *Second planking at interface with counter.*

the soaked planks had been pre-bent with plank nippers, and for the rest of the length I used PVA. The back edge of a scraper was used to stroke the planks into position, this having the effect of spreading the adhesive over the entire area to be glued and assisted in attaining a rapid initial grab. A word of warning is necessary about the procedure; since the grab is almost instantaneous on the wet areas and because even though the planking strips are 1mm thick, the cyanoacrylate will permeate through to the outside of a wet plank and stick to the fingers.

Laying the first plank in the specified position, it was seen that it needed to be tapered at the ends and also angled at the front end to sit snugly against the stem and at the back end, to match the edge of the lower stern counter pattern (372). The problem the model maker is faced with is not getting each of the end shapes correct, but getting the shapes combined with the correct overall length. It was easy to finish up with a plank too long which wouldn't sit down correctly, or one that was too short which wouldn't reach the stem or stern pattern! This was a difficulty that was persevered with for the first plank laid each side. From then on, planks were laid in two pieces with a butt joint amidships at one or other of the bulkhead positions.

This process has several advantages. Two short lengths of planking strip are easier to handle than one long one, especially the length required for the subject model. The butt joints amidships (never on the same bulkheads for adjacent planks), are below the waterline and in any case will subsequently be covered by the

Fig.4.16   *Lower second planking complete with stern post in place.*

Fig.4.17   Upper gun-deck in position.

Fig.4.18   Upper deck with mainmast sleeve.

copper plating. For areas above the waterline, any butt joints may be covered by the main wale, or positioned in such a manner as to be covered by the fenders, **(Fig.4.14)**.

The first stage of the second planking was such *as relate to* the length of the bottom edge of the lower stern counter pattern, starting from the outside rounded, corner and working inwards to the stern post aperture, **(Fig.4.15)**. This area was covered on both sides of the model before moving on to the lower planking.

The lower planking, or second stage was, for the most part, laid in full-length strips since there was overhang at the aft end. Several stealers were required to permit the planks to take their natural run without distortion. This stage was completed on both sides of the model before trimming the ends at the sternpost seating then gluing the post in place, **(Fig.4.16)**.

Planking above the recommended start line and moving upwards was put on entirely with cyanoacrylate; again stroking each plank into place to ensure that is was properly seated. This section of the planking includes the two lower rows of gun-ports. The lengths of the intermediate planks between ports were cut to leave a minimal amount, about 0,5mm, for trimming each side. It was worth spending time to do this, because when trimming the ends of the planks it was helpful to have a better sight of the gun-port pattern beneath to use as a guide for final sizing. At a later stage, these ports had to be lined and it was particularly important to keep them all to the exact size of the ply gun-port patterns so, having the least amount of material to remove, reduced the opportunity for error. Light cuts with a sharp scalpel were the order of the day.

Fig.4.19   *Continuing the second planking.*

The gun-ports on the two lower decks were ultimately to be lined differently to some on the upper gun deck, so the second planking had to be suspended before moving any further upwards.

The upper gun deck

The false deck, six beams and two inner bulwark gun-port patterns were acquired, care being taken to ensure that the right beams were selected and then mounted correctly to either the fore or aft side of the respective bulkheads.

Putting the false deck in place was relatively easy. Although the position of the locating slots had been very accurately produced, because of the distortion required to fit the deck into place, this accuracy was, in fact, something of a disadvantage. Accordingly, before attempting any trimming of the outside edges, it was found necessary to open out in both width and depth the slot in the rear edge of the deck that fitted over the central protrusion of the false keel. This helped to avoid jamming the deck while doing the trial and error work to attain final fit. The freeing operation could have proved disastrous! The rear edge of the false deck was another feature for early attention for the same reason. Alternatively, if you feel that the repeated removal of the deck is too hazardous, then cut the deck carefully down the centre line and fit each side separately. If you choose this alternative do all the adjustments to the *outside* edges; do *not* touch the edges at the centre line. It was worth noting that the fit between the edges of the deck and the inside of the hull was not critical since the joint would ultimately be hidden within the

cavity provided by the inner bulwark patterns.

The inner bulwark gun-port patterns also needed some trimming to accurately match the gun-port positions on the outside patterns. The slots in the upper edges of the inner patterns were already elongated to attain true position fore and aft, but I needed to remove about 2mm from the bottom edges to get alignment of the top and bottom sills.

As a double check that all was well, I made up a basic gun carriage with barrel. Then, standing it on a piece of 1mm scrap to represent the thickness of the deck planking, I could then see that the barrel was central within the height of the gun-port aperture. The upper gun deck in place is shown in **Fig.4.17**.

Planking the upper deck

I followed the same procedure as that used for the middle gun deck, the exception being that when I got to the outside of the deck, the last couple of planks were laid in two parts. This made it easier to accommodate the outer shape of the hull, the butt joint between the two pieces being made coincident with the centre of a gun-port, thus being hidden when the gun was in place. The planking was then scraped and sanded smooth before applying a few coats of matt varnish, **(Fig.4.18)**.

The mast sleeves were assembled in the same manner as for the middle deck.

Before lining the 8 gun-ports without lids I prepared two strips of the 4x1mm walnut for planking the inner bulwarks' patterns by painting them yellow ochre. These were to be used for the lowest plank each side and avoided awkward painting where the planks met the deck

Fig.4.20   The wales at the beak deck.

surface and would be further hindered by the quarter deck support extensions above.

Lining the ports without lids was simplified by the fact that the apertures, being pre-cut in the patterns, were all of the same size. The sidepieces were cut first using the 1mm x 16mm material provided, ensuring that the grain ran vertically. PVA was used to stick them in place, all sixteen ports being attended to and left to dry. The outside and inside edges were then trimmed flush with the inside and outside patterns before cutting and placing the upper and lower sills in place. After trimming the sills, the inside and outside patterns were sanded to smooth off the edges of the linings.

Planking the inner bulwarks

The two previously painted strips were cut to size and glued into place tight down onto the deck. Further planks were added, covering the edges of the 8 lined gun-ports. The planking was trimmed at gun-ports as progress was made upwards until the top of the apertures were reached. At this stage, the deck beams for the quarterdeck were temporarily clipped in place using small clamps, in order that the uppermost inner bulwark planks could be cut to fit.

Continuing with the outer hull planking

The second planking was continued so as to cover the upper deck gun-ports, **(Fig.4.19)**. However, this was not proceeded with beyond the bottom edge of the ports for the quarterdeck.

The lidded gun-ports for the upper deck carriage guns were now lined using 16x1mm strip, pre-painted red. The front edges of the linings were set back 1mm from the outer surface of the hull, as instructed.

However, the front edges of sides and most sills had to be angled and this was best done by marking with a pencil line during the initial dry fitting stage and cutting before permanently fixing the pieces in position. The inside edges were trimmed and the inside bulwark planking sanded and painted yellow ochre.

The wales

A lot of care was taken to ensure that the lines of the wales were correct and for starters, I marked the position of the top of each onto the hull with a pencil, checking all the while that port and starboard were identical. Guidance as to their true position was given in the manual and, of course, on the drawings. Eyeballing the bows and stern to make sure that the lines met at the same height at stem post and quarter galleries was also done. The front end of the top wale has a very specific position relative to the beak deck which is a good starting point for getting things correct, **(Fig.4.20)**.

The first (top) plank of each wale was laid to the pencil line previously marked and medium cyanoacrylate was used as the adhesive. In order to maintain the true conformity of line the whole strip was laid in one piece, going across gun-port apertures where necessary. When adding further strips, I cut shorter pieces as required leaving about 1mm over-length for trimming, making sure that they were fixed tight up against the lower edge of the previously laid strip. With such minimal amounts left for trimming, the tidying up of the gun-ports was much less hazardous.

The lowest strip in each wale proved to be the most difficult to fit, inasmuch as the strips were a constant width to keep the wale width constant, thus providing a

Fig.4.21   Lined gun-ports.

tendency for the bottom edge of the strip to lift from the surface of the hull. However, using cyanoacrylate and concentrating on fixing a few centimetres at a time the problem was overcome. Any gaps between planks were filled and the wales sanded smooth. Special attention was paid to the edges to keep them clean and square for the later ease of painting.

Lining the lower and middle deck gun-ports

I concentrated on the lower deck gun-ports first, all of which used 6x1mm strip for the lining. No doubt, every modeller will have his own favourite method of doing gun-port linings, but for those who have not yet had the dubious pleasure of having to line ports in this manner, I offer my system as a starting point and basis for personal development. The main problem with this type of lining process was that the two side pieces, fitted first, were supported only by the 1,5mm thickness of the gun-port patterns and the accuracy of a push fit described below.

I calculated that I would need approximately one strip of wood for each row of gun- ports. These were sanded on one face and one edge and these two surfaces then painted with the appropriate red paint.

When I did the second planking, it may be remembered that I mentioned that when trimming, it was important to maintain the size of the ports as presented by the gun-port patterns. Now, during the lining operation, was when the consistency of size paid dividends. I carefully measured the height of the gun-port apertures and cut a length of strip slightly oversize (about 0,2mm). This piece, held in tweezers, was located into the bottom left corner of the gun-port, 1mm back from the hull surface, then pivoted anti-clockwise into

the top left corner. It was seen that the over-length interference was just about right to hold the lining in place, although some may prefer a little less or maybe even a little more. All vertical sides were then cut to this length for lining the lower deck gun-ports on both port and starboard sides.

Each sidepiece was held in tweezers and PVA adhesive applied with a toothpick before fitting into position as described above, with the painted edge to the front. The problem lay in the fact that, when attaining the required 1mm depth of the front edge of the lining from the face of the hull planking, there was only the aforementioned 1,5mm thickness of the gun-port pattern on which to glue the lining. However, I managed to complete the thirty openings losing only two pieces into the bottom of the hull.

Having got all of the sides in place, I then concentrated on the sills, top and bottom. The same approach was adopted; a slight interference fit, located to match to front edges of the sidepieces and glue applied with a toothpick. The only difference was in the fitting of the top sills where the unpainted edge was to the front. Advance reading of the manual indicated that the gun-port lids would later fit and be glued against this edge and I didn't want to contaminate an already minimal joint with paint. The reason for the minimal glue application was to avoid getting too much excess in the 1mm recess. Any that did appear was immediately removed before tackling the next gun-port. Lined gun-ports are shown in **Fig.4.21**.

The bottom sills were fitted first then the hull inverted to do the top sills. This provided a more positive means of putting them in place. On the subject of the

Fig.4.22   *Setting out the copper plates.*

top sills, as mentioned, their front edge provides the surface to which the back edge of the gun-port lids fit. It was important to fit the front edges to a *maximum* depth of 1mm from the hull surface; any more than 1mm might mean that the gun-port hinges prevent the lids actually coming into contact with the sills, thus providing an inadequate joint.

The first gun-port on each of the middle and lower gun decks were presented as closed gun-ports and, as such, had to be marked and cut into the second planking by hand. The positions were marked with a pencil then the outline gently cut with a sharp scalpel. A second cut, about 0,5mm inside the first, was then made. The thickness of the scalpel blade was sufficient to ease the wood away from between the cuts, leaving a neat outline to the gun-port.

The holes for the dummy gun barrels were now drilled, keeping the drill square, in line and central within the gun-port apertures.

Painting the hull sides

It seemed a bit odd painting the hull at this stage, before the second planking had been finished. However, the upper gun deck would have to be fitted out before further progress on planking could be made and protruding gun barrels would not be very convenient when wielding a paintbrush; even less so if masking before the use of an airbrush was contemplated.

I used Humbrol enamels throughout. For best results it was essential to make sure that the paint was properly mixed; a quick shake of the tin was not good enough if the paint was to maintain its correct colour, key properly and flow well from the brush. Several minutes of good stirring were well worth the effort, particularly when preparing the black paint with its seemingly heavier pigments. If you really want to take the effort out of the paint preparation, then a Badger paint mixer is a very useful and effective tool.

I decided that I would first paint the three yellow ochre bands all a bit wider than required. The width and position of each band was taken from the photograph in the manual as instructed and, after the first coat any blemishes were filled and sanded out. Further coats were applied until a satisfactory finish was attained. When thoroughly dry, the bands were masked using Tamiya tape and the remainder of the hull was painted black from the waterline up to the lower edge of the upper yellow band. A minor problem arose in the selection of the black paint, in that the list of paints refers to Humbrol 85, which is satin black and the painting instruction refers to matt black, which is No.33. Having listened to the arguments for and against the use of satin paints many times, I am still of the opinion that matt is best. The edges of the gun-port linings were touched up with red as required.

Copper plating

Plating the bottom of the hull was not particularly difficult, but it was tedious work and, if extended sessions are involved, could prove hazardous due to exposure to the fumes from the thick grade cyanoacrylate used as the adhesive. The ill effects of

Fig.4.23   *The finished copper plates.*

breathing in these fumes should not be underestimated and a suitable respirator should be worn.

The instruction manual advised that the best way to cut the plates was to use a craft knife with the plate laid on a hard, flat surface. This was good advice, but even better was the use of a self-healing cutting mat. What was avoided was the use of scissors, since the shearing action involved tended to curl the copper.

One of the problems mentioned in the manual occurred where the plates came to the waterline. The difficulties of cutting the individual plates to conform to a straight line could be overcome by the painting of a tidying copper paint line as suggested in the manual. However, previous experience showed that the exposed edges of the plates were not an enhancement to the finished appearance of the model. Earlier research had revealed that, in many cases, a 75mm wide batten may have covered the top edge of the plating at the waterline so I took advantage of this to make life a little easier and improve the appearance of the model.

Having set the hull up square and true on the cradle, the waterline was marked in place with a pencil line on both sides of the hull.

To represent the batten, a strip 0,5x1,0mm was required. The obvious solution was to trim a 1,0mm wide strip from the edge of a scrap 0,5mm thick strip. However, this was not as easy as it sounds bearing in mind the coarseness of grain usually found in such materials. As it happened, there was an alternative; it is called cheating and involved the use of Microstrip, available in many small sectional sizes including 0.02 x 0.04in. Yes, I know that it

is not wood, but having done the outer planking in *walnut* and stuck most of it on with *cyanoacrylate*, I could hardly shout about traditional methods and materials, could I? I glued lengths of Microstrip on the upper side of the marked waterline to provide a hard edge against which the plates could terminate and also to prevent the edges from being exposed from above. The beauty of the ploy lay in the fact that when painted black, the strip was virtually invisible whereas, without the strip, the edges of the copper plates would be something of an eyesore.

The manual suggested that the actual plating started at the keel and work progress towards the waterline, this is historically and technically correct for "Victory". However, because no two modellers are going to lay the plates exactly the same, problems might arise as the plating operation approaches the waterline, an area most visible to anyone examining the model.

Experience suggested that four or five plates are laid centrally at the waterline and then several rows below, until a wooden planking strip took up its natural curve to meet the waterline at stem and stern posts, this position being marked with a pencil. On my model this position was thirteen rows of plates below the waterline amidships, **(Fig.4.22)**. A line of plates was then completed from the keel up. The result was historically correct, i.e. no apparent gore line, and with no awkwardly shaped plates at the waterline.

As was found with the wooden planking, there were a number of places where the plating demanded the fitting of stealers. Using the rivet heads as an optical guide was a good way of assessing the shapes to be cut.

Fig.4.24   Upper gun-deck gratings.

Where the underlying surface of the hull was curved, a similar curve was induced into the copper plates by gentle pressure between thumb and forefinger. The aim was to produce a slight over-bend where the ends of the plates touched down first and required a little push in the middle to seat them in place. It was also easier to feel the proper location of the plate end before the adhesive grabbed.

The final areas of plating that needed careful attention were the keel, stem and rudder-post. These features were plated separately, keeping the plates parallel to the keel.

Unfortunately, the sides of the keel proper were wider than the plates therefore a couple of options presented themselves, much depending upon the proximity of the bottom row of hull plating. The plates can be bent to cover the joint between hull and keel or each plate cut into two longitudinal pieces, the former probably being the best choice. Whichever method was adopted, the best presentation of plating was that which involved a row of plates coincident with the bottom edge of the keel, leaving the fiddly bits largely unseen. The edges of the keel were plated last, ensuring that the adhesive totally covered each plate, permitting problem free trimming when the glue had set.

When the whole surface had been plated, it was examined for odd poorly fitted plates, which were replaced. There were one or two instances where two plates had stuck together during manufacture. I then sprayed on a couple of coats of matt polyurethane varnish to take off the shine of the copper plates, **(Fig.4.23)**.

Upper gun deck fitting

There were six sets of gratings to make (seven if you make the largest in two parts), to fit over the various openings in the deck, **(Fig.4.24)**. These were fabricated from the conventional combed strips and the first step was to select strips of the same shade for each grating; one odd one stands out. It is also wise to check for thickness; again the odd one spoils the appearance of the finished item. In this instance, thickness difference was not a problem and the gratings were assembled with little difficulty. Each was given a soaking in dilute PVA and left to dry before trimming and fitting with their respective coamings. It was noted that the ledges ran athwartships and the battens, which were fully seen, went fore and aft. It was important to get them all correct since should one grating be made the wrong way round it would rather stand out.

The largest grating could be made in two parts but, with a bit of thought and interlacing of the combed strips, one integral assembly could be constructed, which certainly produced a better job.

The companionway ladders were assembled as instructed in the manual with no difficulties. Accurate measurement of the width of companionway into which the ladder was to be fitted was essential to cut the ladder treads to their correct length for a snug fit. Treads were sanded to a clean and smooth finish before cutting from the strip, as were the sides before assembly. The 0,25mm natural thread "handrails" were attached to the eyes of the stanchions at the bottom of each ladder assembly before putting the ladders in place and left to

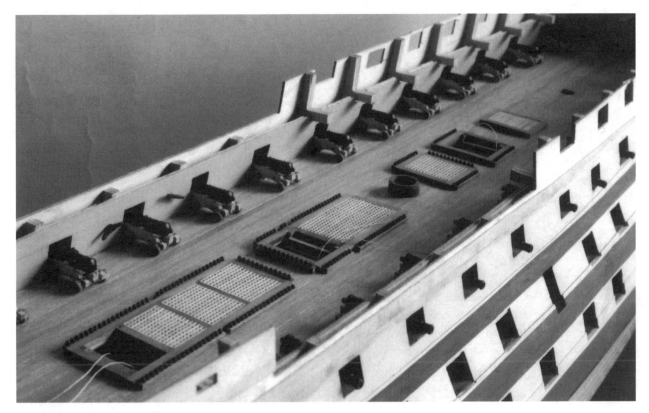

Fig.4.25   *The upper gun-deck 12-pounders.*

lie on the deck until the remaining companionway assemblies were fitted.

The pre-cut shot garlands were identified and glued in place against the coamings and the cannon balls glued into position with cyanoacylate. A toothpick to place a spot of adhesive into the hole in the shot garland was found to be the best way, using tweezers to place the ball itself.

The four large cleats were painted and positioned on the inside walls of the bulwarks.

One over-riding consideration that was not to be forgotten when fitting out the upper gun deck, and particularly when it came to the gun carriage assemblies, was that once the deck above had been fitted, access was largely denied.

Etched brass parts

The work from now on increasingly featured parts cut from the several sheets provided in the kit. Looking at the forthcoming tasks it was seen that basically the sheets were to be painted yellow ochre or black on one or both sides. I decided to

paint all parts in one go and, where necessary, touch in after assembly.

All sheets were carefully cleaned with cellulose thinners and then sprayed with an etching primer followed by a couple of coats of the appropriate colour enamel. All gun barrels were mounted on spigots pushed through a piece of board and similarly treated. I chose to spray or airbrush these items rather than brush paint because of the greater control on the amount of paint applied. Some of the etched brass parts are very fine

and by using a conventional brush, I could envisage finishing up with more paint than part.

Having got all the sheets nicely painted, it was not forgotten that paint would have to be scraped off again in those places where adhesive was to be used.

Removing the parts from the etched sheets was best done with a sharp craft knife, cutting down on to the smooth side of a piece of hardboard. Avoid the use of the self-healing cutting mat, the surface is too springy and could distort the parts as they are cut off. Depending upon the thickness of the material, the final trimming of holding tabs can frequently be better effected by using cuticle clippers. I keep a pair specifically for this task.

The upper gun deck 12 pounder long guns

Each gun assembly comprised 23 separate parts; some pre-cut wooden pieces, the barrels, some parts cut from etched brass sheets and some from wire. This was an indication that making the guns was not merely a one afternoon job, in fact, it was quite an extended task.

The carriage sides, axles, bed bolt, stool bed and quoin were assembled taking note of the correct position of the quoin relative to the carriage sides. Only the thirty carriages for the upper gun deck were assembled at this stage so as not to confuse them with others of a subtly different design. Strips of double-sided Sellotape were laid on a sheet of card and the carriage assemblies put in place for airbrush painting. These were coated with two coats of yellow ochre and when dry, the ends of the axles painted black before assembling the wheels, which were left in varnished natural wood. The line-up of finished guns is shown in **Fig.4.25**.

Again, bearing in mind the later inaccessibility to

Fig.4.26   *Ready for adding the quarterdeck.*

the upper gun deck, the carriages were firmly super-glued to the deck. A favourite method of enhancing the strength of this union was to gently pass the assembled carriages over a sheet of fine abrasive paper laid flat on the bench. This action has two beneficial results; it removes any rock from the seating of the carriage to the deck and, secondly, it provides four very small flats rather than point contacts for the wheels to be glued. However, before permanently fixing the carriages to the deck, the eyelets for the rigging were put in place on the inner sides of the bulwarks and into the deck 20mm behind the carriage positions. I found that due to the inaccessibility of the eyelet for the traversing tackle at the rear of the gun carriage, it was helpful to make up and attach the tackle before gluing the unit to the deck.

Whether to rig the guns or not is a matter of personal choice, but the kit does include sufficient blocks and thread for the task. However, the photograph in the manual depicting the finished tackle in place, shows rigging of a very doubtful style and one that I had not come across before. I completed my gun rigging using the traditional method, although only for those carriages that would be seen on the finished model.

Companionway handrails

There was nothing very difficult about setting these up, but it was important to adhere to the proper sequence of applying the handrails. There were three distinct items used in the supporting of the handrails - etched brass stanchions, support pillars and stair balusters. The use and application of the stanchions needed no comment but, in the case of the turned wooden pillars and

balusters, it was important to recognise that the bottom ends had 1mm diameter holes which were very convenient for fixing wire dowels. These parts also required shaping at each end, reducing a round section to a square one. In some cases it was noted that the handrails passed through the pillars, thus it was imperative that holes should be positioned and drilled before fixing in place.

The position of the supports on the hatch coamings was best taken from the skid beam assembly and the quarterdeck, both to be assembled during the next stage. At this juncture, the advice in the manual concerning the dry assembly of parts for positional checking prior to getting the glue out, was very pertinent and should not be ignored.

Completing the upper gun deck fitting

At this stage it was most helpful to ensure that the false quarterdeck could be readily dropped into place and was equally easy to remove. This was necessary so that the remaining items such as the support pillars, deck beams and smoke box, could be correctly positioned before permanently fixing the deck, **(Fig.4.26)**.

The steam trunk was assembled noting the correct attitude of the box sides as indicated on the drawings.

On Sheet 3 of the drawings, reference is made to item 711 just aft of the steam trunk. This is not a feature of the instruction manual but, in fact, represents the chimney from the galley passing upward to the underside of the forecastle deck. It is made from 8mm dowel and painted black.

The skid beam assembly was put together having squared out the slots in each of the beams. It was

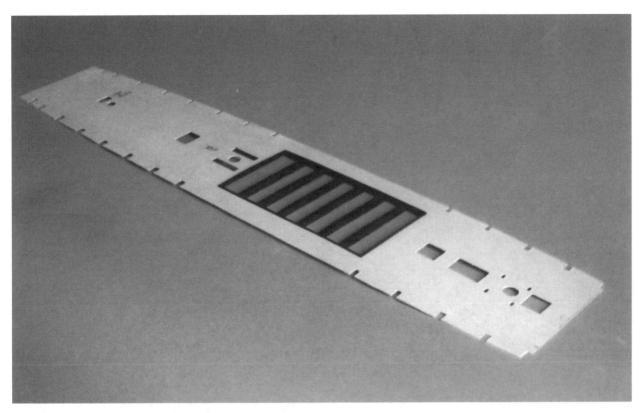

Fig.4.27   The skid beam assembly.

essential to ensure that all the beams sat down on their bottom flat surfaces after putting the sides in place, thus minor adjustments were required to the depths of slots. If, as suggested in the manual, the fit and removal of the false deck has been made easy with no tight spots, I found that the skid beam assembly could, in fact, be fitted before putting the deck in place, **(Fig.4.27)**. The remainder of the deck fittings, bitts, support pillars and the elm tree pump were all fabricated and dry fitted with 1mm brass wire pins to their relevant positions on deck. After a final dry run with the deck to check nothing fouled or needed further adjustment, the deck was permanently glued and pinned in place together with all fittings.

The beakhead bulkhead

Having cleaned up the piece, it was dry fitted in place and its height checked relative to the deck and edges of the forecastle bulwarks. It was then painted with a couple of coats of matt blue enamel and put to one side for later assembly. This deviation from the instruction manual sequence was done to permit better sanding of the forecastle deck and inner bulwark lining after planking.

Planking the quarterdeck

The quarterdeck screen assembly was made up and its position verified and marked before removing the relevant

Fig.4.28   Laying planks at the quarterdeck level.

Fig.4.29   The inner gun-port patterns in place.

bulkhead uprights. Some adjustment was required, particularly with regard to the height of the screen parts, to attain the correct fit. Planking strips were placed on the false deck to bring the screen to its correct height. The use of the false poop deck was also useful to check the final height of the various parts. The assembled screen was then put to one side until later.

Working from the centre outwards, all apertures for gratings and companionways were cut as the planks were laid, **(Fig.4.28)**. This was far easier than covering the holes completely before re-establishing the shapes of

the cutouts. The deck was then sanded, brushed off and varnished.

The inner gun-port patterns were then put in place ensuring that their bottom edges were tightly down on to the deck planking and that the gun-port openings were in correct alignment with those in the outer skins, **(Fig.4.29)**. A small amount of adjustment was required to fulfil these conditions, although nothing more than that could be done by sanding.

Apart from the last three gun-ports on the quarterdeck, all gun-ports were lined and painted red ochre on their inner faces. The inner surfaces of the

Fig.4.30   The fitted out foc'sle deck.

Fig.4.31   The fitted out quarterdeck.

bulwarks were given two or three coats of yellow ochre. It was important to do this at this stage to avoid an awkward painting job after fitting the bulwark capping.

Finishing off the second planking

The outer hull planking was completed up to the tops of the bulwarks in the manner described earlier; trimming the gun-ports as the covering proceeded. Great care was needed when rubbing down so as not to knock the gun barrels off the upper deck battery. The last three gun-ports were then lined leaving a 1mm deep recess from the surface of the hull.

The capping of the bulwarks completed the main hull construction. This was relatively straightforward but a little advance thinking made the task a lot easier. The vertical edges of the bulwarks at the rear of the forecastle deck and the front end of the quarterdeck were first faced. The inner and outer edges of the capping for the forecastle and quarterdeck were to be flush with the bulwark sides; I sanded the inner edges first to properly match the shape of the bulwarks and painted this edge black. When dry, the strip was glued and pinned to the bulwarks so that all overhang was on the outside of the hull and I had a nice straight, contrasting line between the black of the capping and the yellow of the inside of the bulwarks. The outer edge of the capping was then pared and sanded down to the hull side.

The capping at the waist of the vessel was aligned to the inner edge of the bulwarks at both ends then, having painted the inner edge earlier, the two strips were pinned and glued in place.

The previously painted, upper yellow band on the hull was now masked off to delineate its upper edge and the remainder of the second planking and the bulwark capping painted black.

Fitting-out the quarterdeck and forecastle

This part of the construction provided a pleasant change from the more robust procedures of building the hull proper. Each item was dealt with as a separate mini-project as the fitting-out process progressed. The fitted out forecastle deck is shown in **Fig.4.30** and the quarterdeck in **Fig.4.31**.

Consideration was first given to the forecastle gratings. The basic gratings were made up as described for the upper gun deck fitting above and were sized to fit the apertures in the deck. Placing the gratings into the deck and maintaining the required 1mm above deck level was a bit of a fiddle. An alternative method was to use scrap 5mm x 1mm strip to make ledges and stick them to the underside of the deck, leaving seatings 2mm wide on which to drop the gratings. The protruding gratings were then coamed and sanded.

The base for the galley chimney was put in place and the chimney casting fettled and cleaned. I found that opening up the chimney outlet, by drilling a hole 4mm diameter to a depth of about 5mm, enhanced the appearance of this item.

The forecastle breast beam and the quarterdeck barricade assemblies benefited from a bit of careful planning, the final results being seen in **Figs.4.32**. Bearing

Fig.4.33   *The quarterdeck barricade.*

Fig.4.34   *The beakhead area.*

in mind that these assemblies were to be painted black, to avoid getting paint on to the deck, the edges of the capping for the skid beam end pieces were painted before assembly as were the breast beam supports. The trickiest job was making the eight supports for the quarterdeck barricade. It was imperative that all were of an identical 6mm length and that the ends were flat and square. Failure to attain these conditions would provide a result that was both unsightly and weak at the joints.

The waist ladders and the remaining two companionways were made up as described earlier. For added strength, the corner balusters for the main companionway were both pinned and glued.

The kevels, pinrails and shot garlands were made up as instructed and painted black before assembly to the insides of the bulwarks. A secure fit of these joints was essential to take the strain of later rigging and each kevel and pinrail was fixed with two pins.

To complete the fitting out of the forecastle and quarterdeck, the ship's wheel and binnacle were assembled and fitted.

The quarterdeck and forecastle cannons

These were constructed in a similar manner to those for the upper gun deck, the main difference being the length of the barrels and the position of the quoins. All guns were rigged and, as before, the trail tackle was fixed to the rear of the carriages before anchoring the units down to the deck. I also found that it was easier

Fig.4.35   Hair brackets and rails with the four head timbers.

to make up the side tackles on the bench before attaching them to the carriages. This was purely a personal choice and the procedure adopted would largely depend upon the digital dexterity of the model maker.

Beakhead capping

Having put the pre-cut cat-tails in place, the two corner shot garlands could be prepared. Great care was required to remove them from the sheet since they were cut into solid walnut rather than ply. One "leg" was cross-grained and this coupled with the weakened section created by the holes, made them very vulnerable. All of these parts were painted before assembly.

The plank sheer was checked for length and glued in place. The timberheads and fiferails were dry fitted to verify their lengths and joints, then also glued in position. Temporary packing pieces were used between the plank sheer and the underside of the fiferails to maintain camber and correct spacing of the fiferails. The final assembly was painted black.

The roundhouses

The patterns were removed from the sheet and the tenons on their back edges cleaned up to provide a close fit into the slots in the beakhead bulkhead. It is imperative that each set of three patterns are perfectly aligned in the vertical plane so that the planking that follows sits properly across their edges.

The planking strips should have slightly bevelled edges, like barrel staves, to avoid a major filling operation after assembly and before final shaping. The top ends

were left over-length and finally trimmed before fitting the top pieces to each roundhouse. After finish sanding, each unit was painted blue.

The hole for the bowsprit was cleaned out and sized to accept a 12,7mm diameter dowel before planking the beakhead deck. In fact, I found it useful to leave a short piece of dowel in place while I planked the deck in order to attain a more accurate elliptical hole.

The beakhead pilasters, doors and gun-ports

The brass etched pilasters had been previously painted before removal from the sheet. The centre piece was now dry fitted to check position and flatness against the face of the beakhead bulkhead. When satisfied with the fit, paint was scraped away at salient points and the part glued in place. The same procedure was adopted for the two pilaster parts that fitted around the roundhouses. This operation needed quite a bit of care to ensure that after bending, the pilasters remained truly upright. All three parts required some adjustment at the bottom end of the pilasters to attain the correct height and to sit tightly down on to the deck.

The doors were hinged as outlined in the manual and, in my case, were assembled in the closed position. Experience has shown that if doors are left open, at some time in the future, exploratory fingers will investigate as to whether or not they will close - frequently with disastrous results.

The gun-port lids were fitted and touched in with yellow and blue paint to concluded this stage of the construction, (Fig.4.34).

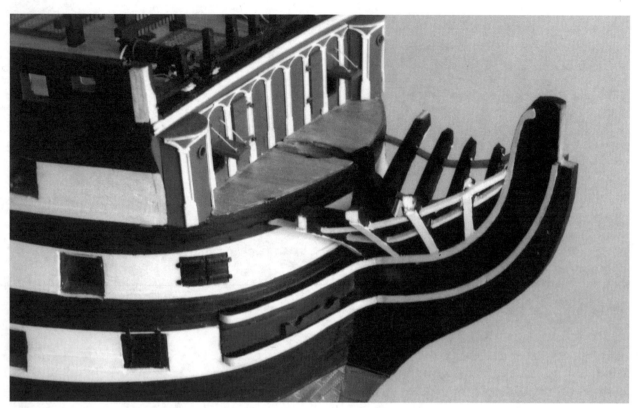

Fig.4.36   Head-rails in place.

The bows and head rails

On most models, this part of the construction is arguably the most challenging of all. While getting all the various shapes and sizes correct is demanding enough for the average modeller, reproducing each part in the opposite hand to achieve that essential balanced structure is really demanding. However, experience of previous kits from this stable had encouraged me to think that once again the task would be presented as simply as possible. Unfortunately, I was a little disappointed. The drawings lacked part identification numbers and cross-referencing to the manual, and the manual assumed that all model makers would have knowledge of the nautical terms involved. On the bright side, once all the delving back and forth between drawings, manual and parts list had been done, all relevant parts had been accurately pre-cut and required only to be properly cleaned up and painted before assembly.

One thing that I found to be most helpful was to look also at the following stage, "The Bow Gratings". The two parts to the beakhead platform were particularly useful in assessing angles and chamfers of the head timbers. It was most important to ensure that all tapers, angles and chamfers were done before permanently assembling *any* of the parts.

The hair brackets (the upper ones) and the lower bow cheek rails all had sufficient width to permit shaping on their rear edges to attain an accurate fit against the hull. Unfortunately, no mention was made anywhere of the lining that should fit against the hull between the upper and lower rails. This was a reinforcement of the

hull planking thickness at that point to add strength around the hawseholes for which I used three 4x1mm strips.

The hair bracket and rails were all painted as required before assembly. The hawse bolsters were then fitted and the hawseholes drilled. A final touching in coat of paint was applied before moving on to the next stage, (**Fig.4.35**).

The four head timbers were removed from the sheet and cleaned up ready for painting the faces and top edges black. The side edges were left unpainted at this stage. The bottom edges were angled to fit tightly down against the top edge of the upper bow curved rails and the bottom and sides of the slots to take the head rails. The timbers were then dry fitted to the stem and the bow main rails (394), offered up to assess the degree of chamfering required to the side edges of the timbers. The bow, main rail timberhead (395) was glued in place onto the side of the inner timberhead (125) and chamfered together with the edges of the head timbers. The two beakhead platforms (321 and 322) were most helpful in assessing the position and degree of chamfering required. The thin forward ends of the bow main rails were cut and angled to fit against the upper bow curved rail.

Attention was then given to the slots for the head rails. These were provided undersize in order to be able to angle the sides and bottom to suit the curve of the rails. The bulk of this work was done on the bench finalising the fit of the rails after assembly to the stem. Having attained the desired seating and fits for these

Fig.4.37   Temporarily fitted knightheads and boomkins.

parts, the head timbers were permanently glued in place maintaining squareness and alignment. The bow main rails were then painted and put to one side until later.

The head rails, made from 2mm square flexible beech proved to be the most difficult part of the project, the problem being that there are compound angles to be cut at each end of the rails and, at the same time attaining the correct length around the curve. I first established the fore end angle then, after a number of dry fittings and trimming, got the other end correct where it sits against the hull. I had to make six to get the four pieces but fortunately there was ample beech in the kit to cater for this potentially difficult task, **(Fig.4.36)**.

The beakhead platforms were then put in place together with the stools, or "seats of ease". The handrails were reasonably described in the manual but do not appear anywhere on the drawings. The back-end fixing can just be made out in Photo 032 but nothing to indicate the correct position to the fore end. This was assessed on the basis that the handrail should run parallel to the edge just above the profiled area of the bow main rail (394) and approximately 2mm above it, **(Fig.4.37)**.

The figurehead and bow decoration

The castings for the 5 pieces that comprised the bow decoration were crisp and well detailed and the first task was to paint them. I chose to apply grey primer to seal and prepare the surface for the colour coats. This was very lightly sprayed to avoid clogging up the cast detail of the parts. The colour was applied using well-mixed Humbrol enamels.

On the subject of mixing, a cocktail stick swirled about in the tin for a few seconds is totally inadequate if you want a nice, dense and opaque colour job. I use a Badger electric paint mixer, which is absolutely ideal, especially for the heavily pigmented black and metallic paints.

The only colour guidance provided is provided by photographs in the manual. Unfortunately, the lighting used appears to have highlighted some of the gilded areas and changed the gold to white. Some parts are supposed to be white, so a little care is needed not to get confused.

The slot across the edge of the stem locates the figurehead in its correct position. The upper end of the bow curved rail (lower) should be trimmed and angled to suit the lower end of the blue sash bearing the inscription "Dieu et Mon Droit." Two-part epoxy was used to fix the figurehead in place and, when set, the port and starboard scrollwork was added. These, in turn, established the positions for the seraphim and cherubim respectively. Needless to say, all these parts were painted before assembly, **Fig.4.37**.

The knightheads and boomkins

The manual gave explicit instructions as to how the boomkins and knightheads came together and the drawings showed all dimensions for tapering the boomkins.

Again, there were left and right handed assemblies to consider and the first task was to make the knightheads and fit brass wire dowels to reinforce the

Fig.4.38   *The catheads.*

joint at deck level. These were then dry fitted in place in order to assess the correct angle for the boomkins. When satisfied with all positions and angles, they were cyanoacrylate glued to the outside face of the knightheads at the correct height. When the joint had thoroughly gone off, I drilled a hole 0,7mm diameter through the joint and pushed in a brass dowel. These two vulnerable assemblies were then put to one side for later fitting. Temporary fitting is seen in **Fig.4.37**.

The catheads

The main body of each cathead was made by laminating seven strips of timber together with three intermediate pieces being shorter in length to form the sheaves in the outer end. The dimensions given in the manual established the basic vertical plane angle. The knee (129) was next used to mark the horizontal plane angle so that the butt end of the cathead could be compounded. The knee was then glued in place and its rear edge sanded to match the compound angle on the cathead. The support bracket (130) does not match the compounded face since the hull is shaped at this position.

Making the first cathead was not too difficult, but the second one needs a degree of concentration and care in order to match the first with regard to size and angles, but to the opposite hand, **(Fig.4.38)**.

Having completed both assemblies by adding the cleats, they were painted before fixing in place on the side of the hull and the pre-painted crown casting put in place.

An eyebolt should be positioned in the under-face of each cathead just inboard of the sheaves to take the standing end of the cat falls.

Finally the brass profile was cut and bent to run from the bottom of the support bracket round to the end of the upper head rail each side of the hull. The actual bending process was enhanced by the application of heat, and a section of old broom handle around which to shape the brass. I had been warned not to overheat the brass since the sectional pattern of which could thus disintegrate.

Fig.4.39   *The fitted out poop deck.*

Fig.4.40   Stern fascia parts preparation.

The shaped pieces were then cleaned and painted yellow with a blue central stripe before assembly.

The marines' walk and the supporting pillars were added to complete the assembly of the front end of the hull.

The poop deck

Bearing in mind that this deck is enclosed on three sides, it is worth considering removing the upright stubs from the bulkheads first and planking the deck before assembly. This certainly made the finishing of the deck simpler.

The inner lining and planking to the bulwarks were added, remembering to paint the planking yellow before cutting and fitting in order to get a clean line of demarcation between deck and bulwarks. The plank sheer was painted on its edges before gluing in place; the upper face was left unpainted to better facilitate the glued joints when assembling the barricade assembly later. The edges were painted purely to attain a nice clean line between the sheer and the deck.

Note that the pre-cut bulwark capping strips come down to deck level at the fore end, **(Fig.4.39)**.

The flag lockers

If anyone needed confirmation of the accuracy of the pre-cut parts in this kit, the pieces for the flag locker assemblies provided it. Each locker comprised sixteen parts, which all fitted together as instructed without any need for trimming, adjustment or other tweaking. Very impressive. See **Fig.4.39**.

The skylight

Do read the seven lines of instruction in the manual before using the glue pot. As before, I used polyurethane varnish to stick the glazing material in place.

The fifty-two window frames were all painted brown before removing them from the sheet of etched brass parts. The skylight can be seen in **Fig.4.39**.

I keep two pairs of small cuticle clippers in my tool kit; one for the close trimming of rigging knots and the other for cutting small brass parts from the sheet. I have found over the years that, in most instances, it is possible to cut sufficiently close so as to avoid any subsequent filing.

The poop deck barricade assembly

I chose to make this assembly before the poop deck ladders and extensions because of the vulnerability of their inner handrails.

The barricade assembly was a simple enough structure at first sight but, in fact, making the rail supports needed quite a lot of patience. They had to stand upright on the cambered plank sheer which meant that the angles, top and bottom, had to be different for each support while still retaining the correct 5mm height. For added strength, a brass pin was used at the joint between the plank sheer and each support, the upper rail being used to mark the correct position for the holes. See **Fig.4.39**.

The rail itself was pre-bent before gluing to the tops of the supports. The bucket pegs were fixed in position before painting the whole assembly black.

The brass buckets needed to be drilled to take the thread handles. The hole position was centre-popped near to the top of the bucket and drilled 0,5mm diameter, drilling through both sides of the piece. A length of 0,1mm thread was threaded with all the buckets, the thread being raised by a piece of 2mm dowel across the top of each bucket in turn. The thread was then pulled down tightly onto the dowel and cyanoacrylate applied to the holes each side, the removal of the dowel leaving all handles the same size. All 21 buckets were prepared in this manner and left on the thread ready to be spun and sprayed with black paint before trimming each bucket from the thread. The buckets were not put in place at this stage.

The poop ladder assembly

The manual was followed meticulously for this stage of the construction, remembering to drill the balusters

Fig.4.41   Main mast channels.

to take the brass eyelets before gluing them in position. The inner, shaped, handrails were made "off" the model as suggested using cyanoacrylate to stick the scarfed pieces together. The rails were then stained and, when dry coated with cyanoacrylate to strengthen the assembled parts. They were left over-length for final fitting between the balusters.

The stern fascia and quarter galleries

The corners of the window apertures in the outer fascia were cleaned out using a scalpel, to get a really sharp corner, rather than a file as suggested in the manual. The sills and the areas around the windows were then painted yellow and, when dry, masked off to paint the black vertical panels between the frames, (Fig.4.40).

The glazing was put in place on the surface of the inner fascia and the outer skin glued in place. Clamps were used to bind the two skins tightly together. The outer edges were then trued up and faced on top and sides. Having trimmed all round, the black areas were painted.

The etched brass window frames were cut one by one from the sheet and gently pushed into place in their respective apertures. I found a piece of 5mm square strip about 80mm long and cut one end flat and square to act as a pusher. The accuracy of fit was such that glue was not necessary for fixing the frames into the stern fascia although the depth of the seating recesses, in the quarter gallery skins, prompted a touch cyanoacrylate. Each frame was located onto the bottom sill of the aperture and gently pushed in with the pad of the index finger. The end of the pusher was then used

to seat the frame down against the glazing material.

In order not to spread adhesive except where necessary when fixing etched brass decoration in place, the various pieces were trimmed and hung on pins. When I was satisfied with their position, the parts were easily removed, the adhesive applied and the pieces replaced on the pins to be dropped back into their correct place. All items were, of course, painted before assembly.

An easy way to produce the black line in the upper and lower grooves on the baluster rails was to use an Edding draughtsman's pen. This gave a very clearly defined line, far better than any attempt that I might have made with a paintbrush.

Castings were offered up, any adjustments to seating faces carried out, painted and put in place. It was known at the time the kit was produced that the Prince of Wales feathers were not correct for the Trafalgar date, but were salvaged from H.M.S. "Prince" and fitted much later. However, when ongoing research can define what was there in 1805, JoTiKa will provide all registered customers with the relevant new casting.

Probably the most taxing task in this section of the build was the fitting of the No.1 brass profile. The angular ends at specific lengths on a curved piece of brass called for a lot of patience and dry fitting to ensure everything was right before committing to the glue. I think that the best tip I can pass on is that unless you have particularly good lighting and sharp eyes, it is a job best done in daylight. It also helps to prime and paint the brass strip before fitting and touch in any marks and scratches afterwards.

The four lanterns, including the Admiral's lantern,

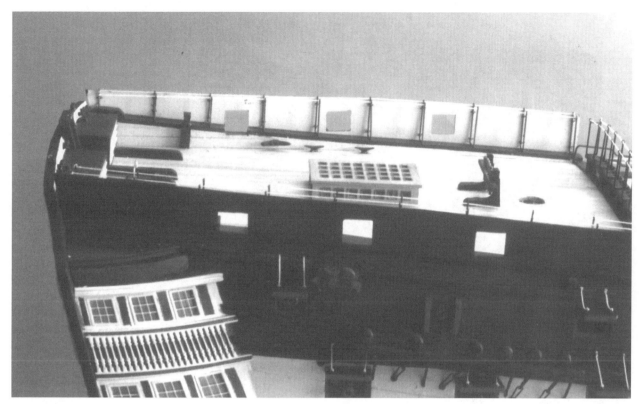

Fig.4.42   Mizzen channels.

were assembled at this time although not fitted in place on the model. Following the detailed instruction for this stage of the proceedings produced excellent results.

The side entry port and steps

The cast parts for the entry ports were cleaned up and painted before assembly. The central coat of arms was located above the entry; this, in turn located the top canopy and thence the sides.

Vertical alignment was the most important thing to watch when adding the steps. I found that a length of 2mm square strip lightly pinned to the side of the hull provided an ideal guide against which steps with common alignment could be pushed. There were ten different lengths of step each side of the hull which, unfortunately, were not numbered on the drawings. However, it was found that the numbering started at the top (181) and followed in sequence to (190) at the bottom.

The steps were painted after fixing with the colour of the hull surface upon which they were fixed.

Brass rails

I had, in fact progressed to making the channels when I realised that there was some considerable advantage to putting the brass rails on first. Feeding the brass pieces under the channels and through their support brackets was always going to be a fiddly job and an even worse one after the chain plates had been assembled. Cutting and filing short lengths adjacent to the fenders and chesstrees would also be awkward.

Rails were primed and painted with one coat of the appropriate colour for their full length before cutting and fitting, the second coat being applied after assembly - another good reason for fixing the rails before the channels and chain plates.

It was also easier to cut the brass rail with a saw rather than crop it with side cutters. The resulting pinched ends from side cutters are difficult to file square afterwards and the saw provides a better control on the lengths being cut.

It was important to check the position of the chain plate fixings when fitting the brass rails to avoid any interference, although there is one link under the mizzen channel that has a specific fixing through the brass rail.

I also found it very easy to put the brass strips on upside down, particularly when using artificial light. Profiles 2 and 3 are especially easy to overlook the correct attitude.

Fenders and chesstrees

Wales and capping strips were slotted to accept the fenders and chesstrees and slots cut to fit over the brass rails. One point not mentioned in the manual is that the chesstrees needed to be drilled with a hole to take later rigging. I chose to drill a hole 1mm diameter, 7mm down from the top edge. I also chose to fit the bower and sheet anchor palm blocks at this stage. Parts were painted after assembly.

Channels

The manual gives timely warning about getting the channels the right way round so that the deadeyes are in their correct position - a warning that is ignored at your peril.

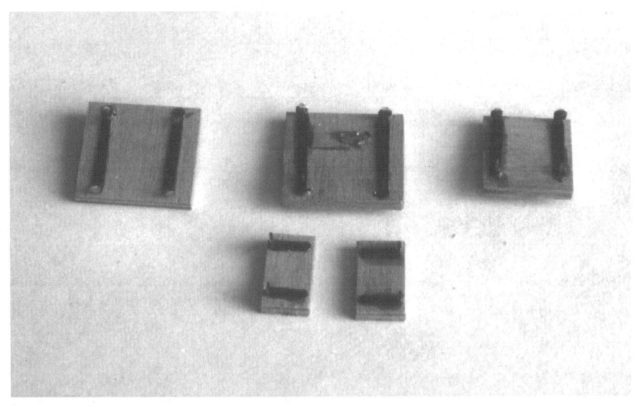

Fig.4.43   *Gun-port lids.*

The curve on the back edge of each channel needed little adjustment to seat tightly against the side of the hull and, having done any tweaking required, two pins were inserted into the back edge of each channel. The hull was drilled to accept the pins and the channels dry fitted, again checking that they were the right way round before removing to fit the deadeyes and strops. A drop of thick grade cyanoacrylate was put into each slot before assembling the strops. This was definitely a belt and braces technique; the strop design is such that they will not pull out under the strain of rigging the shrouds. However, if you have ever had the experience of "pull out" and its consequences, you will understand

the desire to take that extra precaution.

Deadeyes were rotated at this stage so that the holes were in their correct orientation for rigging the lanyards.

With the deadeyes in place and the slots capped along the front edge of the channels, the assemblies were again dry-fitted to fit the support brackets (626). Mention of these had been omitted from both manual and drawings. They were glued only to the underside of the channels before removing each assembly from the hull for painting.

Copper eyelets were added to the upper surface of the channels before permanently fixing the

Fig.4.44   *The rudder.*

Fig.4.45   The rudder assembly.

complete sub-assemblies to the hull.

The chain plates

The etched brass chain plate assemblies were numbered sequentially from the fore end of the fore channel to the aft end of the mizzen channel, each being unique to its numbered position. *Each assembly was cut from the sheet, as it was required to avoid mixing them up.*

The design of links was excellent with no wire parts to bend or shape. All parts were painted on the sheet and touched in after assembly.

I found that a relatively easy way to fit the chain plates was to first slip together the two (or three) parts together and pass the open top link through the loop in the bottom of the deadeye strop. A scriber was then located in the hole of the bottom link (or the upper hole of the bottom link on a three-part assembly) and, keeping the assembly taut, the position of the securing pinhole was marked on to the hull with the point of the scriber. The hole was then drilled to be a light press fit for the pin. The pin was passed through the hole in the bottom link and entered into the drilled hole, dabbed with a touch of cyanoacrylate and gently pushed home. On a three-part assembly, the bottom link was then rotated for correct alignment and its lower hole pinned in the same manner. The top link was then closed and the joint glued.

After fixing the first two or three assemblies, the sequence of fitting felt comfortable and no difficulties were encountered. The main and mizzen mast channels and chain-plates are shown in **Figs. 4.41** and **4.42** respectively.

Dummy gun barrels

The fitting of the dummy gun barrels was quite straightforward and my only thought was that it was more convenient to do them before adding the gun-port lids, but that was a personal choice and might not suit everybody's way of working.

The gun-port lid assemblies

There was nothing fundamentally difficult in making up the lids, but the sheer number of them demanded a routine to counteract the monotony. There were at total of 78 top-hinged lids, 32 of them comprised nine parts, each of the remainder having seven pieces. The various types and sizes are shown in **Fig.4.43**.

I worked on one side of one deck at a time. I trimmed and sanded the basic wooden parts, trimmed and glued the hinges in place, drilled holes for the eyebolts then fitted all the upper eyes first. At this stage it was wise to remember that the bent portion of the hinge be set back from the rear edge of the lids by a *minimum* of 1mm. Failure to do this could result in the hinges preventing the correct mating of the glued rear edge of the lid with the front edge of the top sill. I then fitted the lower eyes and, in the case of the lower deck lids made and assembled the scuttles and their hinges. After all lids had been made, the undersides and three exposed outer edges were painted red, then the tops black.

Bearing in mind the vulnerability of the port lids on the side of the hull it was worth considering putting at least one pin into the rear edge joint for added strength.

The lid rigging was then added together with the

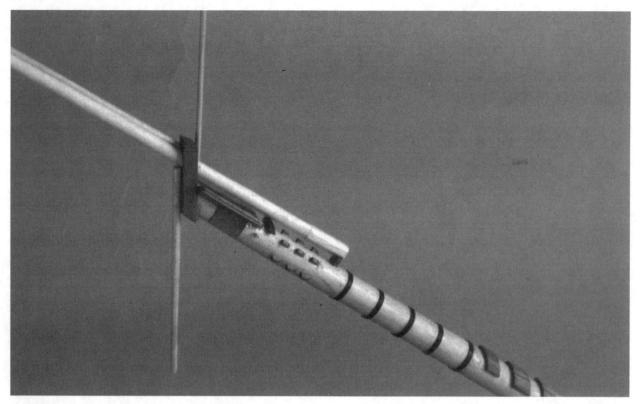

Fig.4.46   The bowsprit, ready for painting.

rigols. Which was done first? I chose to do the rigols before the rigging, but again, that was my personal choice.

The rigging of the lids was a rather tedious job, but there were one or two dodges, which helped speed up the process. First I made a drilling template using a piece of 0,5mm thick Plasticard. This was 10mm wide with two holes set 6mm up from one edge and spaced to match the distance between the lid hinges. I laid the template on top of the lids and drilled through the holes into the hull thereby keeping all the holes reasonably in line. Secondly, I drilled the holes 0,8mm diameter rather than the 0,5mm recommended, but tied a small knot near the end of the thread used for rigging. The larger hole made it easier to locate the end of the thread and the knot was a neat push fit with the aid of a scriber. The result was a sound mechanical as well as glued joint.

The rudder

Before plating the rudder, the internal upper corners of the hinge apertures were cleaned out sharp so that the pintles, (the parts with the pin), could seat snugly into the corners, **(Fig.4.44)**.

The assembly of the rudder to the stern post was also made much simpler by deciding that it would not actually swing on its hinges. This permitted the whole hinge assemblies, (pintles and gudgeons), to be fixed in place at the same time, thus allowing far greater accuracy when spacing out the holes for fitting to the stern post, **(Fig.4.45)**.

I chose not to make the rudder move on the basis that if known to move, there will be fingers that will move it with the consequence of potential breakage.

The waist deck stanchions and hammock cranes

There is little to say about this stage of the hull fitting except that it is imperative to properly read the instruction manual; apart from the spacing of the relevant parts, the identification of the various styles of etched brass pieces is basically descriptive text rather than drawn detail.

All the hammock cranes were rigged with 0,1mm natural thread and I recommend that the thread be fixed only at each closed hammock crane, leaving the intermediate cranes free of adhesive. My reason for this lies in the vulnerability of the cranes to being bent out of alignment during the later, rigging operations. If the thread is glued at each crane and one gets knocked, the whole line goes astray and it is almost impossible to get the thread properly taut again.

Having read a little further into the instruction manual, I had realised one or two potential problem areas concerning the fitting of the poop deck bulwark barricade. The barricade itself is fitted to the outside arms of the hammock cranes and it was seen to be important that the position of the hammock cranes needed to be accurately established but only permanently fitted in conjunction with the barricade itself.

There were three unused gun-ports in the barricade, the aftermost one each side being partly in the barricade and partly cut down into the bulwarks. I decided to determine the position for this port and cut into the bulwarks before fitting the hammock cranes. I assumed that the inside surfaces of the cutaway portion would be painted red, as were all other ports.

Making the barricade was probably the final serious challenge of the hull construction, the problem being the thickness of the material to be used. I understand that the full size thickness was 1.5 inches thus requiring a scale thickness of 0,5mm. The manual required five strips of 0,5 x 4mm material to be glued together edgewise. Unfortunately, the quality of the edges of the strips provided was not good enough to effectively perform this operation and one edge of each strip had to be re-qualified with a scalpel to obtain an adequate gluing surface. In consequence, six strips were required to attain the 20mm total width needed.

The are alternative procedures of course and the choice is largely dependant upon your craftsmanship or dedication to scale. 1mm thick material can be used which, if left at that basic thickness, will simulate a barricade 3in. thick (and stimulate a great sucking in of breath from the purists). The 1mm can be reduced by half by careful sanding or, you can choose an alternative material, the latter probably not being wood, bringing forth a further sharp intake of breath from the super critical.

Whatever process is adopted, one further recommendation would be to establish the top edge of the barricade first, then cut in the gun-ports before producing the bottom edge. Following that procedure safeguards the integrity of the very thin bottom edge of the middle gun-port. The barricades were clipped against the hammock cranes while black thread was used to tie them to the cranes. Passing a length of thread around the crane upright, then through holes either side of that upright effected each tie. The thread was super glued and trimmed flush with the outer surface of the barricade.

One final point about the barricades; according to research reported in the manual, although the six carronades formerly on the poop deck were removed prior to Trafalgar during the 1803 re-fit, the barricades remained.

Anchors

The four identical anchors were assembled from the various wooden and cast parts provided and painted black all over. After an adequate number of coats had thoroughly dried, the rings were added and puddened. The bower and sheet anchor palm blocks had been added at an earlier stage.

The anchors were put to one side for later rigging and the model, as constructed that far, was put to one side while the masts and spars were fabricated.

The bowsprit

The tapering of the bowsprit and the jibbooms was carried out in the manner described in the manual, shaping first from round to square, then octagonal and so on, until finally sanding smooth. As with most dowel rod, a David plane could be used for three sides of the square section but not the fourth due to the way the grain ran. A Perma-Grit file was found to be a suitable alternative to the plane in these areas.

The tapering was done first before tackling the assembly of the bowsprit cap. The cap is provided plain, without holes and needed careful marking out to attain the correct orientation and offset. Once assembled the upper and lower edges of the cap were angled to follow the line of the bowsprit.

A flat was filed on to the top of the bowsprit on which to seat the bowsprit bee flat.

It was essential to get the bee flat the right way round, the forward, staggered, cut-out being to starboard and its front edge being chamfered to sit snugly against the rear face of the cap. Before gluing in place, flats should be cut onto the port and starboard sides of the bowsprit to seat the sheaves 417 and 418, both locating centrally under the cutest in the edges of the bee flat. This should bring the angled front edge of the starboard sheave tight up against the rear face of the cap.

The three rows of cleats at the fore end of the bowsprit were simplified in their application by positioning five strips of 1,5mm square sectioned timber, each strip long enough to cover the entire length of three cleats. The gaps were then cut between the cleats after the glue had dried and the back of each cleat chamfered. By adopting this procedure I avoided the difficulty of trying to keep short pieces of material in their correct position and alignment.

The position of the gammoning saddles was taken directly from the model rather than from the drawing. The bowsprit was put in place and a vertical line taken from the slots in the prow upwards to the bowsprit. One long length of 1,5mm square timber was laid centrally on top of the bowsprit to cover the total length of the three saddles. Shorter lengths were then added in a staggered manner to form the three separate pads, the ends of these being trimmed to final shape after the glue had set.

The cartridge paper simulated bands were put in place, copper eyelets added and the whole assembly given a coat of sealer prior to painting, (**Fig.4.46**).

When the paint job had been completed, the various blocks and deadeyes were tied on and the bowsprit put to one side.

The foremast

Before doing any practical work on this stage, it is wise to read the *whole* of the instructions including those for the fore topmast, the fore topgallant mast and the painting. There was considerable overlap in the procedures to be adopted and it was seen that doing something out of sequence could prove disastrous. Having said that, the fabrication and assembly of the lower foremast proved quite straightforward apart from the

Fig.4.47   *The fore top assembly.*

boarding pikes, which were left until after the mast had been painted.

The making of the topmast and the topgallant mast can be quite a challenge for those modellers who do not have access to a lathe. Reducing tapers that suddenly swell out to larger sizes are not easy to produce, particularly if there is a combination of round, square and octagonal sections involved. A way round the problem is to make each section as a separate part and dowel them all together with 1,5mm brass wire. True, you have to keep all your ends square and all your holes straight and in line, but the process does work. Glue all the doweled joints with cyanoacrylate and no weakness results.

The 6mm dowel required to make the topgallant mast with its 4mm square butt end and hounds meant that the fore topmast cap (88) could not be assembled from *either* end of the mast, the hole in the cap being only 4mm diameter. If the mast had been made as outlined in the manual, the only option would be to *split the cap from front to rear* then re-assemble it on either side of the mast, similar to the procedure for the mizzen mast

where the cap had been pre-cut in two pieces. If the mast had been fabricated in its various pieces as outlined in the above paragraph, then it would have to be assembled to the mast prior to doweling on the butt end.

Having made the fore top, I decided that it would be far easier to fit all the eyebolts prior to assembly with the masts. Eyebolts were added to the masts after assembly and prior to painting as were the futtock strops and deadeyes, ensuring that the holes in the latter were in their correct attitude before using just a spot of cyanoacrylate to hold the strops in place. The fore top and the fore topgallant assemblies are shown in **Figs. 4.47** and **4.48** respectively.

The mainmast

The fabrication of the mainmast followed the same procedures as for the foremast; again the main topmast cap (89) required to be split to facilitate assembly. Similarly the boarding pikes were not put in place until after painting. A hole, 0,7mm diameter, central in the back edge of the main top, was drilled ready to take the Admiral's lantern.

The mizzen mast

Again, the making of the mizzen followed a similar pattern to that for the two previous masts. However, with smaller diameters involved, more care was needed and the fitting of the topgallant mast required greater precision to attain the proper alignment and attitude.

Stepping the masts 1

The various mast sleeves were identified and checked for fit and the small cleats put in place at the foot of the main and fore masts. The masts were dropped into their respective holes and the rake and alignment checked. They were not permanently glued at this stage and put to one side until all rigging blocks had been added.

This was also a good time to look ahead and note where eyebolts were to be fitted on the deck. Some of them are quite close to the mast positions and it was seen that fitting the eyebolts before stepping the masts would be to advantage. Plan sheet 18 shows the relevant placements.

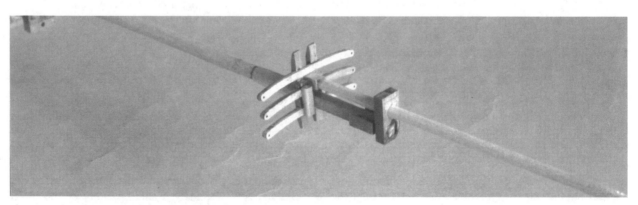

Fig.4.48   *The fore topgallant top assembly.*

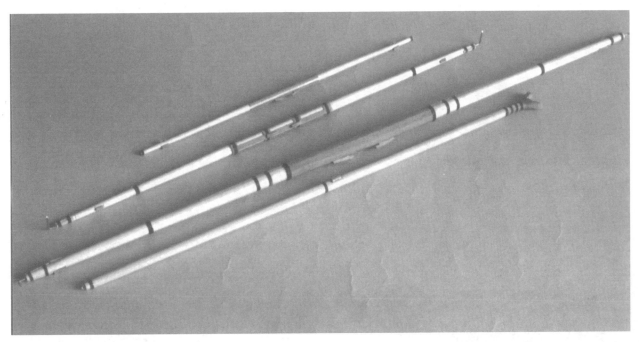

Fig.4.49 **Yards and spars ready for painting.**

The yards and spars

A considerable amount of careful handwork would be involved in the absence of a lathe. Dowel was required to be reduced on diameter as well as being tapered and a degree of skill keeping everything straight and true was necessary. If tapering is done by use of plane, file and sanding, it is a good idea to cut the overall length of dowel about 10mm longer than finished size. This allows for the inevitable few millimetres of increased taper, induced by hand sanding at the small end of the tapers, to be cut off at the end of the tapering process.

Cleats were made from 1,5mm square strip. A lot of fiddly work was saved by cutting slightly over-length pieces and gluing them onto small flats filed on the surface of the yard or spar. Final shaping was done *in situ* after the glue had thoroughly set.

The sling cleats were, for the most part, provided as pre-cut parts, which was a nice touch since, although simple in shape they can be demanding to fabricate.

The lower and topmast yards were all fitted with stuns'l booms. Part of the "ironwork" were the stuns'l boom straps that fitted over the end of the yards and through which passed the ring supports. These etched brass straps were centre-popped before fitting to facilitate drilling down the end of the yards after the straps had been glued in place to take the 1mm brass wire used for the supports. A selection of unpainted yards and spars can be seen in **Fig.4.49**.

The stirrups for the footropes were made and fitted

Fig.4.51 **The finished boats.**

Fig.4.52   *Position of shroud ties.*

were marked with the part number before removal. In fact, I numbered each of them twice, once to port and once to starboard, in case the vulnerable area around the slot separated the part into two pieces and it was necessary to match up the correct bits.

Obviously, it was important to get the bulkheads in the right order and equally essential to get them all lined up. I put the first and the last bulkheads on first and glued them squarely in place. This provided a good eyeballing line for the rest. The assembled framework was left overnight to thoroughly set before attempting the planking.

One of the problems encountered with the first layer of planking was the fact that the edges of the ply bulkheads seemed to soak up the cyanoacrylate too quickly thus robbing the joint of adhesive. I found that the solution was to soak the planks in water first, taper to size, then apply the cyanoacylate. Wet planks equalled instant grab of course, and it was easy to stick fingers to boat since the adhesive quickly soaked through the plank thickness. However, with practice, I realised that fairly accurate tapering, plus pulling the plank through the fingers to induce the bend, kept the handling time and the risk to a minimum. The second planking was more straightforward, having total area contact for gluing. This was started about a third of a plank width above the top edge of the bulkheads so that the joints with the first planking were not coincident.

After completing the second planking the shell was well brushed with diluted PVA inside and out before fitting the floor, the ribs and the rising plank (or riser).

using 0,75mm wire. The spritsail yard has three per side, although these were not shown on the drawings in earlier kits.

All yards were painted matt black before fitting the stuns'l booms, which were left natural.

The ships boats

I decided to make the boats at this stage mainly because their position on the skid beams is a little bit critical, both to their relationship with each other and to the positioning of some of the rigging. So, although they would not be permanently positioned at this juncture, I did want to fix the boat cradles, which would have been more difficult after the rigging had been completed.

These four small craft probably presented the greatest challenge of the entire project and, unless you are used to very late nights, I think that the two weeks of evenings mentioned in the manual is a bit optimistic.

It was absolutely essential to study the manual and the drawings contained therein in their entirety before making a start.

The slots in the keel and bulkheads needed some easing to attain a comfortable fit and, as far as possible, this was done before removing them from the sheet, using a scrap of material to validate the fit. All bulkheads

Fig.4.53   *Futtock shrouds and ratlines.*

The interior and exterior surfaces were then painted with several coats of the appropriate colour before fitting the thwarts and doing any fitting out desired. In order not to cover up too much of the interior detail, in most cases I only fitted a token number of oars, (Fig.4.51).

Mast and yard blocks

Using the appropriate drawings, all blocks and eyelets were tied on to masts and yards. Note that the thread size for the brace pendants has to be found in the manual rather than on the drawings.

The rails on the rear edges of the tops were assembled after fitting blocks, as was the small Admiral's lantern centrally on the rear of the main top.

The tackle pendants

Bearing in mind that these hang down under their own weight, this was something not easy to simulate on the model and so I felt that a better attempt could be made if they were put on before stepping the masts. Once seized to the masthead, they were coated with dilute PVA and clamped against the sides of the masts until dry.

Stepping the masts 2

Only the masts were stepped at this stage, the bowsprit being left until later in order to reduce the risk of damage when turning the model during the rigging of the shrouds and ratlines.

The standing rigging

It was worth looking forward on the drawings and in the manual to identify and fit any further eyelets and blocks that could be fitted before actually starting the rigging.

It was also required that the deadeyes for the shrouds be painted black. That job was something of a nuisance and the easiest way I found was to pin the 5mm and 7mm pieces to a board and spray one side. When dry, the heads of the pins were removed, the deadeyes removed and turned over ready for spraying the opposite side. The smaller sizes were dealt with a black marker pen after seizing to their respective shrouds but before rigging the lanyards.

Before getting hands and fingers in amongst the masts and spars to do the rigging I have always found it wise to remove my wristwatch and rings, and roll my sleeves up. Getting your watchstrap accidentally caught in the rigging can cause horrendous damage to the nearly completed model!

The shrouds

The sequence of fitting the shrouds to each mast was clearly shown on the drawings and a workable process of applying the deadeyes described in the manual. Again, to avoid unnecessary turning of the model, I chose to rig the first pair of shrouds to the starboard side of each of the masts, before turning to repeat similar pairs to port.

I adopted this basic procedure throughout the

rigging of both the lower and upper shrouds, thus making only about a third of the turns of the model I might otherwise have made.

A further point worth remembering when tying each pair of shrouds together at the masthead is to correctly position the tie. In order to attain the correct convergence of the shrouds, each tie should each be positioned above and aft of the previously tied pair, rather than in a vertical straight line up the face of the masthead. This positioning is illustrated in **Fig.4.52**.

The lanyards were prepared by positioning a knot at one end as a stopper and applying a smear of cyanoacrylate for about 8mm at the other to provide a sort of built-in bodkin to assist in threading through the deadeyes. It was helpful not to stiffen any more than an 8mm length or the end would interfere with the side of the hull when threading the lower deadeyes.

The futtock staves

Cut over-length from 1mm brass wire, these were initially positioned using small "crocodile" clips, one on the foremost shroud and one on the swifter. The position was determined by cutting a gauging strip from a piece of scrap to the distance from the main top to the mast cap. This was then used below the top down to the stave. The main mast was done first, reducing the length of the strip for the foremast, then the mizzen. Four pieces of 0,25mm thread were cut, two to tie intermediate shrouds and the other two for the end shrouds. These were then sealed with dilute PVA and trimmed when dry. The remaining shrouds were then tied. This avoided getting the ends of the ties all mixed up and pulling things out of line.

Catharpins

The main problem found when putting on the catharpins was attaining equal tension in each. Probably, the simplest way is to permanently fix the starboard (or port) side first and do all adjustments to tension on the opposite side.

Futtock shrouds

The small, etched brass hooks were seized to the ends of the shrouds and a check made to ensure that the holding tabs had been cleanly removed. Similarly, the holes in the deadeye strops previously assembled to the tops were checked to be clear.

Having put the hooks in place, the shrouds were pulled down behind the futtock staves below and their ends seized to the lower shrouds to about 4mm below the stave. Equal tension in each set of shrouds should be attained before sealing the seizings with dilute PVA.

The topmast and topgallant shrouds

These were set up in the same way as the lower mast shrouds and presented no difficulties.

For each topmast and topgallant mast, there was a 3mm single block to be fitted between the first two

Fig.4.54   *Mouse and eye with snaking on main stay.*

shrouds just below the relevant tops, both to port and starboard. I found that by stropping the two shrouds together at a position above where the block was to be rigged, the block could then be slid up into place and held by the tension between the shrouds. A second strop was then added below the block and dilute PVA applied.

Ratlines

This part of the project, as stated in the manual, calls for a great deal of patience and care if best results are to be achieved. There never has been a satisfactory "quick" way to do ratlines that looks anything other

Fig.4.55   *Open and closed hearts rigged at lower end of main stay.*

Fig.4.56   ***Standing rigging to the bowsprit.***

than a bodged job. However, I have always found that to try and do the lot in one go (in this instance, involving over 2600 knots), was not a sound approach. To that end, I do one flight at a time then rig one or two stays to break up the task into more manageable stages.

The spacing was critical, not only from the accuracy point of view, but from the general appearance of the finished job. Spacing that varied would be immediately apparent, particularly when the basic distance between each "rung" was only 4,5mm.

A strip of Plasticard provided a very useful spacer. When laid on the knots of the previously tied ratline,

Fig.4.57   ***The figurehead and bobstays.***

Fig.4.58   The forecastle deck.

the knots of the ratline currently being tied could be eased down to the top edge of the spacer with a pair of tweezers, thus keeping everything in line and at the correct spacing.

A piece of white paper between the mast and the inside of the shrouds, sprung vertically between the deck and the underside of the top, helped to keep the eyes in focus and reduce any strain; another good reason for breaking up the task into several stages.

How much length to cut for each ratline? With the number of ratlines in question it would have been easy to waste a lot of thread. So, with that in mind, I cut a test length, then tied it on to the shrouds as my first ratline at the bottom to determine a practical length for the remainder. This length was gradually shortened due to the convergence of the shrouds as the application of the ratlines progressed upwards.

All knots were sealed with dilute PVA adhesive. I keep a pair of cuticle cutters for trimming the ends of rigging, (not for wire or etched brass), and over the years have found the cutters to be a sound investment for producing clean and close trimming. Futtock shrouds and ratlines to the mizzen mast are shown in **Fig.4.53**.

Fitting the bowsprit

Having checked that all deadeyes and blocks had been put in place, the bowsprit was glued into position. The gammoning was rigged as outlined in the manual. I would, however, add a couple of notes:

The gammoning was rigged with a built-in twist. The thread first passed over the bowsprit to the rear of the space between the saddles then passed down through the head rails to the forward end of the slot through the stem. This procedure continued for all nine turns of the gammoning working forward over the bowsprit and rearwards through the slot.

The nine, frapping turns were applied above the beakhead deck, then pushed downwards to a lower level with tweezers before coating with dilute PVA.

The copper eyelets for rigging the travelling guy, the guy pendant and the flying jibboom guy were mounted on the front edge of the beakhead plank sheer before fitting the knightheads and boomkins in place. With regard to the knightheads, some thought was given as to the attitude of the copper eyelets in their front faces and whether they should be positioned horizontally or vertically. Rigging hooks are ultimately used at these points and have to be manipulated into place in a fairly restricted space, so getting the eyelets into a convenient attitude was helpful.

Completing the standing rigging

The sequence and descriptions given in the manual were well defined and when used in conjunction with the relevant drawings, the standing rigging was put up without difficulty. However, it is important to read the manual carefully in order not to miss anything. **Fig.4.54** shows the top end of the mainmast stay and its preventer. Note the mouse and eye feature and the snaking between the two. The heart and collar rigging at

Fig.4.59   Head-rails and beak deck.

the bottom end is shown in **Fig.4.55**.

Standing rigging to the bowsprit can be seen in **Fig.4.56** with bobstays and figurehead shown in **Fig.4.57**.

The running rigging

I worked strictly in accordance with the manual as regards to the sequence of applying the rigging. It worked with the minimum of difficulty and, although there were some areas that I personally may have chosen to do differently, my advice would be to stick to the instructions for good results.

The rigging that attaches the yards to the masts was the first to be put up; slings, jeers and truss pendants for the lower yards with parrals and ties for the topsail and topgallant yards. The jeers to the main mast were particularly difficult to belay, having to pass the running

Fig.4.60   Anchors.

Fig.4.64   Poop deck.

end down through the quarter deck and tie off on the bitts on the deck below. Using a wire messenger as suggested in the manual does work, but choose a time of good humour and patience to carry out the belaying!

This stage of the rigging was completed by the attachment of the spritsail yard and the spritsail topsail yard. The next stage featured the lifts, buntlines and leechlines, to all spars, nothing too difficult here, just a matter of patience. The main thing that needed watching was whether the lines dropped to their belaying points through the tops or to the outside; something not always apparent at first glance. Some of the rigging that goes to the outside of the top, belays to the pin rails on the inside of the bulwarks, and thus has to pass through the shrouds and ratlines. Patience was required to ensure that rigging lines were not "bent" at these points but re-directed to a straight run as necessary. This particular stage was the one where you get to finally square up all the yards, so additional care was necessary to balance tensions port to starboard.

The next set of rigging involved the cluelines and sheets. The drawings showing the cluelines need careful study and the sequence of rigging them is important if you are not to deny yourself access to other ongoing rigging. One of the valuable suggestions in the manual was to start some lines at the belaying point and work backwards. This helped considerably where the system had to be tensioned up and where finishing at the belaying point would have been hazardous. In fact, depending upon the dexterity of your fingers, you may find working backwards advantageous with lines other than those recommended. On the subject of tension it

was important not to over-tension. If the lifts are seen to slacken, you've overdone it!

The braces were the next part of the rigging to install. Again, close attention to the details in the manual and the belaying points shown on the drawings was given.

The driver gaff

A check was made to ensure that all the rigging blocks and pendants had been put on the gaff before shipping it to the mizzen mast via the parrals.

The throat halyard and the peak halyard were rigged but not belayed. I chose to then rig the vangs, in order to balance the system for both tension and alignment. All lines were then permanently tied off before rigging the braces to the mizzen topmast and topgallant yards.

The driver boom

Rigging the driver boom was done in a similar manner to the gaff, the topping lift and the sheets being belayed simultaneously in order to retain the boom in its required position.

Mounting the ship's boats

I decided to put the ship's boats in place before rigging the cluelines, tacks and sheets to the foremast and mainmast as it was apparent that they would somewhat restrict access to the waist of the ship.

One end of each of the boat lashings for the launch was tied to the relevant skid beam and the launch then mounted on its supports. The trailing ends of the lashings were tied off before starting work on placing the pinnace using a similar procedure. The pinnace provided the

Fig.4.62 **The main mast and quarterdeck barricade.**

means of tidying up the stay tackle, the hooks of the tackle being attached to eyebolts fitted fore and aft. This permitted tension to be put into the system before permanently belaying the running ends. The positioning of the barge and finally the cutter completed this stage of the model.

Cluelines, sheets and tacks

This part of the rigging was approached in a somewhat different manner to the rest in that the clue lines, sheets and tacks were all first rigged without belaying. This was done for a number of reasons, to ensure that the balance

Fig.4.61 **The ship's boats.**

Fig.4.63   Mizzen mast and poop deck barricade.

of the system was correct and that the clue garnet strop hung directly and vertically below the yard. Care was taken to route the tacks and sheets through previously rigged lines but you have to be prepared to re-route since interference may be found when the slack is taken up. All lines were permanently belayed. The positioning of the spider through which the main sheet pendant passes was a bit tricky. I found that the easiest way was to pin the top bracket in place first, thread the pendant through the ring and then make sure that the alignment of the pendant is correct before pinning the bottom bracket in place.

The quarter davits

These were made up as instructed in the manual using 1,5mm square strip to make the seven cleats on each davit. I glued a continuous strip over the length of the davit and cut away between the cleats to leave the length required. The backs of the cleats were then tapered off.

The boat falls, and hooked block were assembled before putting the davits to the side of the hull. The cast cleats to which the falls were belayed have to be angled so as not to foul the hull when the davits are raised to the stowed position.

It was noted also that the lift, thimbled to the span between the davits should pass to the forward side of

the mizzen shrouds and not through the ratlines thus making them inoperable.

The anchors

Holding the anchors in place was an airy-fairy business since there was not enough weight in the set-up. However, having put the span on each anchor in place, I then rigged the cat falls and cable to each of the bower anchors using an inside clinch to secure the cable to the anchor rings. Now that everything was in place, I put a touch of two-part epoxy between the anchor and the anchor palm blocks and hung some weight on the anchor while it set. This added some stability to the system and took out any slackness in the falls and spans, **Fig.4.60**.

Finishing off

Hanks and coils were the only things left to make and fix, making sure that the correct size of thread was used at each of the positions. This is always something of a hazardous process and requires a lot of care and once again calls for the removal of watches and rings. I admit to using model-maker's licence here and fit only a symbolic number of hanks and coils.

Figs.4.58 through **4.69** show various views of the completed model.

Fig.4.65   *Stern view and lanterns.*

Conclusions

This kit costs a lot of money in anybody's terms. Is it expensive, and is it worth it? The answer lies in what it is you expect from a kit, that being largely determined by what skills and facilities you have available for your model making. You certainly do not need an all singing and dancing workshop, and a fairly basic tool kit was more than adequate to build a superb and accurate model of "Victory" in all her glory. The extensive pre-cutting of parts and the provision of a vast amount of etched brass-work had considerably reduced the actual craftsmanship needed. However, there were one or two aspects of the kit about which I would raise some criticism.

On the whole the quality of the materials was good, and the drawings were well drafted. More identifying part numbers and terminology would have been useful, particularly for defining the various parts of the rigging. There was only limited instruction and drawn detail for the head rail assembly, a notorious feature for many modellers.

The manuals, all three of them, were a great attempt to portray what to do and how to do it. They were there to be read in order to facilitate the construction and rigging and *not merely for reference if things went wrong*. By and large they were a success.

The description of the rigging and its application in the manual was accurate and precise, but you need to have some knowledge of rigging terminology to relate what you read in the manuals to what you see on the drawings.

The outstanding aspect of the kit was the vast number of pre-cut and drilled parts, all very accurately produced in extremely good quality ply.

The eight sheets of etched brass parts provided the means with which to portray the vessel in a manner not possible for the average modeller just a few years ago.

So, we get back to the question of value. Bearing in mind the depth of research, the provision of the etched brass parts and the myriad of accurately pre-cut pieces (with no charred edges to remove), I guess that for the modeller who doesn't have the ability, or has only limited kit, to produce similar items from sheet or strip, the answer has to be, yes, it is good value.

There will inevitably be over ambitious modellers who may want to build a "Victory", but do not know their jeers from their truss pendants; for these people the kit construction could be a major challenge. I would suggest that a successful build of several kits would be required before attempting this one. But, if you really do want to rise to this particular challenge, don't forget to decide where you are going to put it before you go to the shop! In order to participate in JoTiKa's up-date programme do remember to register your kit after purchase.

CHAPTER 5

H.M.Cutter "Lady Nelson" – 1800

Victory Models is a new-comer to the market place and on the basis of the quality of this beginners' kit, has all the potential of being a major player on the period ship modelling scene.

The cutter, as modelled here, is a design that evolved from the vessels used by smugglers around the British coasts. Further developed by the Royal Navy, it was used extensively to counter smuggling activities. Having a large sail area for its size, it was very fast and ideal for patrol and despatch duties.

The original vessel was 52' 6" long at the keel, 17' 6" wide and carried a complement of about 30 officers and men. Her armament was ten 3-pounder carriage guns and twelve swivels on her bulwarks. At a scale of 1:64, the model has an overall length of 54cm.

The kit

The "Lady Nelson" kit has been designed with the beginner or the intermediate modeller in mind and to be an ideal introduction to plank on bulkhead techniques. The contents include laser cut parts in birch ply and walnut, metal and wooden fittings together with very comprehensive drawings and instructions created in English. The strip wood is of high quality and the laser cut sheets are finely produced with the minimum of effort required to remove parts cleanly from the sheet. The whole presentation gives the kit an air of quality right from the time that you open the box.

Tools required

The tool requirements are very basic and I list the essentials below:

- Heavy-duty craft knife
- Razor saw
- A selection of needle files
- Pin vice or small electric drill
- Small wood plane
- Drills from 1mm to 3mm diameter
- A selection of paint brushes
- Pliers/wire cutters
- Various grades of abrasive papers
- Tweezers
- Steel rule
- Masking tape

Consumables

- White PVA wood glue
- Dark wood dye
- Cyanoacrylate adhesive
- Dark wood filler
- Black Indian ink
- Matt polyurethane varnish
- Black paint
- Red paint
- White paint
- White spirit

Making a start

Before starting to cut pieces from the laser cut sheets, it was, as always, a good thing to properly read the instruction manual and study the drawings. It is unfortunate that many modellers tend to look at the instructions only when things go wrong instead of spending a little time to familiarise themselves with the construction procedures and getting to know what goes where, and when.

Constructing the hull

This kit employed the conventional technique of slotting the bulkheads into the false keel and adding support pieces at bow and stern to provide fixing points for the ends of the planks. These latter pieces were roughly bevelled prior to permanent assembly, as were the edges of the first three and last three bulkheads, (Fig.1). The bulkheads all slotted into the false keel snugly and without any adjustment. Having glued them in place, the false deck was dry fitted to hold the keel/bulkhead assembly square and true while the PVA adhesive dried.

The walnut prow, keel and rudder post were next glued in place, (Fig.2), ensuring proper alignment, remembering to use a damp cloth to wipe off any residual glue from the exposed surfaces of the walnut. Failure to

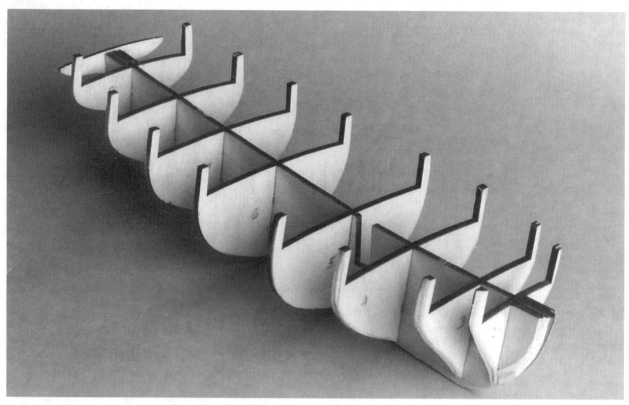

Fig.5.1 *The basic hull carcase. Note that the edges of the first and last few bulkheads should be bevelled before assembly.*

do this will result in stains that will be seen through any varnishing that has to be done later.

Once all the joints so far glued had set, the false deck was removed and the tops of all frames bevelled as necessary to recognise the curved line of the deck and to provide proper seating. A pencil line was drawn down the centre of the false deck as an aid to the later deck planking operation. The deck was then returned to the framework and permanently glued and pinned in place, taking note that it had to be fitted the right way round with the two square holes to take the bowsprit support side frames to the port side of the centreline. With the four counter frames glued in place, the edges of the bulkheads and false deck were sanded and bevelled to

the lines of the hull and to ensure full and proper seating for the first planking.

First planking

The two gun-port strips were removed from the 1mm ply sheet and put in soak preparatory to pinning and gluing them to the upper sides of the hull, **(Fig.3)**. It was important to recognise minor differences between these two parts and fit the one with the cut-out for the bowsprit on the port side.

The first planking was done in 1mm x 5mm lime. All planks were soaked and all required a degree of tapering to permit them to fit totally flat against the edges of the bulkheads. However, it was remembered that the

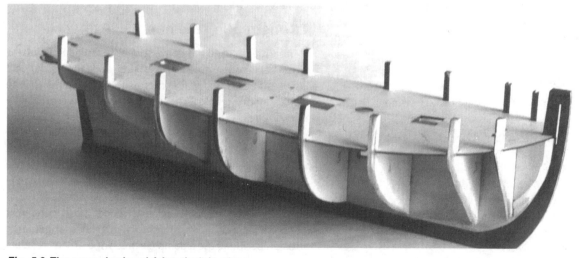

Fig. 5.2 *The prow, keel and false deck in place.*

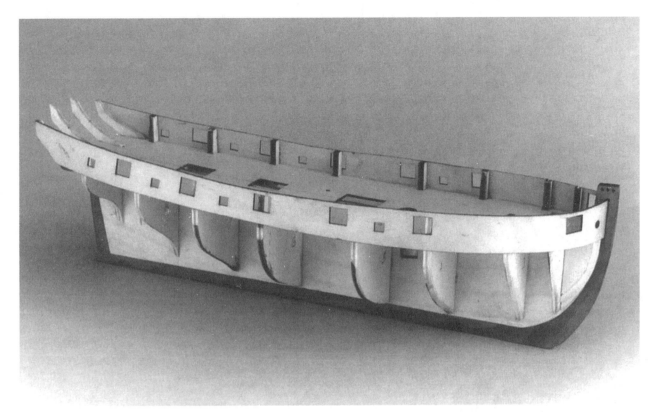

Fig. 5.3 The pre-cut gun port patterns need to be carefully aligned with the port and starboard being correctly identified.

cosmetic appearance of this first layer of planking was relatively unimportant, its prime purpose being to lay down a firm basis upon which to apply the second planking strips.

The amount of tapering was determined by offering a strip amidships against the underside of the previously laid plank, then gently bending it around the bow, it was marked where overlap started, this being the point at which the taper should commence. This procedure was followed at bow and stern.

All planks were pinned and glued in place, the pins being left proud for easy removal. Glue was applied to both plank and bulkhead edges. Planking started at the underside of the gun-port strips and continued down towards the keel. Neat bevelling of the plank end at the stem was attained, whereas at the stern, planking strips were permitted to overlap for later trimming.

The completely planked hull was then left for twenty-four hours for the glue to thoroughly harden before sanding all surfaces with course, then medium grade, abrasive papers. The ends of the planks at the stern were trimmed as required and the stern counter glued into position. The exposed face of the last bulkhead was planked with walnut strips leaving the hull ready for the second planking, **(Fig. 4)**.

Second planking

The second planking involved the use of 1mm x 4mm walnut strip. This demanded fairly accurate preparation in terms of tapering and bevelling in order to attain a neat job. However, the quality of the material was great

for producing nice clean cuts and the task was more about care and patience than difficulty of application. All planks needed a thorough soaking and this, in conjunction with a plank nipper, solved all bending problems.

It was important not to cover over the oar and gun-ports, but to rough shape them as the planking proceeded. This permitted access for tools for finishing the apertures later.

All planks were laid using cyanoacrylate to avoid pinholes in the finished surface. For newcomers to the hobby, I would suggest that the adhesive be applied to the hull, using the last laid plank as a guide for the nozzle of the bottle. This will help to control the flow of the

Fig. 5.4 The first planking completed.

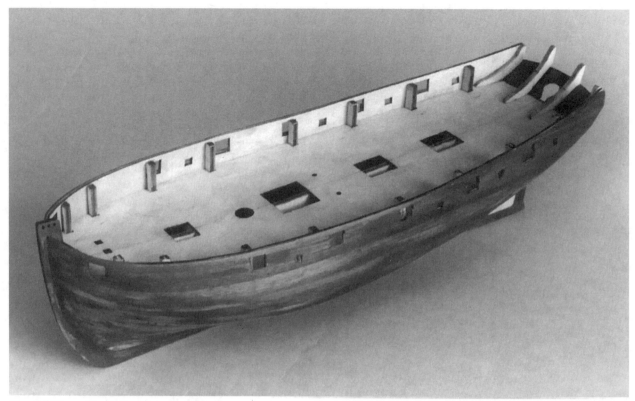

Fig. 5.5 The second planking completed.

adhesive, make the positioning of the plank on the hull easier and avoid getting too many planks stuck to the fingers.

It should also be comforting to remember that in the final analysis, the underside of the hull, where the bending and fitting problems are most severe, is to be painted. Thus, the use of filler can help to overcome the cosmetic faults of less experienced plank laying. The completed second planking is shown in **Fig.5**.

Bulwark inner planking and deck planking

Some modellers may find that it is easier to lay the deck before planking the inner bulwarks, but this is a personal choice and depends on how you prefer to work.

The bulwark ears apparent above deck level were twisted off using a pair of pliers, and the remaining stubs trimmed down flush.

The deck was laid using 0,6mm x 3mm beechwood strips starting at the previously marked centre-line and working outwards to the bulwarks, any slight gaps around the outside of the deck would be covered by the thickness of the bulwark planking. The deck openings were not completely planked over but were trimmed to size before rubbing down. A coat of clear matt varnish was applied to seal and protect the deck during the ongoing construction.

The inner surface of the bulwarks was then lined using 1mm x 4mm walnut strips. The first strip was pre-painted red so that it made a clearly defined line with the deck. It was found that there were advantages in using several pieces at each level of planking using the

gun-ports as convenient break points; it certainly provided better access for a scalpel when trimming the sides of the ports.

The top edges of the bulwarks were pared to shape and the inner surfaces rubbed down and painted red.

I used a pair of odd-leg callipers running along the top edge of the bulwarks to mark the position of the top of the main wale, which was then made up using two strips of 1mm x 3mm walnut. The stern side finishings were then trimmed to shape and glued in place. The construction to this stage is shown in **Fig.6**.

The bulwark capping rails

A check was made to ensure that the top edges of the bulwarks were flat and true to line so that the capping rails would sit snugly. Crocodile clips were of immense value for this part of the construction and were used at each gun-port position to hold the rails tightly down in place. A dry run was made and the ends of the rails trimmed to size and shape. PVA was applied to the underside of the rails before clipping them in place to dry. After rubbing them down and putting a radius on the corner of each upper edge, the timberheads and gun-posts were put in place then painted black, see **Fig.7**.

The upper wale

The position for this wale was marked in a similar fashion to that used for the main wale. The 1mm x 2mm walnut strip was applied in one piece, (rather than separate pieces), using cyano acrylate for the adhesive. The strip was then carefully cut away at the gun-port positions, again see **Fig.7**.

Fig. 5.6 Deck planking and inner bulwarks lined. The planks for the main wale were painted before assembly.

The catheads and the bow inner knee were fitted in conjunction with each other to ensure a proper fit. Any adjustments required were done to the knee and the bulwark capping rather than the catheads that had an unfriendly direction of grain.

Deck fittings

Many of the fittings were from the Amati standard listings and some needed to be made up from parts provided within the laser-cut sheets. The following comments were found to be pertinent.

All parts should be painted or varnished as necessary before assembly to the deck.

It should be remembered that paint and glue are not good friends, so paint should be scraped away where necessary to ensure a sound joint; this was particularly relevant to fixing the cleats.

Copper eyelets should be painted black. To do this, a series of holes was drilled into a piece of scrap timber and, into each hole, an eyelet was housed up to the

Fig. 5.7 The bulwark capping in place with together with the upper wale. Alignment is most important for optimum results.

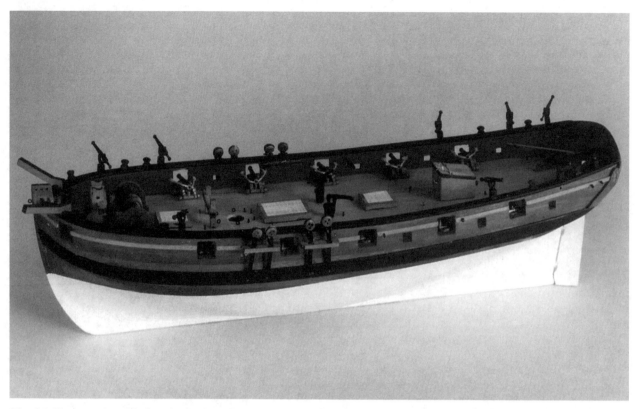

Fig. 5.8 The completed hull with all deck fittings in place. The swivel guns are only temporarily fitted at this stage.

underside of its eye. They eyes were then painted and left to dry. This method leaves the shanks clean for gluing.

Gratings should be made such that the strips that run fore and aft are seen in their entirety.

Bitts, belaying pin racks and channels should be glued *and* pinned for total security.

Dragging each gun carriage gently over a sheet of fine sandpaper produced a small flat on each of the four trucks or wheels. This substantially added to the effectiveness of the joint when gluing the carriages to the deck.

The gun carriages and barrels seemed somewhat small when making reference to the drawings, this I suspect, being the result of choosing the nearest size from a standard listing. Incidentally, it was important to look carefully at the gun barrels; there was a top and bottom to them, the top being identified by a very small dimple representing the touch-hole. The guns were rigged with breeching ropes only, for which 1mm natural thread was used. The completed hull can be seen in **Fig.8**.

The Stand

For as long as I can remember, I have, in my reviews, been critical of kit manufacturers who do not provide a stand on which to display the model. In this kit we have two, one being assembled from laser-cut parts and an ideal cradle during construction, the second being an Amati base with a pair of brass pedestals. Full marks for a bit of foresight since the finished model when made

properly, is more than deserving of being well mounted.

The mast

This presented one of the more difficult parts of the model to make due to the hounds. These are the two swellings toward the top end of the mast that, in one case, prevent the shrouds from sliding down the mast and, in the other, support the lower of the two mast caps. The problem can be overcome to a large extent if you have turning facilities with adequate supports for stabilising long thin work. If not, then there are two other options to consider. Make the mast in several parts using dowels to keep everything in line at the glued joints, or carefully carve and file, using an electric drill to spin the mast for the finishing operation.

I chose to make my mast in three main parts. The main stem of the mast was tapered from the butt end to the underside of the top hounds. The lower of the two hounds was made as a cylinder and glued into place on the mast and shaped *in situ* after the glue had dried. The third part, the masthead and upper hounds were made in one piece and doweled to the top end of the mast. This might sound difficult but, provided that you carefully mark and drill the axial holes for the dowel true and on centre, the result is extremely good.

A similar procedure was adopted for the topmast although, with smaller diameters involved, the accuracy of the drilling had to be more precise.

It was essential in all cases to wipe round the glued joints to remove any excess adhesive or, when you come to do the staining, pale patches will result where the glue has sealed the surface of the wood.

After assembly, the four eyelets and two cleats were added before painting the doublings matt black. The remaining bare wood was then stained.

It was found helpful to add all rigging blocks, not only to the mast, but also to the deck, before stepping the mast to the hull. The main reason for suggesting this is purely for ease of access. Advance planning of the rigging process is always worthwhile, bearing in mind that the further you proceed into the task, the less access for hands and fingers there is.

The bowsprit yards and spars

These were all simple to make even when filing the tapers by eye. The bowsprit was stained before adding rigging blocks; the yards and spars all painted matt black. It was helpful to insert a pin centrally in the back face of each yard and drill the mast in the appropriate place to mechanically fix yards to the mast. These joints may be made before or after stepping the mast. As with the mast, it was helpful to add the rigging blocks at this stage.

The butt end of both the boom and the gaff attach to the mast using parrals. These were made up and one end tied to the jaws before shipping these spars.

Rigging

The black rigging thread used for the standing rigging was a bit on the hairy side. Running the thread through the fingers smeared with PVA helps to lay the surface fibres and prevent the later adhesion of dust.

Any line that was seen to pass through a rigging block had its leading end treated with cyano to form a built-in bodkin about 12mm long. Other than for that purpose, all knots and lashings were sealed with dilute PVA.

The shrouds and ratlines were put up first. The ratlines were of 0.1mm natural thread and needed to be

Fig. 5.9 The standing rigging. Do not leave the tedious job of tying on the ratlines until later; it's easier at this juncture.

blackened with Indian ink. Adequate protective covering was used to cover the deck in case of accidental splashing. The remainder of the standing rigging, the backstays, fore stays and bowsprit rigging, were then done before moving on to the running rigging. The completed standing rigging is shown in **Fig.9**.

Fig. 5.10 A view of the deck forward.

Fig. 5.11 A view of the deck aft.

The running rigging was extremely straightforward and, when applied in the sequence indicated by the numbered belaying points, all went well. The belaying of rigging at the fore end is shown in **Fig.10**.

Newcomers to the hobby may find that when it comes to rigging the boom and gaff, it will be helpful to rig two or three lines simultaneously. In the case of the boom, the topping lift (6) and the boom sheet (Starboard 13), applied together, assisted in keeping the rigging system balanced and the boom in its correct attitude relative to the mast and hull. Belaying of the running rigging at the aft end is shown in **Fig.11**.

Similarly, for the gaff, the throat halliard (7), the topping lift (9) and the peak down-hauler (Port 13) were tensioned up together to set the desired gaff angle.

Conclusions

The *Lady Nelson* made up into a cracking little model and was fairly easy to construct. In spite of its lack of size, it has many of the features that can be found in larger vessels. For that reason it is an ideal model with which to introduce the less experienced to the various disciplines involved in period ship modelling. The strip materials were good and the laser cut sheets clean and accurate. The drawings were well detailed with many exploded views to assist in understanding the various bits of tackle employed in the running rigging.

H.M. Cutter "Lady Nelson"

CHAPTER 6

H.M.S. "Mars"

H.M.S. "Mars" is another kit in the Caldercraft Nelson's Navy series and has been produced with the novice and intermediate builder in mind. An 18-gun brig sloop, "Mars" was heavily armed for her size carrying 18 carriage guns and a number of swivel guns. She was built in Holland in the 1770's and commissioned as a Dutch privateer, her sleek lines making her one of the fastest armed vessels afloat at the time. Eventually captured, "Mars" was fitted out for Royal Naval Service and, in 1792, her eighteen carriage guns were changed from 9-pounder to 6-pounder and her swivel guns reduced from twelve to ten in number. The kit features this latter configuration. H.M.S. "Mars" was of 396 tons and had a complement of 120 officers and men. She was lost at sea when she foundered in a hurricane in the Indian Ocean in December 1799.

With a length at the deck of 100ft 11in and a width of 30ft 4in the scale of 1:64 produces a model with an overall length of 790mm, a height of 590mm and a width across the foreyard of 310mm.

The kit

Seven sheets of drawings illustrated the building and rigging processes. These were supported by an instruction manual which included a numbered parts list and illustrated layouts of all the pre-cut sheets and photo-etched parts for easy identification of all the parts.

Virtually everything that could be pre-cut had been accurately routed in varying thickness of ply and walnut sheet. The routing process included third axis cutting by which means halving joints could be produced where required.

The quality of all materials was extremely high, the strip walnut and lime being straight and true. Four reels each of black and natural rigging thread of the appropriate thickness were provided together with a box of fittings that included nearly three hundred rigging blocks.

The extras

As with all kits, there are certain paints, stains and adhesives that have to be purchased in order to build and finish the model. These are listed below:

White PVA wood glue
Walnut wood dye
Cyanoacrylate adhesive (thick and thin)
Walnut wood filler
Indian Ink (black – for the ratlines)
White spirit
Polyurethane varnish (matt)
Black paint (Humbrol 85)
Red paint (Humbrol matt 60 mixed with 50% matt 70)
Yellow paint (Humbrol 74)

As an alternative to matt varnish, a shellac sanding sealer had quite an appeal, since it also provided a sound base for any painted surfaces. For the natural wood finish, it gave a hard, dead flat, surface when rubbed down with very fine abrasive paper.

Recommended tool list

The standard of design of this kit permits building with a very basic tool kit and those items recommended are copied herewith from the manual:

Craft knife
A selection of needle files
Razor saw
Small wood plane (David plane)
Pin vice or small electric drill
Drills from 0,5 to 2,0mm diameter
Selection of glass paper and a sanding block
A selection of good quality paint brushes
Pliers/wire cutters
Tweezers of good quality
Dividers and compass
12in steel rule
Clothes pegs or "crocodile" clips
Tee square
Masking tape

In addition to these items I found that the range of

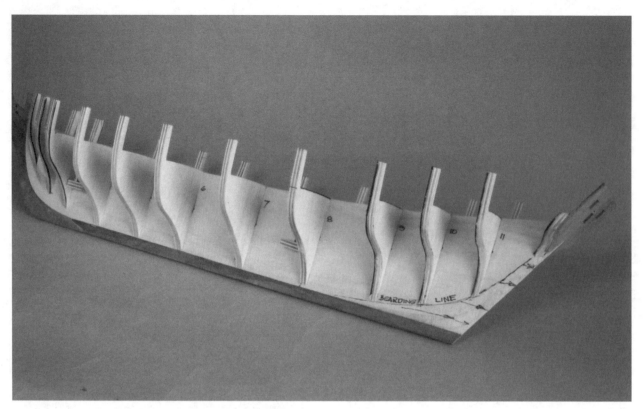

Fig. 6.1 The hull carcase with bearding line established.

PermaGrit abrasive tools was a definite advantage.

Making the hull carcase

This basic construction follows the well-proven process of slotting bulkheads into a false keel, which is first edged with stempost, keel and sternpost. A considerable amount of dry fitting is to be recommended before thinking about getting the glue pot out. I checked the slots in both the false keel and bulkheads first, finding that a slight easing of both was necessary to attain a nice sliding fit. A tight fit is of no real advantage, in fact, more liable to cause a bend in the false keel. Once all the joints could be assembled with easy finger pressure, I set about rough chamfering the edges and angling the tops of the first and last four bulkheads.

The edges had to be chamfered in order to provide the best possible seating for the planking to be put on later. The tops were angled to match the line of the top edge of the false keel so that the false deck could sit properly. I used the edges of the dry assembled false deck in order to eyeball the degree of chamfer that needed to be applied to the edges of the bulkheads. Removing this material was much easier than trying to do it after everything had been glued together. Similarly, the plank termination patterns at the bows were chamfered before assembly.

Earlier study of the drawings had revealed a potential problem that the less experienced modeller may have found a little difficult to get around. Both false keel and sternpost were from 5mm thick material and, bearing in mind that both the first and second planking uses 1mm thick timber, it will be readily seen that finished thickness

at the ends of the planks adjacent to the sternpost will be zero to properly blend. The method that I use to solve this problem is to dry assembly the last four bulkheads to the false keel and draw a line on to the face of the keel that passes through the bottom edges of those bulkheads. This is called the *bearding line*, (**Fig.6.1**). I then chamfer from that line to the back edge of the keel to reduce the thickness to about 3mm. This means that the thickness of the planking would thus be reduced only to 0,5mm, which is a far less hazardous situation.

Thus, the false keel, having been so chamfered, was edged with the stempost and keel but leaving the sternpost off until after both layers of planking had been applied later.

The bulkheads were then glued in place followed by the plank termination patterns and mast clamps. The whole structure was then put to one side for the glue to thoroughly cure.

Using one of the lime planking strips, the run of the chamfers on the edges of the bulkheads was checked and corrected by sanding as required.

The first planking

Some tapering was required at both ends of the hull and soaking, particularly at the front end, was helpful. Although the rigidity of the hull carcase was, in this case, extremely good, it was worth adopting the standard practice of laying two or three planks alternatively each side to be absolutely sure that no distortion was induced. A few stealers were also found necessary towards the stern. These triangular lengths

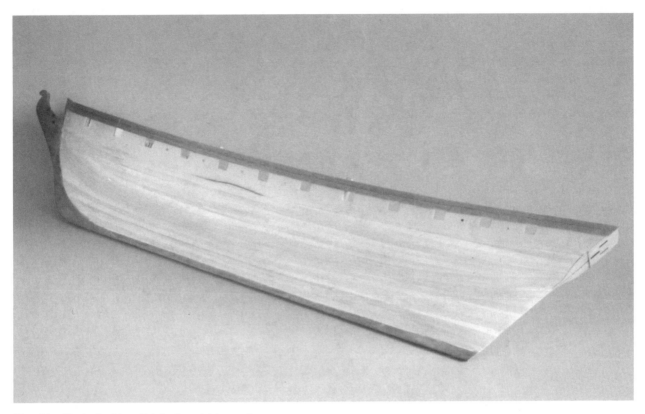

Fig. 6.2 First planking finished and trimmed.

enabled the run of the planks to sit firm on the edges of the bulkheads and thus make the subsequent rubbing down much easier. All strips were laid with overhang at the stern and trimmed flush with the transom and the back edge of the false keel, **(Fig.6.2)**.

Planks were glued and pinned to each bulkhead and glued to each other along their edges. This provided a firm structure that was then sanded to give a strong shell on to which the second planking could be laid.

The outside of the stern bulkhead was then planked as shown on the drawings.

The second planking

There was a choice to be made with regard to the method of fixing the planks; the same principle of pinning and gluing as used for the first planking or avoid the pin-holes and use either a contact adhesive or cyanoacrylate. I chose the latter, applying the adhesive

Fig. 6.3   Second planking completed and rudder post fitted.

Fig. 6.4. The working cradle as provided by the kit and my bespoke display stand.

to the back face of each plank carefully handling them using thumb and forefinger on the edges. Accurate preparation was important to avoid unsightly gaps and first time positioning was essential when placing each strip. The same procedure with regard to stealers was adopted as for the first planking, all planks overlapping the stern edges.

After an initial rough rubbing down, any gaps and

cracks were filled, the overlaps trimmed and the rudderpost fitted, **(Fig.6.3)**. A final finishing treatment with fine abrasive paper was then carried out.

Before moving on to the next stage I found it convenient to drill the oarports from inside the bulwarks through to the outside of the hull. If this is not done before planking the inside surfaces of the bulwarks, their position is lost.

Fig. 6.5. Wales and upper rails painted before assembly.

Fig. 6.6. Deck planking, with marker pen caulking on one plank edge only.

The stand was then constructed. The unit as provided in the kit was more than adequate to support the model during the ongoing stages of construction and would, if properly stained and finished, have resulted in a reasonable display stand. However, this was not to my personal taste and I subsequently made a different design to exhibit my model, using the profiles of the original as a guide to the proper support. The two stands are shown in **Fig.6.4**.

A note on painting

It may seem strange to talk about painting at this early stage of the building process. However, there are some parts and areas that if painted at a particular juncture or before assembly, will provide some very definite advantages. In this particular case there are yellow head rails that sit on a black stem piece and painting the rails before assembly permits a nice clean line between the two colours. So, a look at the drawings allows you to decide where such advantages are to be found. In my model, all exposed timber was covered with two coats of shellac sanding sealer and rubbed down whether it was to be painted or not.

The main wales

These two strengthening features along each side of the hull comprised three, 4mm wide strips. It was remembered that they were to be painted black and lie on the natural wood surface of the hull. It was therefore found very helpful to pre-paint the strips on both edges and one face before assembling to the hull sides. This provided a very clean-cut line on top and bottom exposed

edges in a manner far easier than if I had left them to be painted afterwards. Obviously, the outside faces would require a second or third coat but this was readily done without having to worry about the shaking hand problem!

Similarly, the 1.5mm square rails along each side of the hull were given an initial coat of yellow paint before finally fixing in place, **(Fig.6.5)**.

Deck planking

To further make life easier, I decided to plank the deck before the inner faces of the bulwarks. This made the fit of the outer deck planks against the bulwarks less critical, since the run of joints would ultimately be covered by the thickness of the bulwark planking.

The kit depicted the deck planking in straight planks with no butts and thus careful preparation of each plank is essential so that end shapes and overall lengths are exact.

To simulate caulking, I blackened one edge of each plank with a marker pen, **(Fig.6.6)** but only after testing the procedure on a short length. Some timbers are too absorbent and the ink will run into the grain. There are two alternatives, use a soft pencil or pre-varnish the strips with matt varnish before using the marker pen. Or, there again, if you think that caulking is a bit over the top, then like many modellers, don't bother at all.

The choice of adhesive was again important. The planks are 0.5mm thick and can sometimes warp if white PVA is used. Bearing that in mind, I decided to use cyanoacrylate albeit that handling long glued strips takes a bit of practice if they are not to stick to the fingers rather than the model.

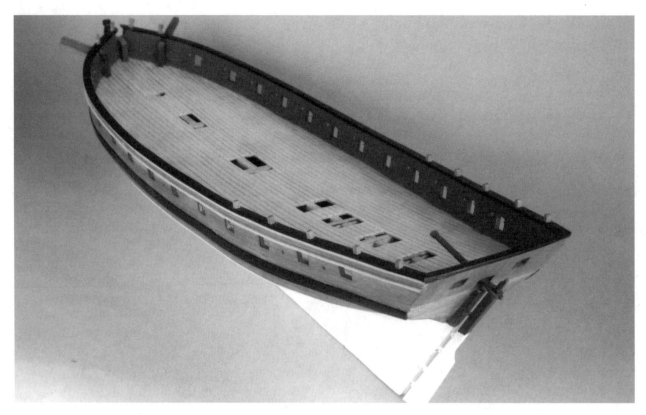

Fig. 6.7. Bulwark capping rails and timberheads in place.

In order to get the sort of finish I like on a deck, I scraped the surface with a spare Stanley knife blade before sealing with matt varnish.

Bulwark inner planking

Again, to make the later painting job that much easier, I pre-painted the lowest plank each side so that I attained a nice crisp line between the red of the planks and the natural wood finish of the deck, again see **Fig.6.6.**

If you choose to use short lengths at gun-port level, do try to ensure that they all come from the same strip of wood. Even the best quality timber can vary in width due to manufacturing tolerances but even the smallest variation can play havoc with the edge butting of subsequent full-length adjacent strips.

After sanding the entire inner surface to the required finish, I painted it with the 50/50 mixture of Humbrol 60 and 70, **(Fig.6.7).**

Bulwark capping rails

Unlike so many other kits, JoTiKa recognised that you cannot easily bend 6mm wide x 2mm thick walnut across the width and therefore they pre-cut the rails to shape. In addition, slots were also pre-cut to take timberheads and swivel gun posts. Very little tweaking was necessary to attain the right fit before pinning and gluing in place. However, this was yet another instance where there was great advantage in painting before assembly in order to preserve a nice sharp line between the black edge of the capping and the yellow of the hull upper rails, **(Fig.6.7).** The stern capping merely needed trimming to

length for a snug fit between the side capping rails. The boat davits were then put in place.

Fig. 6.8. The head rails.

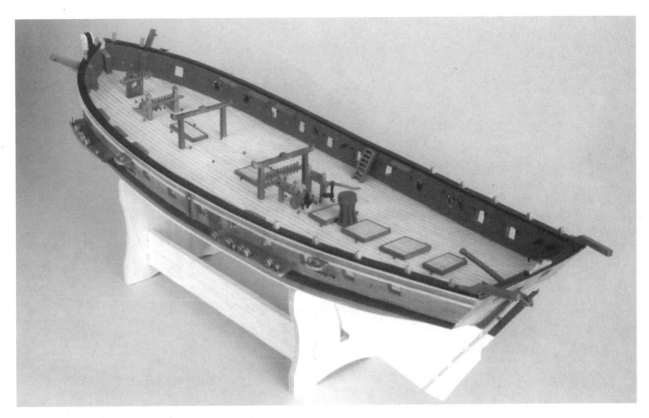

Fig. 6.9. Deck layout. Pumps, capstan hatches and gallows.

The head rails

The stempost above the waterline was first painted black and left to dry while the ten pieces that went to make up the total head rail assembly were removed from the sheet, sealed and painted. All parts were very accurately pre-cut and needed only minor trimming to fit against the stem and hull, (**Fig.6.8**). This was a gradual process of trial and error and required some patience, but really there was nothing difficult in the operation. If only the head rails on many of my past models were as simple to do!

Deck fittings

The first of these items to be made were the hatches, features that in so many cases spoil an otherwise good model. From the decorative point of view perhaps it didn't matter too much, but looking for technical accuracy, then it paid to give attention to correct laying of the two main components, the ledges and the battens. The ledges laid across the hatch opening and the battens laid on the ledges fore and aft. It is the latter that would be seen in their entirety when looking straight down on the deck; a point not missed by judges if you subsequently choose to submit your model in competition. A further note for consideration; it is almost better to get all the hatches wrong than get a mixture of correct and incorrect attitude, the error is far less noticeable.

The jointed hatch strips provided in the kit were of excellent quality, all being of similar thickness and colour and requiring no sorting. It was important not to make hatches oversize because the two adjacent to the

capstan position were critical in their separation in order to leave room for the capstan base.

This was particularly pertinent in my case because the capstan base and top were pre-cut oversize, a matter that JoTiKa has now put to rights. I liked the manner in which the capstan was built providing truly square holes to take the ends of the capstan bars, another small point that gives the model a little bit of something extra. The finished assembly was painted red, the same shade as the inner bulwarks.

The stern davits and, indeed, the catheads should each be drilled with four holes and not two as shown on the drawings and fitted with eyelets on one side to attach the rigging for hoisting the cutter or the anchors. The deck layout is shown in **Fig.6.9**.

Chain plates and channels

You may find, as I did, that the channels are more easily assembled with the relevant deadeyes and eyelets before fixing them to the side of the hull. Thus the pre-cut channels were first checked for fit against the side of the hull then drilled to take the fixing pins, two in each assembly. Incidentally, it said something for the accuracy of the pre-cutting, that virtually no adjustment was required to the curved rear edges of the channels to attain the correct fit.

The etched brass sheet was sprayed with matt black paint and left to thoroughly dry before proceeding to the next stage.

The deadeye strops were taken from the etched brass sheet, fitted with deadeyes and then put into the slots in the outside edge of the channels. The design of

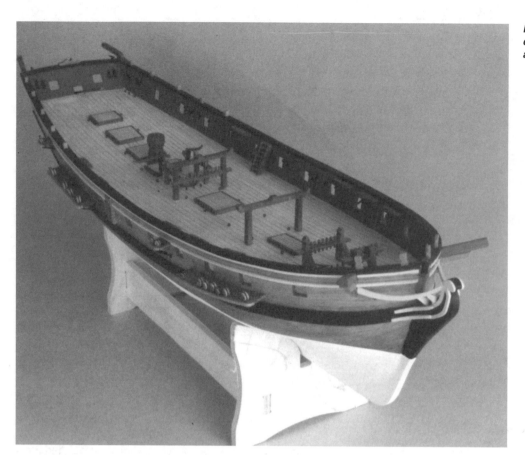

Fig. 6.10. The capped channels assembled to hull.

these parts was such as to provide a self-locking system and it was found to work extremely well. The "spiky" bits were fed into the slots at about 45 degrees with the lower "spikes" resting against the underside of the channel and the upper one digging into the back corner of the slot. The strop was then compressed and pushed home against the back of the slot. A dab of epoxy was considered a bit "belt and braces," but I did it anyway, this being one place that you don't want things failing during the rigging process later on. Having got all of the deadeyes in place, the capping strip was added before finally gluing the channels to the sides of the hull, (**Fig.6.10**).

The chain-plate straps were then bent and pinned in position. A piece of dowel dropped into the mast positions permitted a length of thread to be tied at the relevant height and then draped down to the channels so that the correct angle for pinning the straps could be eyeballed.

The guns

The barrels were painted first and allowed to dry while I made up the carriages. The carriage parts were coated with shellac before removing them from the sheet after which they were assembled using cyanoacrylate. It was important to place the shorter axle at the front and the longer one at the rear of the carriages. The 1mm diameter, wire cross-bars were then put in place to stabilise and strengthen the structures before adding the wheels. The pre-cutting of these parts was sufficiently accurate to permit the wheels to be push-

fitted to the axles having previously applied a very small dab of adhesive. It had to be remembered that the larger of the wheels had to be fitted at the front of the carriages.

The quoin beds and quoins were put together before adding them to the carriage assemblies, which allowed for the easier tapering of the quoins.

The barrels were then assembled and the trunnion brackets put in place using cyanoacrylate. When thoroughly set the brackets were used as templates to drill down into the carriage sides in order to take the head-end of shortened pins.

At this stage, the carriages can often be found not to sit squarely on all four wheels. A simple remedy for this condition was to take a sheet of fine abrasive paper and lay it flat on the bench then, taking each carriage assembly in turn, place it at one edge of the paper then pull it once across the sheet. Not only was the uneven seating cured, but also the resultant small flat increases the area of contact for gluing the carriages to the deck. The mounted guns can be seen in **Fig.6.11**.

The cutter

The kit was classified as being suitable for a novice or intermediate modeller. However, with respect to this particular part of the kit, I felt that the novice just might have a few difficulties. Like most boats at this scale, it was difficult to make.

The parts were numbered before removing them from the 1,5mm sheet and the slots in the keel, bulkheads and floor, filed clean and sized. This needed quite a bit

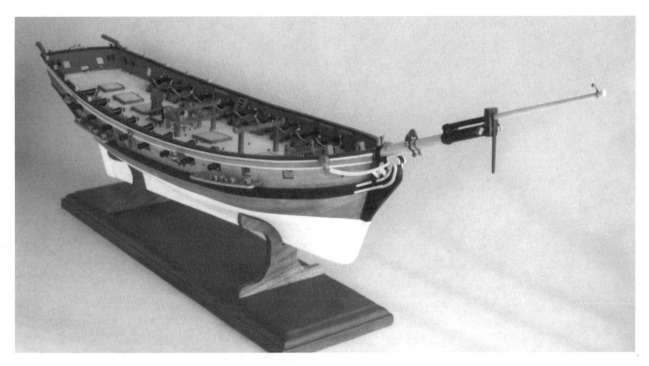

Fig. 6.11. The armament in place together with the assembled bowsprit.

of care due to physical size of the pieces and the inherent weak spots. Dry assemble these parts *and make sure that the bulkheads are in a shipshape order*. The best way to do this is to eyeball the lines of the boat from stem to stern and do not totally rely on the sequence of bulkhead numbering. Once everything appeared to be presenting the right lines *and* the top curve to the bulwarks, the assembly was thoroughly coated with dilute PVA and left overnight to dry.

Having shaped the edges of the bulkheads to follow the curves of the boat, the first planking in 0,5 x 3mm strip was put on using cyanoacrylate. I applied the cyanoacrylate sparingly using a toothpick and, where possible, used small crocodile clips to hold things in place. Even so, somewhere along the line, planks inevitably got stuck to fingers. Each plank needed shaping carefully so as not to leave gaps between them. When the entire shell had been covered, it was well brushed with dilute PVA and left to dry before doing the odd spot of filling prior to rubbing down.

The second planking required a bit more attention. Whereas the first layer was put on primarily to provide a sound base, the second really needed to reflect the lines of the craft, particularly since the finished boat was not to be painted. I also chose to cut down the width of the strips from 3mm to 2mm to make for easier working and started a little way down from the bulwarks, where the first strip would lay completely flat from stem to stern without any distortion.

I also planked to the edges of the false keel, then, after filing a narrow flat from stem to stern, I added a combined keel and stem post square strip (1,5mm square).

A further refinement I made was the addition of bulwark capping strips fashioned from scrap, 1,5mm thick

walnut sheet. I traced the outline of the bulwarks on to the sheet and, having cut the outer shape, produced the inner edge 2mm parallel to the outer. These were stuck on after gluing the ribs in place, thus covering the top ends.

The manual suggests a week of evening work to complete this stage of the kit. I think that should include a few late nights as well!

The anchors

The four identical anchors are simple to make following the instruction manual guidelines. A minimum amount of work was necessary to clean up the castings before painting. The wooden stock halves required a little opening out of the slots to ensure a snug fit on the anchor shank before gluing together and applying the black cartridge paper simulated iron hoops. A feature not often mentioned in period ship kits was the puddening; the binding that went round the anchor ring. This was one of those minor things that add that something extra to the standard. Once completed, the anchors may be mounted on to the hull or put to one side for later rigging according to your own preference.

The bowsprit

The drawings provided all dimensions necessary to prepare each of the individual components that went to make up the bowsprit. For the less experienced, the main thing to watch was the relevant angles of the cap and the dolphin striker, both of which should be vertical and square to the waterline, thus involving modifying the holes in the cap to take the bowsprit tenon and the passage of the jibboom.

A similar procedure had to be adopted with the hole in the forward bitt into which the butt of the bowsprit

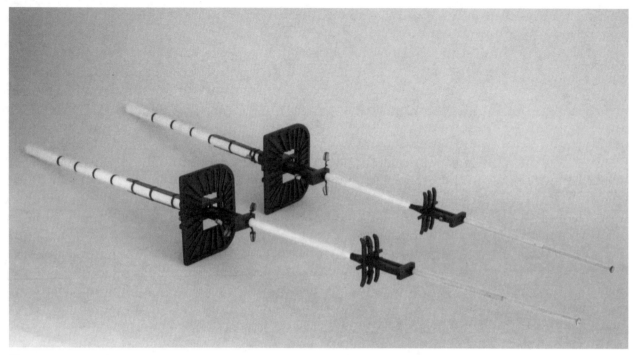

Fig. 6.12. The masts ready to be stepped.

was housed. The assembled bowsprit is shown in **Fig.6.11**.

The masts

The instruction manual again provides an adequate guide as to how to construct the masts. This was another area where the model maker should not be in a hurry to get the glue into action. Dry fit all parts first to ensure that the correct fits and alignments are have been attained. It was also found that this gave the opportunity to note the sequence of fitting since it is possible to get things wrong and finish up with a part that cannot be assembled!

The topmasts were probably another area where the beginner might have had some difficulty. The hounds below the masthead involved some very careful file work if a lathe or some other sort of turning facility was not available.

The masts were painted matt black at the doublings and all blocks identified and put in place using dilute PVA, **(Fig.6.12)**. Earlier dry fitting had established proper mast alignment and rake angles and so stepping them into the hull with a spot of glue was quite straightforward.

The spars

Four of the yards had a central octagonal section. If the modeller has not made yards with this feature before, it may be of help to follow the following procedure.

I cut a length of the appropriate diameter dowel rod making it 6mm longer than the finished required dimension, then, using a small plane, I planed the total length to an octagonal section. The length of the centre section was marked on, and then the eight faces tapered from those marks to each end of the yard. The resultant edges were filed off to leave a roughly round section, which was then spun in an electric drill to finish.

The ends were then cut to length, (3mm from each

end) and carefully rounded.

It may be questioned why the dowel was cut over-length in the first place. The reason is that if the tapers are sanded by hand, the last couple of millimetres usually gets different pressure and hence an incorrect and excessive taper. Depending upon how each person works, the 3mm may be found insufficient, but in general terms, it is a factor worth considering.

Similarly, the cleats were cut off a couple of millimetres longer before fixing in place with cyanoacrylate. When set, they were then trimmed to their correct length with a sharp scalpel. This avoided having to position them over-carefully when gluing them to the yards, their lengths and relative positions being attained with the scalpel.

The instruction manual suggested that the yards be fixed to the masts prior to stepping the masts into the hull. As a purely personal choice, I assembled the masts to the hull first, and did not fix the yards in place until after I had done the standing rigging. This left more "finger space" particularly for tying on the ratlines. However, the method of attaching the yards using 1mm diameter wire pegs was a sound move and was a definite advantage when, later on, I came to do the running rigging.

The yards were painted matt black and when dry, blocks were tied on as required and the completed yards put to one side, **(Fig.6.13)**.

Standing rigging

Tying on of blocks, lashings and belaying all needed a touch of adhesive to permanently secure them. Probably the safest and least hazardous preparation to use is dilute PVA. Do not be tempted to use cyanoacrylate, since an over-enthusiastic application can soak right through the thread and knot and, when dry will make the line brittle

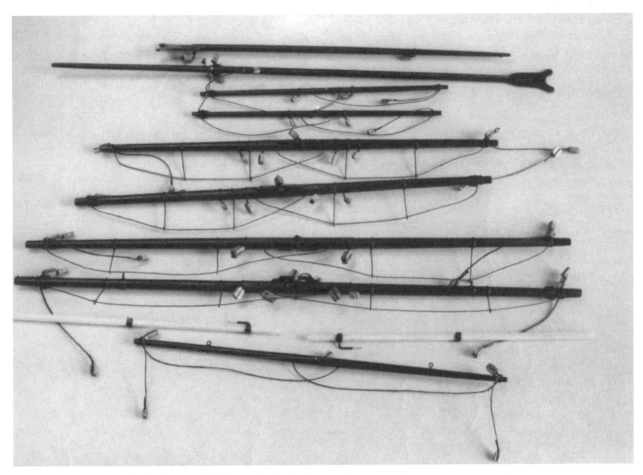

Fig. 6.13   *Blocks lashed to yards before rigging to the masts.*

with disastrous results as and when load may be applied. It also dries shiny and needs touching in with paint or varnish, so any time that was saved before trimming knots can be offset by extra work with the paint brush.

As mentioned earlier, I normally do not put the yards and spars in place until after I have done most of the standing rigging and certainly not until the ratlines have been tied on.

The lower shrouds were the first to be rigged followed by the upper shrouds and then the ratlines. A degree of tension in the shrouds was useful to prevent distortion when doing the ratlines. Nothing looks worse than the outer shrouds having that "pulled in" look! Fortunately, the design of the deadeye strops is more or less self-locking and the whole shroud system will sustain quite a bit of tension, so there isn't too much excuse for getting things distorted.

The fore and aft stays were then rigged, this time not applying too much tension, **(Fig.6.14)**.

Note that all standing rigging is done with black thread except the lanyards between the deadeyes, which are rigged using natural thread. There is often confusion about this amongst modellers, but, if it is remembered that the tension in the shrouds occasionally has to be taken up during the life of the vessel, running tarred rope through deadeyes would not be possible. Natural rope thus becomes the order of the day, **(Fig.6.15)**.

Running rigging

Natural thread was used throughout for this part of the rigging. I worked from the centre of the vessel outward and upward to avoid, as much as possible, obstructing access for fingers, scalpels and tweezers. The rigging of the lower sheets and tacks was left until the very end specifically for this reason. Various views of the running rigging can be seen in **Figs.6.16** to **6.21**.

It was also remembered that at the termination of each line of running rigging, there had to be a coil or hank of rope. These were made up and put on afterwards rather than attempting to make the coils as a direct continuation of the rigging line.

Once everything was in place, a careful inspection of the model was made to identify any untrimmed knots, areas where paint needed touching in, or odd bits of detritus lurking in corners or under gun carriages.

Enhancements

There were two omissions in the kit that I thought were worthy of doing something about. There were no lower stuns'l booms to go with the upper booms fitted to the foreyard, and there was no cat tackle fitted to the anchors. The additions were easily made; the booms, with the gooseneck fitting on their butt end were lashed to the gallows and an eye added to the edge of the fore channels from which the lower booms would have swung out when in use. The cat tackle was rigged using a 7mm double block to which I fitted a spare hook from the etched brass sheet.

Conclusions

This was a thoroughly delightful kit to build and, apart from the ship's boat hanging on the back, one well within the range of those kits suitable for the less experienced.

It produced a most attractive model, not too large, but properly detailed and having that proper ship-shape feel about it, in fact, one of the most attractive vessels kitted for some time.

The kit itself was of a high standard in all departments. The quality of the timber was good and was complemented by a comprehensive set of fittings and rigging materials.

Fig. 6.15. The lanyards to the lower shrouds.

Fig. 7.17 The forward end with anchors rigged. Note the eye on the fore-channel to accept gooseneck of lower stuns'l booms stowed on gallows.

Fig. 6.18. Amidships view. Note hanks of rope at belaying poins and the breech rope to all guns.

Fig. 6.16. The running and standing rigging to the bowsprit.

CHAPTER 7

"Endeavour"-J Class-1934

Sir Thomas Sopwith's 1934 UK challenger for the America's Cup is one in Amati's America's Cup Series of kits for famous yachts. The double-planked model is at 1:35 scale and finishes up at 1150mm long. It is primarily a static model but recognition has been made of the possibilities of sailing the model under radio control.

Endeavour was a "J" Class yacht of 143 tons displacement and sported 7560 sq ft. of sail. She was designed by Charles Nicholson and built at Gosport by Camper and Nicholson in 1933. Sopwith designed a double-clewed jib to give him an aerodynamic advantage over the America's Cup defender "Rainbow" but unfortunately, during trials, the Americans noticed the ploy and rigged "Rainbow" in a similar fashion, thus negating Sopwith's advantage. This, coupled with crew problems effectively scuppered his challenge for the trophy.

The kit

The kit itself was extremely well presented, offering five sheets of excellent drawings and good illustrated instructions showing exactly what was to be done and, in some cases, what was not to be done! The laser cut parts were in high quality ply sheets, the strip material had been labelled for instant identification and all these items were supported by a wealth of other brass and wooden fittings. The instruction manual was in two parts. The first provided written instructions (In good English) identifying by part number all parts used in the construction of the many sub-assemblies and also a recommended sequence of working. The second provided excellent exploded views of each stage of building clearly indicating the part numbers to be used. The manual, together with the drawings, gave a pretty good picture of the construction process and, obviously, a lot of work had gone into their creation. It was well worth a thorough read *before* starting.

Tools and consumables

The prime tools needed are:
    A craft knife
    Razor saw
    File
    Fine nosed pliers
    Straightedge
    Cabinet maker's scrapers
    A small drill - preferably low-voltage electric type
    Perma Grit abrasives
    Light hammer

White PVA adhesive and cyanoacrylate will sort out all the gluing problems and, in conjunction with the

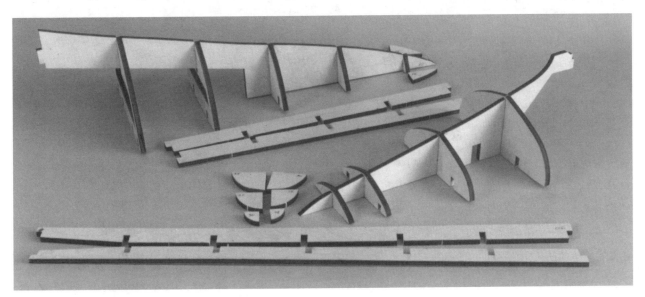

Fig. 7.1 The fore and aft sections.

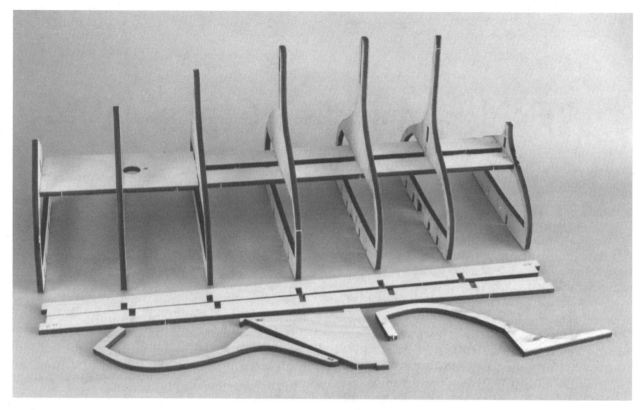

Fig. 7.2 The centre section.

aforementioned files, various grades of abrasive paper will do the smoothing and finishing, including fine grit wet or dry paper.

Depending upon how you will wish to finish the model, fillers, paints and varnishes will be required. For this class of model spraying is really a 'must' if you want to obtain that gleaming finish.

Building the hull framework

There was nothing too difficult in constructing the hull framework, but it was helpful to understand the sequence of build before getting the glue out. To that end, I first cut all the relevant parts from the pre-cut sheets.

I then had a totally dry run assembling all of the hull parts. This had two main advantages, in that any joints that needed a little easing could be identified and dealt with and that the most efficient sequence of assembly could be established. The amount of joint adjustment was minimal due to the excellent accuracy of the pre-cut parts.

As instructed, the fore and the aft sections were built first, **(Fig.7.1)**, followed by the centre section,

Fig. 7.3 The fin and its housing within the keel area.

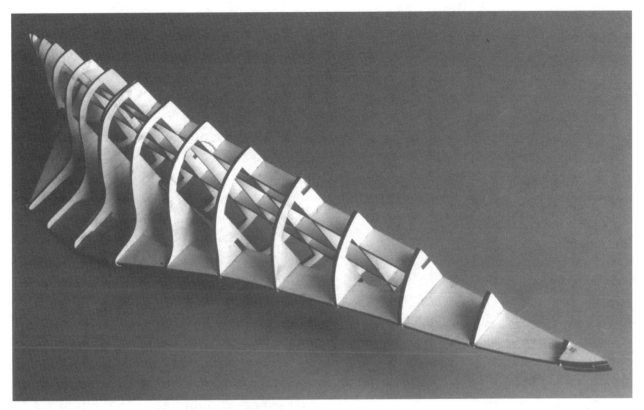

Fig. 7.4 The completely assembled hull framework.

(Fig.7.2). In each case the longitudinal slotted strips were again dry fitted to keep the bulkheads parallel and square with the keel pieces while the glue dried. The strips were then removed and each section of the hull brought together, locking them by replacing the strips, this time with glue. The fin and its housing pieces were fitted between the relevant bulkheads as the centre section was built up, (Fig.7.3).

The keel support pieces and laminated stern blocks were fitted, together with the two side cheeks at the prow, (Fig.7.4). Everything was then left overnight for the glue to completely cure before removing the fin ready for shaping the external edges of the framework.

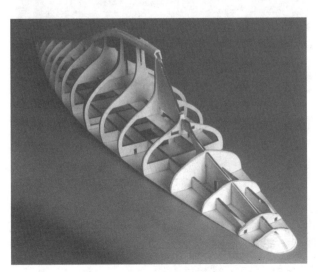

Fig. 7.5 The deck in place stabilises the hull framework whilst the bulkhead edges are chamfered

The instruction manual was most emphatic that the deck pieces should not be glued at this stage, only pinned. I could see the importance of this and the necessity to ensure that the cockpit aperture and the holes for the mast were in their correct position. However, having made those checks, I could not understand why the temporary fixing had to be sustained throughout the planking operation. In fact, it was my opinion that there were distinct benefits to gluing the deck before shaping the outer edges of the bulkheads and the stern and prow blocks, in that the glued deck provided much greater stability to the structure during that operation, (Fig.7.5).

PermaGrit flat and half-round tools made relatively light work of shaping the bulkhead edges. Attention was paid to chamfering of the keel pieces making sure that angles and edges were consistent with providing correct seating surfaces for the first planking. The area around the bulb of the keel was particularly important in this respect.

The first planking

This operation started at the very bottom of the keel in what was referred to as the "bulb" area. Twelve strips of 2mm square material were used either side of centre to cover the area aft of frame L18 back to the false keel L35. The upper part of the hull was then planked with 4 x 1mm starting at deck level and working downwards, (Fig.7.6). Planking was applied fore and aft of the double frame L16/25/26 until well below the waterline, when the length of the given material could be used to cover

Fig. 7.6 First planking in progress.

the entire length of the hull at that level.

When the hull had been completely covered, a coat of diluted PVA adhesive was brushed on and left it to dry before starting the rubbing down process. This completely eliminated any chance of a sprung plank, which, with only 1mm of thickness to work with, would have made the smoothing operation a bit difficult.

Planks were glued at each bulkhead and to each other using white PVA adhesive. Holes were drilled at each bulkhead position through the planks using a drill 0,1mm smaller than the diameter of the pins.

The second planking

The instruction manual gave the option of a total hull paint job or leaving the bottom surfaces covered with mahogany planking. I chose the latter finish, but I would like to make a comment about the planking for that option that is not covered in the instructions. Having used the 3 x 0,5mm strips to plank the bulb area as recommended, I then positioned a key 4 x 0,5mm strip from the step immediately above the top of the rudder, then forward until the whole length of the strip just overlapped the underside of the forefoot. It was

Fig. 7.7 Second planking below the key plank.

Fig. 7.8 The hull masked below the waterline.

important to ensure that it followed the natural curvature of the hull and lay completely flat against the first planked surface, **(Fig.7.7)**.

Planking was continued downwards towards the bulb, carefully shaping the forward end of the planks to match the earlier laid bulb planking, (again see **Fig.7.7**). It will be noted at this juncture that planking has been carried out using whole length planking strips without any butt joints. Working above the key plank, this cannot happen because the strips provided are not long enough. So, to avoid a central line of butt joints like those resulting from the first planking, full-length strips were laid alternately from the bow and the stern, cutting shorter lengths to complete the run. In this manner, the butt joints made a diagonal pattern that gradually moved upwards and towards the centre of the hull at the waterline from both bow and stern. The stagger of the butts above the waterline was much less, but still avoided a straight line. In any case, these would not be seen due to the several coats of primer and paint.

Tapering was minimal although there were just one or two instances where a stealer was needed. One side at a time was worked, carefully trimming the overlapping ends as work proceeded. This avoided mishaps when moving the hull around on the bench to conveniently present the surface in the right attitude for effective planking. Before starting the second side, the edges of the first side planks were gently filed to match the angle of the surface of the second side in order to get the best possible overlap condition. Even so, after finishing the hull planking operation, a gentle dribble of superglue was run along the centre-line joints and allowed it to completely cure before attempting any rubbing down.

For fixing the second planking, Thixofix thixotropic contact adhesive was used applied to both the hull and the plank. I discarded the serrated spreaders; the best way was undoubtedly to finger spread the adhesive on to both parts. Working on two planks at a time, the first was ready to position by the time that the second was coated.

The strips of 3x1mm were put in place around the top edges of the hull staggering the butt joints and the vertical pieces of the same size material were added using cyanoacrylate.

At this juncture I decided to deviate from the sequence suggested in the instructions and proceeded to make and fit the rudder and prepare the hull for painting and varnishing before laying the deck. I did this for two reasons; first to make masking a lot easier and, secondly, to avoid any possible over-spray onto handrails, which would now be positioned later together with the deck planking.

The rudder was assembled and offered up to the hull where it was found that its thickness needed to be reduced by at least one ply. This was to ensure that when planked, the rudder would not be thicker than the sternpost. The planking, 3x1mm mahogany was laid parallel to the sternpost and not horizontally in line with the lower hull.

Hull finishing

The whole surface of the hull was first scraped using both flat and curved cabinet-makers' scrapers. The pressure from this operation was particularly pertinent to planks laid using a contact adhesive, providing extra bedding-in facility. A light sanding with two reducing grades of fine abrasive paper was all that was required to prepare the hull for varnishing and priming.

The waterline was marked on and the lower hull

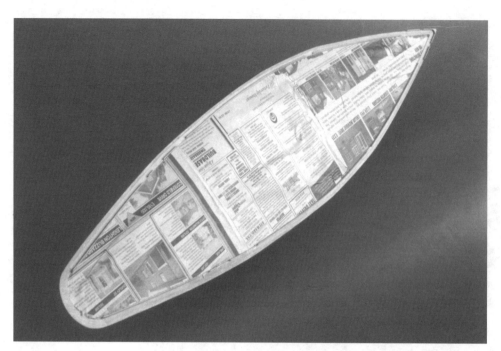

Fig. 7.9 Deck masked within the edge rails.

and the deck area masked, **(Figs.7.8** and **7.9)**, while the above-waterline area was sprayed with a couple of coats of grey primer/filler. The first coat revealed a few gaps and indentations that needed to be attended to. After filling, the surface was rubbed down with wet and dry paper then the second coat applied. Another rub down prepared the surface for colour coating.

Dark blue was sprayed on to the hull sides and top rim. A minimal rubbing with wet and dry paper took off the few high spots and a second coat applied. This was allowed to thoroughly dry before masking off the top half in order to varnish the under-surfaces. All masking was removed after about twelve hours.

White, self-adhesive car body trim strip was used to line the upper hull and waterline.

Planking the deck

This was one place in the construction where the drawings had to be used rather than the visual detail in the manual. The manual shows two planks between the lipped edge of the hull and the handrails whereas a much greater width was necessary in order that the various cleats could be properly positioned later on. Dimensions taken off the plan view solved the problem, **(Fig.7.10)**.

I also reasoned that it would be difficult to angle the ends of the planks to neatly butt up against the 4x1mm centre strip positioned before starting the planking. Accordingly, I marked the line of this strip with a pencil and merely overlapped the ends of the planks then cut a 4mm wide slot after the planking was finished. All of the pre-cut holes on the deck were kept open as

Fig. 7.10 Rails in place. Check drawing for distance from the edge of the hull.

Fig. 7.11 The stand

planking proceeded in order not to lose their position.

Thixofix contact adhesive was used for all deck planking except for the centre strip, which was secured with white PVA adhesive.

The stand was made up, **(Fig.7.11)**, and it was found that the seating points for the hull sides needed a bit of padding to properly support the hull. In fact, one supporting arm seems inadequately shaped and I finished up with a three-point seating.

Fittings

The pictorial presentation of the making and the siting of the fittings was very clear. However, there were one or two points that I think are worthy of mention.

The diameter of the drill required for the deck ports

and the winch drums was 6mm and the drill size for the eyelets was 1,5mm.

The wire provided for the boom tackle arch was 1,5mm diameter and would not enter the eyelets placed in the deck. This had to be replaced with 1mm diameter.

The three skylights have a central longitudinal strip specified to be 3x1mm. This thickness was not sufficient and it should be doubled up or replaced with 2mm thick material in order to be able to do the final roof shaping.

The fitting out of the deck is shown in **Figs.7.12** to **7.16** inclusive.

The mast

Considerable care was required to make the mast and the initial lamination of the six half-round sectioned

Fig. 7.12 Deck cleats and port-holes in position.

Fig. 7.13 The forward winch and skylight.

Fig. 7.14 The binnacle and skylight amidships.

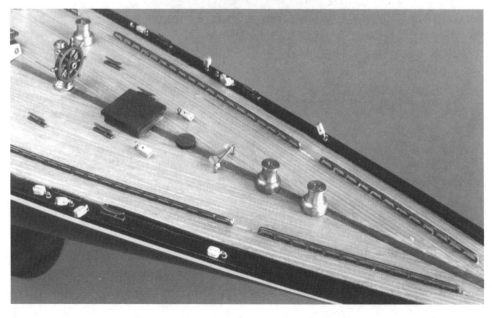

Fig. 7.16 The boom tackle arch and aft winches.

pieces was critical to ultimate success. Obviously it was essential to get the pieces in the correct relative position within the 146cm length, but it was also imperative to get them assembled straight. The use of a long straightedge was helpful and, the occasional rolling on a flat surface as each piece was added, provided an indication that things were in line. The use of white PVA adhesive had an adequate grab time to permit any adjustments as the construction proceeded. Each piece was allowed to grab before adding the next and, when complete, the assembly was left for 24 hours before moving on to the next stage.

The instruction manual suggests filing the taper prior to sanding. Even using the rough side of PermaGrit tools, this would be quite a formidable task, and I decided to plane the taper, first to square section, then octagonal, before taking the corners off with a file and finally rubbing down with reducing grades of abrasive paper.

The central joint line was used as a guide to fitting the tracks fore and aft in their correct orientation. Again, straightness was the order of the day and this time I used cyanoacrylate, applying it over short lengths at a time to maintain a constant check on alignment.

Holes for the three tubular spreaders were drilled. Having drilled the first, I slid a length of the tubing into place to act as an eyeballing aid to getting the second and third in correct alignment. The holes for all of the small eyelets and the boom pivot were then drilled in position and the spreaders fitted prior to painting satin white, filling as necessary, then rubbing down before applying a final coat of paint.

Painting was done before the fitting of the eyelets, **(Fig.7.17)**, primarily to avoid filling them up with paint and making it more difficult to glue the actual eye pins securely in place, but also for the cosmetic presentation of brass fittings on a white background.

I was puzzled as to the term "counterbalance" in respect of the two brackets and their attachments that fitted at the bottom of the two tracks on the front of the mast. At the size depicted, they would not have enough weight to counterbalance any of the sail rigging. In fact, investigation revealed that almost certainly these

Fig. 7.17 The upper spreaders assembled to the mast with eyelets in place.

were spinnaker holsters or pouches to house the spinnaker, which would then be hoisted up the track to the required height.

The boom

This item might also have been a bit tricky to make if I hadn't taken the trouble to give the process some thought before I started to pick up my tools. The boom was basically of rectangular section and a length of such timber was provided in the kit. However, the under-edge should be tapered upwards towards each end and, similarly, in plan view, the sides also taper to fore and to aft, while at the same time maintaining a true triangular section.

The starting positions of all tapers were marked and then, using a David plane, I planed the tapers on the bottom as seen in profile. This produced two triangular facets on to which I drew the centre line of the boom. I then planed the side tapers square to the top surface so that I now had a boom that looked right when viewed both from the top and the side. The plane was set to a very fine cut and the triangular section re-introduced using the top edges as gauging lines together with the pencil marked centre lines below.

The "I" section plastic strip was then cut into pieces and attached to the top surface of the boom. The cutting needed to be fairly accurate since there was only just enough material to do the job and I found that about 0.5mm overhang each side was about the right size to aim at. Each piece was stuck on with cyanoacrylate and when thoroughly cured the ends were trimmed to match the width of the boom.

Holes were then drilled to house the several eyelets and the pintle/gudgeon pivot unit fixed to the fore end. The boom was painted before inserting these fittings.

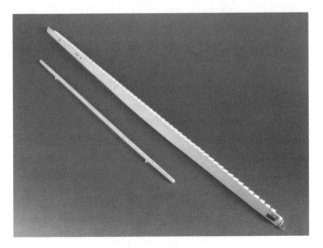

Fig. 7.18 The finished boom and spinaker pole.

Fig. 7.19 The belaying of some of the standing and running rigging.

The finished boom is shown in **Fig.7.18**.

The standing rigging

Having stepped the mast, the standing rigging was set up. For the most part, the rigging instructions were adequate although you do have to carefully consult drawings, instructions and illustrated manual to obtain the complete picture. For me, this stage of the building process could have been made clearer but I hasten to add that this is a personal comment rather than a severe criticism. There are several ways in which rigging instructions can be portrayed, they all have some disadvantages and there will always be model makers for whom the chosen method is inadequate.

The hairiness of the 1mm black thread needed to be sorted out and PVA adhesive was applied by pulling the material through gluey fingers!

Tension on a model of this size had to be sufficient so as not to sag under the weight of the sails to be fitted, but not so great that it would distort the mast alignments or pull out the eyebolt fixings. Passing the ends of the rigging through the relevant eyebolt, doubling and lashing did all fixing.

The sails

The suggested procedure for making the sails worked well. However, I felt that there were a few points that might help make things a bit easier.

Ensure that the material is adequately sealed to avoid excessive fraying at the edges and is well stretched to make subsequent handling easier.

When ironing the material make sure that the iron is set fairly low. The setting for rayon or silk is about right. Higher temperatures will tend to soften the fabric and make it stick to the iron.

For marking the seams, I used a flat lead pencil (0.2mm thick) to retain a constant thickness of line and grade HB for density. An ordinary pencil will do the job just as well but, of course, the lead has to be constantly trimmed.

The vertical seam was wired with soft brass wire to assist in forming the concertina effect simulating the furled down condition.

The running rigging

The running rigging was basically the same as for the "sails up" condition, except that most lines needed to be rigged slack.

The rigging to the two foresails was quite straightforward and although I chose to portray the vessel with the sails furled down; the rigging would remain attached as described in the manual. However, the rigging to the mainsail is almost certainly not shown correctly in that the halyard that runs through a sheave at the top of the mast would not be tied off to the aforementioned spinnaker holsters, but to a cleat via a block and winch. To raise or lower the sail a considerable length of rope would have been employed and would have been coiled after belaying to the cleat.

As a matter of interest, the area of the main sail was around 412 square metres and, in 1934, before the advent of today's lightweight materials, would have had considerable weight and would certainly have had to be winched up rather than manhandled.

Should you wish to rig the sails furled down as I did, the two foresails were rigged to their respective stays with just three or four rings. The mainsail was fixed to the rear of the mast by the same method as shown in the manual but the holes for the split pins were grouped 6mm apart except for the upper four which were spaced by increasing amounts, 15mm, 20mm and the last two at 30mm. The bottom pin was put in place first and the sail edge concertina'd to bring the next pin into position. This procedure was repeated until the uppermost pins had been fixed. The sail was then draped and lashed to the boom. Some of the belaying of running rigging can be seen in **Fig.7.19**.

The dinghy

This represents the most difficult aspect of model making in the entire kit and the method shown in the illustrated manual is not very practical. Putting pins through 2mm wide strip to secure them at the prow is bad enough, but most of them had to be tapered to a size less than that, making the task unworkable even with carefully drilled holes.

I solved the problem by adapting the basic framework, **(Fig.7.20)**, such that I was left with only that part that was relevant to the shape of the boat shell, all the supporting part having been cut away. When planking, I glued the planks permanently to the framework using cyanoacrylate which avoided the use of pins altogether. Of course, this method could only be used if the inside of the boat was not being displayed and was to be lashed upside down to the deck as shown on the box art, (Fig.7.21).

Conclusions

As a model maker whose area of interest lies primarily in the 18th century, I tackled this project with some trepidation. However, from a constructional standpoint, I found the kit both interesting and enjoyable to build. There was nothing *really* difficult involved but what there was required quite a lot of patience.

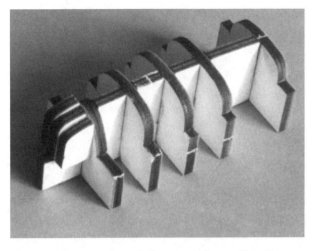

Fig. 7.20 The un-adapted framework for making the dinghy.

The instruction manuals were relatively clear and straightforward and the one or two typographical errors were never really a problem. The illustrated guide was particularly good and easy to follow. However, it should be stressed that at each stage, it was wise to consult both manuals and the relevant drawings for total clarity.

The design of the basic hull framework was excellent and provided a strong and stable foundation for planking the hull. All major parts were accurately laser cut in good quality material and required little attention prior to use.

The making of the mast tested both eye and hand and was certainly not a job for the dining room table. Fittings were excellent and the inclusion of photo-etched brass grills for the glazed areas was a nice touch. Sails are always a bit of a problem but the suggested procedure for making them was pretty good if followed to the letter.

I had no serious complaint at all concerning the kit as a model-making exercise; my main criticism reserved for the rigging of the main sail halyard, which even with my sparse knowledge of yachts and yachting, was obviously incorrect. Nonetheless, for £200 and with a reasonable paint job, the kit produced a most impressive model of a classic yacht.

Fig. 7.21 The finished dinghy lashed down on deck.

CHAPTER 8

The Armed Transport "Bounty"

The Admiralty purchased the "Bethia" in May 1787. She had been built and completed on the River Hull some two or three years earlier, although at the time of her purchase she was lying at Old Wapping Stairs. The Admiralty Board were instructed regarding the vessel's fitting out and in June 1787, it was registered on the list of Royal Navy Ships as H.M. Armed Transport "Bounty". Various changes were made to meet the standards of the day for the Royal Navy and in preparation for a voyage to the South Seas.

I suppose most people are familiar with the famous mutiny that took place in April 1789 about two weeks after the ship had left Tahiti bound for home. The ship was taken over and Captain Bligh, along with a number of his loyal followers, was set adrift in the ship's 23ft launch. Bligh, after a masterful piece of navigation, brought his small boat to landfall after a voyage of some 3600 miles. After his subsequent return to England, he was given command of a naval vessel, fought at Copenhagen and was personally commended by Nelson.

Meanwhile, after several months at sea searching for refuge, the mutineers under Fletcher Christian, a former friend of Captain Bligh, finally ran "Bounty" aground at Pitcairn Island and burned her in January 1790.

The kit

First impressions were that the quality of the strip wood in this kit was excellent. All essential ply parts were very finely laser cut and the range of fittings was as high a standard as I had seen in any kit of this class. The drawings were supplemented by an illustrated instruction manual that were intended to give an extremely clear indication of what had to be done, and when. The manual's text was translated into English in a separate booklet. All in all, a pretty impressive package. The model has an overall length of 760mm.

The kit is described as being of "Museum Standard." Exactly what this is supposed to mean, I am not sure. Certainly, the kit is capable of being converted into a model of such standard but, surely, that is more to do with the skill and craftsmanship of the model maker.

Tools required

The usual craft knife, scalpel and razor saw are the main cutting tools required. Flat and half-round files or PermaGrit tools will fulfil the abrasive needs, backed up by various grades of abrasive paper. A small electric drill will be most useful with a selection of twist drills up to about 2mm diameter, together with a light hammer or pin pusher. A plank nipper should handle any plank bending.

White PVA, contact adhesive such as Thixofix, and a bottle of cyanoacrylate covered the sticking department.

There is a certain amount of painting to do, so surface preparation in the form of sanding sealer will prove advantageous. As for paint, I used Humbrol acrylics. When stirred properly, they cover well and don't get absorbed by the wood, as is the case of some other paint designed, perhaps, more for plastic surfaces. The other big advantage, of course, is that your brushes can be cleaned with water and maybe a touch of washing-up liquid.

Hull construction

The hull construction uses the frames on false keel method with reinforcements at stem and stern. However, right from the word go, there were one or two things that cropped up not mentioned in the instructions, or shown on the drawings, that might have caught the unwary or the beginner. First, it was fairly obvious that the kit had been updated to provide laser cut parts, which now combined what formerly were several individual pieces. But, drawings and instructions did not reflect these changes.

The first job to be done was to cut two slots in the false keel to act as locators for the fore and mizzen masts. I made these 8mm wide for the foremast and 6mm wide for the mizzen mast, both slots being 3mm deep. The 6mm width was measured forward of the front face of frame No.13.

The frames were a good fit on the false keel and needed virtually no work or adjustment to achieve squareness or alignment. I did, however, choose to angle

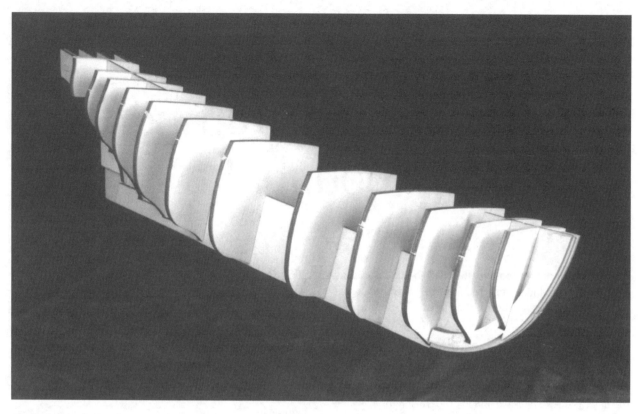

Fig. 8.1 Frames in place on false keel with reinforcing pieces at prow.

the top edges of the frames to match the line of the deck before final assembly. The reinforcing pieces, particularly those at the prow, had to be trimmed for best fit. It is essential to glue these well and leave them to cure thoroughly before attempting to shape them to the lines of the vessel. The assembled frames and reinforcing pieces can be seen in **Figs.8.1** and **8.2**.

The planking of the false deck was carried out using 4x0,5mm walnut material. These were sorted to ensure that truly parallel planks were selected for the task and any that had slight taper were earmarked for the second planking on the hull. The edges of the deck planks were blackened with a felt tipped marker pen to assimilate the caulking and Thixofix contact adhesive was used for mounting them on to the false ply deck.

The deck was glued in place before shaping the edges of the frames and the reinforcing pieces. The assembled deck gave the whole structure much greater

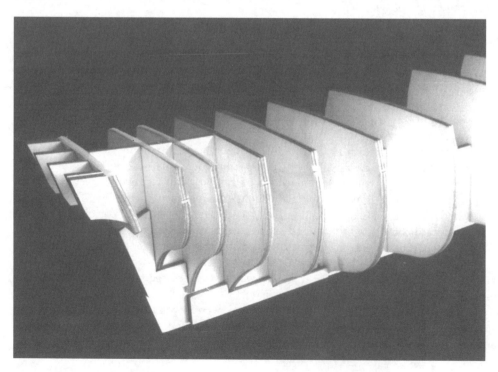

Fig. 8.2 Assembled frames and stern reinforcements before shaping to the lines of the vessel.

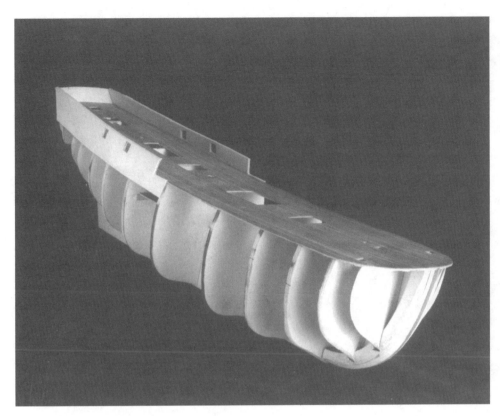

stability for this somewhat arduous operation.

The transom and bulwarks are pre-cut from 1mm ply first checking the width of the bulwark pieces which should, according to the instruction manual, match the depth of the transom and be fixed to the edges of the rear frames. Any adjustments necessary were made before removing the parts from the sheet. The assembled deck and bulwarks are shown in **Fig.8.3**.

The shape of the hull is not too modeller friendly with regard to the first planking and, although I managed to do all bending with an Amati Plank Nipper, I found it necessary to thoroughly soak the timber first. Accurate marking and tapering were essential features of the planking process in order to attain a sound basis for the second planking.

It further paid to study the shape and size of the transom, taking into consideration the etched brass and cast ornamentation provided for that area. A bit of careful measurement paid dividends later on in the construction.

The second planking, in 4x0,5mm walnut, was relatively straightforward and Thixofix thixotropic contact adhesive was used throughout this stage of building. The curves at bow and stern still needed close attention and careful tapering was required to keep the planks flat against the surface of the first planking.

One point worth mentioning at this stage is the fact that "Bounty" would certainly have been copper clad below the waterline. White anti-fouling, as indicated in the kit, would not have proved adequate for a voyage to the South Seas. To simulate the plating, I cut the planking strips into short pieces, having trimmed the upper planking to the waterline, see **Fig.8.4**.

The capping strip that runs around the edges of the

fore part of the deck is indicated as being made from 5x1mm strip. I have to say that bending this size of material on the width around the sort of radius at the bows is ambitious indeed. However, all was not lost, the 1mm ply sheet from which the false deck was cut providing an easy solution. The material adjacent to the fore part of the deck was readily adapted to provide 5mm wide strips with just the right curve.

The main wale was made up from several strips of 2x2mm laminated together. Care was needed to ensure that the position of this feature was correct, particularly at the aft end where several other bits and pieces all come together. The drawings show a rubbing strake just above the wale, but I have reservations about this and believe that the upper part of the wale was actually a band of thinner

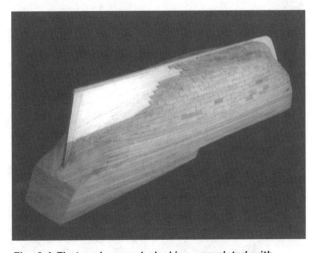

Fig. 8.4 First and second planking completed with partial application of "copper" sheathing below the waterline.

Fig. 8.5 Rails and wales take longer than one might think. Careful measurements are needed to align port and starboard correctly.

material. Accordingly I used a couple of 2x1mm strips.

It was worth making up one gun carriage assembly to check on the position of the gun ports. It presents quite a problem if, when rigging the guns later on, you find that the barrels are too high to go through the bulwarks. Once the position was confirmed the port frames could then be fitted.

At this juncture, I decided to give the hull its first couple of coats of paint. I did this to make life simpler in the later

stages of construction where wielding a paintbrush amidst lots of fittings and protrusions would be a bit of a pain.

The amidships rails and associated pin racks need to be glued and dowelled. They are a little bit vulnerable and certainly need to be strong enough to take the tension of the later rigging. The sketches in the manual rather than the drawing detail, show the correct assembly procedure of rails to pillars.

The 3mm square strip for the pillars for the half-

Fig. 8.6 The basic hull construction completed and painted.

Fig. 8.7 The fitted-out deck. The fife rails around the fore-mast should be parallel to the waterline, not the deck. The head timbers are fitted ready to take the head rails.

pounder swivel guns was painted before cutting each to length, again to avoid fiddly work with the paint brush later on.

The hull construction to this stage is shown in **Figs.8.5** and **8.6**.

Having fitted the channels and boarding steps each side of hull, I decided that further work on the hull would be made easier if the model stood on a stand. I discarded the one provided in the kit in favour of my own set-up. This is not to say that the Amati stand is inadequate, just a matter of personal choice. I also made up an oversize nameplate at this juncture, comprising a piece of thin ply, gloss varnished, to which I applied rub

down lettering. A further sealing coat of varnish was left to dry before trimming the edges of the nameplate to centralise the lettering.

Fitting out

There was a little confusion between the sketches and the photographs in the manual with regard to the direction in which the hatch covers ran, fore and aft in the photograph and athwartships in the sketches. Like gratings, I considered that the ledges would run across the hatch and the visible covers, like battens, would run fore and aft.

The windlass barrel was made up from a set of five

Fig. 8.8 The fitted out deck. The spindle of the ship's wheel should also be parallel to the waterline.

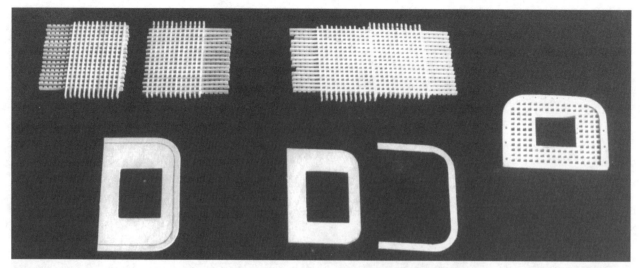

Fig. 8.9 Two pieces of grating assembled then joined together. The pressed ply platform has been marked and cut to remove a 4mm wide band from front and sides.

castings. These fitted very well together into pre-cut wooden trunnions. To enhance the appearance of the assembly, I deepened holes in the barrel parts where indicated.

The chimneystack from the galley also came as a cast part. The stove fitted to "Bounty" was almost certainly a Brodie stove and, as such, would have had a circular sectioned rotateable stack. I therefore made the appropriate modification to the casting, retained the base part and added a wooden upper stack.

The fife rail assembly around the foremast proved to be a bit fiddly and care was needed to observe right and left handed supports as well as those fore and aft, heights having to accommodate the slope in the deck to bring the rails proper in to the horizontal plane.

The space between the uprights of the bitt forward of the foremast should be 8mm in order to house the butt end of the bowsprit. A similar dimension should be accommodated between the uprights of the knightheads adjacent to the stem. These features can be seen in **Fig.8.7**, and the entire fitted out deck in **Fig.8.8**.

The remaining items were relatively straightforward and, treating each unit as an individual project, I found few problems. One feature that was missing from both drawings and manual was the binnacle. This essential housing for the compass should be positioned between the ship's wheel and the aft side of the mizzen mast. My unit was made from scrap 5mm square strip and the top surface faced with 6x1mm and can be seen in **Fig.8.18**.

All fittings were, where practical, dowelled and glued to the deck for maximum strength.

The carriage guns

"Bounty" was equipped with four 4-pounders and ten half-pounder swivels. The kit provides the complete carriages integrally cast with trucks and chock, requiring only the barrel to be assembled. However, as it was intended to fully rig the ordnance, it was necessary to drill the sides of the carriage to mount rings to take the tackle. I chose to keep the rigging of the guns as simple

as possible but, nonetheless, featured the breeching rope, the traversing tackle at the rear, and the gun tackle each side of the carriage to the inside of the bulwarks.

I am never sure that the results of rigging guns, at this sort of scale, is really worth the effort. It is extremely difficult to get a lifelike appearance to the "hang" of the various ropes and I feel that in some ways this detracts from the overall presentation of the model. On the other hand, things do not look complete if the carriages appear to be free to slide willy-nilly across the deck. Maybe the fitting of just the breeching rope would be an adequate compromise?

The head rails

All parts came as soft metal castings, which added considerably to the ease of assembling items that are normally a bit of a headache. The cross-timbers were put in place on the stem post first, followed by the rails. I found that it was best to start with the rail immediately below the cross- timbers, which established a line for the bottom rail. The former rail was in two parts, the upper piece containing the scroll end behind the figurehead. The join was indicated to be just ahead of the front cross-timber, but comparing the two pieces of metal, it was apparent that the sections would not match at this point. Accordingly, I made the join immediately below the scroll. The two upper rails were then added, it being found to be advantageous to start the shaping at the scroll end and then work along the length to the point where it was necessary to cut and shape the thinner end. It was much more convenient to do the total head rail assembly before putting the catheads in position.

The Ship's Boat

Amati provides one of their excellent small boat kits within the main package and this makes up into a very acceptable part of the deck fittings line-up. A finely cast shell is fitted out with wooden floor and thwarts, a little bit fiddly in places, but not too difficult to get a worthwhile

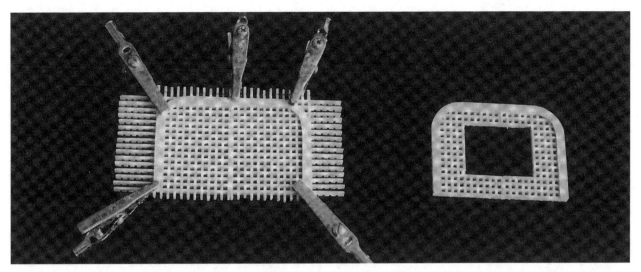

Fig. 8.10 4mm wide band glued to grating assembly. Edges are then trimmed.

result, see **Fig.8.17**. My only adverse comment here is that while the box art and manual photograph show two boats stacked amidships, the kit only provided one.

Masts and spars

I started by making and mounting the bowsprit. The construction was straightforward, the two main items being made from dowel, tapered and cut to required length. The bowsprit cap, together with the main and fore caps, were provided in the kit as soft metal castings. These are fine for the two masts concerned, but some work is necessary to angle the two holes in the cap for the bowsprit, particularly the square hole for the end of the bowsprit proper. Some packing and, subsequently, filling was required to produce an acceptable result.

The little research that I had been able to do indicated that Captain Bligh had required the mast tops to be gratings rather than planked. I assumed that Amati had also come to recognise this feature, and had included

extra grating packs in the kit for the modeller to make this style of top, if he so wished. However, the drawings and instructions in my kit did not specifically mention such modification and I offer the approach I adopted for their construction.

It was apparent that the gratings for the two largest tops would have to be in two parts, the mizzen top just fitting within the area possible with the grating strips provided. I then took the pressed out ply pieces for supplied for the planked style top and carefully marked and cut a 4mm wide band from around the two sides and front edges. The centrepiece remaining was kept to act as a template for sizing and positioning the central cut-out on each top, see **Fig.8.9**. Having assembled two gratings for the main and fore tops, the cut away 4mm band was then glued to the upper surface of the gratings, see **Fig.8.10**. It was important to remember to check that the grating strips all ran in the same direction, i.e., athwartships when viewed from above.

The edges of the gratings were then trimmed to the outer contours of the 4mm band and then covered with scrap strip. The centre cut-outs were then made and lined and holes drilled for the mounting of the futtock shrouds and deadeyes. It was also convenient at this juncture to drill holes along the front edge of the tops for rigging the crowsfeet.

Having made all three tops, I then tapered the various mast parts from the dowel provided and constructed the several cross trees and trestletrees, see **Figs.8.12** and **8.13**. The drawings indicate that the lower shrouds be set up before assembling the upper masts. My own preferred method is to assemble the masts complete on the bench before stepping them into the hull. I find this easier in terms of getting everything at the right angle and in line from butt end to truck. On this model, at least, I could see no real disadvantages with either procedure.

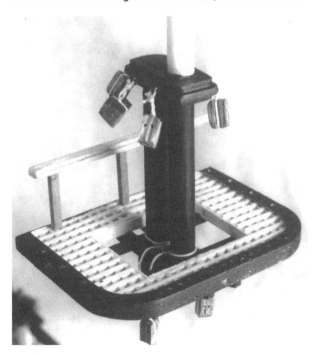

Fig. 8.12 The fore top. It is most helpful to add the rigging blocks at this stage having first ensured that all holes are clear.

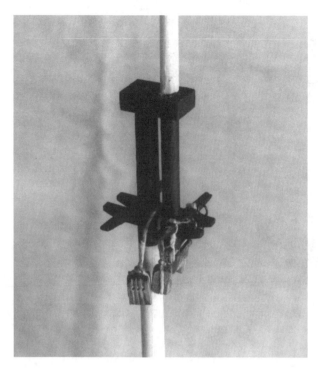

Fig. 8.13 The topmast trestle and cross trees.

Rigging

The instructions and drawings that showed the sequence and run of the various items of rigging were pretty good, albeit that one has to refer to several sheets and the manual, also familiarise oneself with the identification codes. This is not a criticism of the method used, the writing of such guidelines is an horrendous task and considering the amount of rigging involved, Amati have done quite well.

The most pertinent note in the manual regarding rigging, was the advice to start with the standing rigging, working from bottom to top. For the yards and other running rigging, work from the centre to the outside. This was sound advice and would equally apply to the rigging of most other static models of this type.

A further process that many model makers forget or overlook, is to ensure that all of the blocks used are properly drilled. If you happen to miss one, you can be sure that it is always the one in the most inaccessible place on the vessel!

Remember too, that rings and watch straps are potentially hazardous when getting fingers and hands amongst the rigging.

All standing rigging was set up using black thread.

I think that a word of warning is relevant to the setting up of the lower shrouds. The brass chain plate items that hold the deadeyes in place on the channels were on the soft side and would easily distort if the lanyards between the deadeyes were pulled up too tight.

The futtock shrouds were set up using 1mm thread.

The ratlines were added to the shrouds before rigging the backstays, which take up quite a bit of finger room. Actually, I left the backstays until the rigging was almost complete for the same reason; they certainly restrict finger access if you put them on earlier.

The various fore and aft stays were then set up to complete the standing rigging as shown in **Fig.8.14**.

The running rigging shown in the manual relates to a model fitted with sails. If, as in my case, sails were not desired on the model then, obviously, one or two modifications were necessary. The upper yards were lowered to the caps below and the sheets and the tacks to the main and fore courses were hauled up by the

Fig. 8.15 The fore and preventer stays plus other bowsprit rigging

Fig. 8.16 The front end with anchor and buoy rigged to the fore shrouds. Note the clew'd up fore tacks and sheets.

clue garnets as shown in **Fig.8.16**.

All running rigging was put up using tan coloured thread, see **Figs.8.14** through **8.18**.

The identification of the various bits of rigging, where they went and where they were belayed, was a little time consuming. For the most part, the drawings and manual seemed reasonably accurate, but I did need to concentrate hard to follow the codes and symbols.

Neither drawing nor manual showed braces to the crossjack yard on the mizzen mast. A little research indicated that single-block brace pendants hung forward of the crossjack ends and the brace for the starboard pendant started from mid-way up the aft side of the port main shroud. It passed across the vessel, through the pendant block, back to a block on the port shroud and down to the main rail. The brace for the port pendant was similarly rigged across from the starboard main shroud, see **Fig.8.18**.

Finishing off

An additional feature that I felt worth considering was main stay tackle used for hoisting boats and hatches, **Fig.8.17**. Nothing very difficult but something that added that little bit extra.

Coils of rope to hang on the pin rails or lay on the deck as appropriate were made up from the corresponding thickness of thread, see **Fig.8.16**. A tedious

job this, but one that is essential to complete the model.

A good look around the model revealed several untrimmed, or poorly trimmed ends, which needed attention. Odd bits of dust and muck had got into corners and crevices and were blown or brushed out. If you have a camera with a close-up lens, you may find it worthwhile scanning the entire model through the viewfinder. The concentrated eye often picks up all sorts of errors that may otherwise be missed.

Conclusions

The overall quality and quantity of materials was very good. Castings and etched brass parts simplified the construction of features that modellers often find daunting, i.e. the head-rails and stern decoration. The fittings provided were superb and permitted the construction of a very impressive model, but definitely not one for the beginner.

I found the rigging thread extremely good. It took the application of dilute PVA very well for sealing knots and permitted the very close trimming of ends. The twist was well set and didn't open out into several stands when cut.

Value for money? If you want to do a bit of extra research and spend a fair bit of time to build a good "Bounty", you won't do much better than this.

CHAPTER 9

H.M.S. "Agamemnon"

This kit, in the Caldercraft Nelson's Navy series for "Nelson's Favourite", the 64-gun ship of the line, H.M.S. "Agamemnon", has been the subject of the same exacting research and construction techniques established in the earlier kits within the range. One or two innovations to overcome some of the problems that have dogged model makers down the years, like the securing deadeyes to channels and tops, have also been included.

Brief History

H.M.S. "Agamemnon" was built at Buckler's Hard on the Beaulieu River in Hampshire under the supervision of the reputable master shipbuilder, Henry Adams.

Designed by the famous naval architect, Sir Thomas Slade, work started on "Agamemnon" in May 1777 and, this 64-gun, Third Rate ship of the line with an elm keel nearly 132 feet long,

was launched in April 1781. After masting and provisioning at Portsmouth, "Agamemnon" commenced her maiden voyage on the 9th July 1781 under the command of Captain Benjamin Caldwell.

For those interested in the finer detail of naval history, it is interesting to note that one of Caldwell's young officers was Thomas Hardy, later to become Nelson's flag-captain at Trafalgar.

The "Agamemnon's" sixty-four guns comprised twenty-six 24-pounders, twenty-six 18-pounders and twelve 9-pounders. In spite of this considerable armament, in her early years, she was a fast and very manoeuvrable ship.

After seeing action off Ushant, she joined Admiral Sir George Rodney's squadron in the Caribbean where she took part in the Battle of The Saintes in 1782. Later the same year "Agamemnon" returned to England and was subsequently paid off in 1783. She lay inactive for nearly a decade before Horatio Nelson took command in 1793. It was during his three years with the vessel that engagements at Toulon, San Fiorenza and Bastia entered the annals of English maritime history. The siege of Calvi, where Nelson lost the use of his right eye, and action off Hyeres had taken severe toll of the fabric of the ship and in 1796 "Agamemnon"

returned to England for major re-fitting.

After being involved in the Naval Mutinies of 1797, "Agamemnon" was at the Battle of Copenhagen under Captain Fancourt. However, she took little part in the engagement, being hemmed in on a shoal along with the grounded "Bellona" and "Russell".

Captain Sir Edward Berry took command just prior to the Battle of Trafalgar in 1805. Badly damaged during the engagement, "Agamemnon" limped to Gibraltar for temporary attention, then back to England for major repairs. The following year saw her back at sea, involved in the blockade of Cadiz and the subsequent Battle of Santo Domingo.

Now under the command of Jonas Rose, further action at the Siege of Copenhagen was followed by involvement at the blockade of Lisbon in 1807. Then, in 1808, in the company of "Fourdroyant" and "Pitt", "Agamemnon" crossed the Atlantic to Brazil. After the taking of the town of Maldonado, she finally ran aground in Maldonado Bay. The condition of her undersides was poor to say the least and, in the manoeuvring around the shoals, the fluke of one of her anchors had penetrated the bottom. Rose had no alternative but to abandon the vessel to its fate.

Following an extended search by marine archaeologists, divers have recently discovered the remains of H.M.S. "Agamemnon" and, although there is nothing of significance left of the timbers, there are many interesting artefacts that will undoubtedly be treasure to archaeologists and naval historians alike.

The kit

A big box, a full box and a heavy box, in fact, almost needing a forklift truck. Virtually everything that could be pre-cut had been the subject of CNC routing, with spot-on accuracy in top class timber, whether it was ply or walnut. Cross-halving joints for the trestletrees and crosstrees were pre-cut, as were, of course, similar joints for the false keel/bulkhead assembly. The strip wood was of high quality and consistent in size and straightness, with no sign of coarse grain or unacceptable blemish. There were four sheets of etched brass sheet for all the fiddly bits, castings for the decorative pieces and nine hanks of black and natural rigging thread with a total length of 343 metres. An instruction manual that provided a detailed parts list, illustrated identification layouts for all the brass and pre-cut parts as well as the building instructions, supplemented by nine sheets of drawings. I should also mention that there was a pack of 2500 copper plates for the bottom surface of the hull!

A lot of space to work was essential, remembering that it was necessary to push the main carcase to one side occasionally while things like deck fittings and masts etc. were worked on. What was probably the most significant consideration was the facility to turn the model around on the bench easily and safely. The finished model is large and measures 1300mm long, has a height of 945mm and a width of 490mm across the main yard stunsail booms.

Tools required

Because of the amount of pre-cutting and the excellent design of the kit in general, the tool list is fairly simple and I merely copy from that itemised in the instruction manual:

> Craft knife
> A selection of needle files
> Razor saw
> Small wood plane or David plane
> Pin vice or small electric drill, the latter being the recommended item
> Selection of drill bits from 0,5mm to 3,0mm diameter
> Selection of abrasive papers and sanding block
> Selection of good quality paint brushes
> Pliers/wire cutters
> Good quality tweezers
> Dividers or compass
> Steel rule (300mm)
> Clothes pegs or "crocodile" clips
> Tee square
> Pencil or Edding pen
> Masking tape

To this list I would add, for ease of working although by no means essential, a selection of PermaGrit abrasive tools and a couple of cabinet maker's scrapers.

The instruction manual also contains a list of the various paints and varnish required together with the recommended adhesives. These are, of course, added extras not provided in the kit.

> White PVA
> Walnut wood dye
> Cyanoacrylate - medium and thick viscosity
> Walnut wood filler
> Black Indian ink
> White spirit
> Epoxy resin adhesive
> Matt polyurethane varnish
> Black paint (Humbrol 85) – 3 tins
> White paint (Humbrol 34) – 1 tin

> Blue paint (Humbrol 25) – 1 tin
> Yellow paint (Humbrol 74) – 3 tins
> Red paint (Humbrol 60 + 25% Humbrol 70) – 3 tins and 1 tin respectively
> Copper paint (Humbrol 12) – 1 tin
> Gold paint (Humbrol 16) – 1 tin
> Flesh paint (Humbrol 61) – 1 tin
> Brown leather (Humbrol 62) – 1 tin

You may also consider using Humbrol acrylic paint rather than the tins of enamel and take advantage of the easier brush cleaning using water. (The numbers are similar).

Preliminaries

Before making a start, a few suggestions that may avoid problems, or at least pave the way for a smooth running project.

Do make sure that all your tools are sharp and keep an oilstone handy to keep them that way. Ensure that spare blades for the craft knife of your choice are to hand.

It is worth repeating the suggestion in the manual to read the instructions and study the relevant parts of the drawings at each stage of the construction, treating each step as a mini-project in its own right.

Do not let past experience inveigle you into making any wrong moves. There are doubtless many procedures that can be done in a manner alternative to those recommended in the kit, but before you deviate, make sure that they are viable. There was considerable time and effort put into the design to ensure that the sequences suggested provided the required result.

Making the hull carcase

The drawings provided dimensions for a simple building board and it was a wise move to spend a bit of time in making this in order to keep the basic framework of the hull straight and true in the early stages of construction. The only variation to the design that I made was to make three swivelling clamps for easier loading and release of the keel from the building board, **(Fig.9.1)**.

The basis of the carcase was the conventional bulkhead on false keel assembly, **(Fig.9.2)**, and it was during a dry run the size of the model really hit home. The pre-cut slots needed little attention to attain a square snug fit and the overall accuracy of the CNC work came through when fitting the main gun deck. This part has the effect of locking all the bulkheads in place on to the false keel and it slid into place like a dream. This had to be a very gentle operation since the 5mm ply deck had to be fed over the vulnerable upper ears of the bulkheads. But the accuracy was such that I never felt in fear of a disaster.

The dry run served several purposes. It confirmed the squareness, straightness and general stability of the assembly and, for those who want to make something really special, it enables the position of internal surfaces that may require painting to be

H.M.S. "Victory"

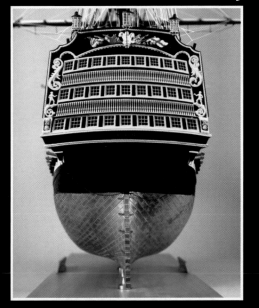

Period Ships
in Colour

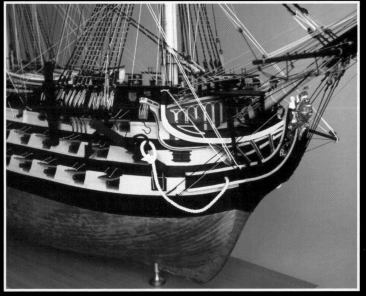

H.M.S. "Victory's" Launch

"Endeavour" J-Class Yacht

English Carronade

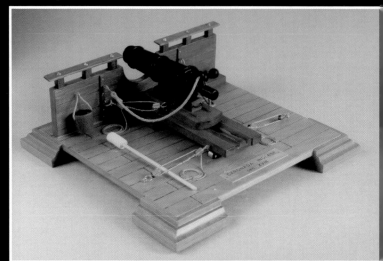

The Armed Transport "Bounty"

H.M.S.
"Agamemnon"

H.M.S. "Mars"

H.M. Cutter "Lady Nelson"

H.M. Barque "Endeavour"

Fig. 9.1 The building board with the false keel held in place with three swivel clamps.

Fig. 9.2 Bulkheads mounted on to the keel. Possibly "seen" edges are painted red.

Fig. 9.3 One of the three trapped nuts for attaching the finished model to stand and pedestals.

Fig. 9.4 Dummy barrel blocks are well jointed but must be firmly glued on to main gun deck.

around the dummy gun positions where someone with a small mirror can peer into the model through the open gun-ports. I kid you not; there are people who carry such a tool in their top pocket alongside the 6in rule, magnifying glass the inevitable row of ballpoint pens and sometimes even the little torch! The point to be made was that it was easier to paint before planking than trying to poke a brush through the gun-ports later on.

There were a couple of other tasks that I considered worthwhile before getting the glue out, the main one being to chamfer the edges of the bulkheads to provide a full width seating for the first planking. Using a short piece of planking material, it was not too difficult to see where the chamfering was needed, and the worst of the material was removed holding the bulkhead either flat on the bench or in the vice as convenient. This avoided, as far as possible, putting the vulnerable ears of the bulkheads at risk. The final chamfering was carried out after the assembly of the bulkheads to the false keel. The relevant edges of the plank termination pieces were similarly treated.

A bit of advance thinking suggested to me that it might be helpful to reduce the thickness of the false

keel at its back edge. This took the form of a taper from the bearding line, (the line that curves up from the keel at the bottoms of the bulkheads Nos.12 to 16), to a thickness of 3mm at the back edge of the false keel. This would greatly reduce the amount of sanding that would be necessary after the first and second planking, remembering that the sternpost and the rudder should both finish up with basically the same thickness prior to coppering. Of course, there are several ways of tackling the requirements of this area; the main thing is to consider it at this stage so that it doesn't become a problem later on.

It seemed a bit premature to start considering the stand at this stage, but if you intend to mount the finished model on pedestals rather than sit it in a cradle, then now is the time to make your final decision and do whatever work is necessary to the false keel before assembly. It was my intention to bolt the model from beneath a wooden base, the threaded screws passing up through the pedestals into the false keel into which I would trap 2BA nuts and washers soldered together. To that end I cut three slots 4mm wide into the bottom edge of the false keel and with a small file made slots for the nuts ensuring a tight fit before using epoxy adhesive to hold them in place, **(Fig.9.3)**. The false keel was edged with the walnut stem and stern pieces and the walnut keel drilled after assembly with holes 3,8mm diameter to take the shanks of the screws. Using this system there were no protrusions from the bottom of the model during the remainder of the construction process. The walnut

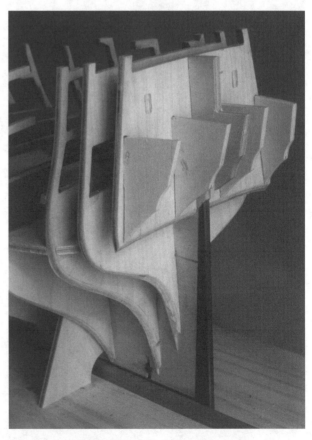

Fig. 9.5 Stern counter/fascia frames in position.

Fig. 9.6 Upper gun deck dry run using dowel rods to check mast alignment.

pieces were a perfect fit around the false keel, a further indication of the accuracy of machining and a most encouraging start to the building process.

It was important to join the bulkheads No's 15 and 16 together with two spacer blocks before gluing to the false keel. The remaining bulkheads were positioned and, before the glue dried, the lower deck was put in place, **(Fig.9.4)**, together with the bow deck and the stern counter patterns, **(Fig.9.5)**. The two outer counter patterns were angled inwards to conform to the outer lines of the hull and to do this the tenons on the rear edge needed a little bit of relief. The result, when the glue had cured, was a sound and rigid framework upon which the rest of the hull construction could be carried out.

The beams for the upper gun deck were then put in place and held with "crocodile" clips while the glue dried. Care was taken to ensure the correct selection of beam and to glue it on to the correct side of its relevant bulkhead.

There was a choice about planking the upper gun deck. The false deck could be sprung into position and then planked *in situ* or it could be planked before assembly. If the latter method was adopted, the planked deck would have to be cut longitudinally down the centre line in order to feed it into position over the bulwark ears. However, the great advantage was the easier deck sanding and finishing operation before assembly.

The planking could be done in one of two ways. Either full-length strips could be laid down and the butt joints marked or cut in afterwards, or the planks could be cut into separate and exactly identical lengths, then

laid according to the correct pattern. I chose the latter method, albeit that a full-length strip was laid down the centre line of the deck first and the glue allowed to thoroughly dry, to provide a good solid edge against which to plank. I also marked one edge of each strip with a chisel pointed marker pen to simulate the caulking. At this scale, I felt that to mark both edges would have made the deck lining too prominent.

To prevent warping of the 2mm ply false deck, it was found advisable to weight the edges while the PVA adhesive dried. Of course, you don't have to use PVA, but a contact adhesive could be a bit messy and cyanoacrylate limits the time available to make sure that everything keeps properly in line. The entire deck surface was planked and allowed to dry before separating into two pieces down the centre line.

Before fixing the deck in place, the holes for the masts were checked for both size and alignment. For this check, the deck pieces were dry fitted and the lower mast dowels dropped in place down through the deck and into the slots in the false keel, **(Fig.9.6)**. Any rectification to the various slots and holes was better done at this stage rather than later when deck fittings and the like had been put in place. The deck halves were glued in place one at a time using "crocodile" clips at each beam to ensure that the deck was correctly seated and that the camber was attained.

The inner walls were next planked, **(Fig.9.7)**. Five planks per side were required for this stage and, in addition to the manual recommendation, I also coated both sides of the planks with diluted PVA before assembly, something that certainly paid off later when I came to

Fig. 9.7 Inner surfaces planked and painted.

cut the gun ports. The bottom plank on each side that sat directly on to the deck, I painted red before placing in position. This provided a nice hard line and avoided the shaky hand problem later on!

Preparation for planking

This part of the construction process is vital in making a really good hull. The top deck and poop deck pieces were eased into position, checked for alignment all round and then temporarily pinned into place, **(Fig.9.8)**.

The rough chamfering of the bulkheads fore and aft done previously now paid off as all edges were now brought into line. PermaGrit abrasive tools came into their own as the bulkhead edges were all trued up using a length of planking strip to check conformity. The aim was to obtain a continuous run of planking bulkhead to bulkhead and, at the same time, provide a full edge seating upon which to glue and pin the planks.

Fig. 9.8 Main and poop decks temporarily pinned in place.

This was not a five-minute job, but the possibility of bumps and dips in the planking had to be avoided at this stage.

First planking

The left hand and right hand bulwark patterns were fixed in place, **(Fig.9.9)**. These had to be correctly positioned since the six gun-ports in each were the location points for the template that governed the positioning of all the other gun-ports. Having satisfied myself that all was well, the planking commenced at deck level, the first five planks not requiring any taper. I also carefully marked on to the outside of the planking the levels of the two lower gun decks at their outside edges. I felt that this might well come in useful when I ultimately came to marking out the positions of the gun-ports.

It was a pleasure to find that even the brass pins provided in the kit were of good quality. True, there were one or two with spade points, but the vast majority were needle sharp and I found that texture of the lime planks, being what it was, there was no need to drill holes for fixing the planking. The pins could easily be pushed into the planks then tapped in sufficiently to hold the planks in place. A minimal penetration was adequate, thus leaving enough to get hold of for easy removal later on.

Having reached down to the level of the beak deck, the front end of each plank needed to be tapered from about bulwark No.6 to about half width at the end. A few minutes soaking was sufficient to be able to induce a bend into the planking strips with thumb and fingers and was better, in this instance, than using a plank nipper. The major problem experienced was the edge-to-edge matching around the curve between bulwark No.1 and the stem plank termination piece and some model makers may find it helpful to block in that area with balsa or obeche before planking so that better control of the bent plank can be achieved. Tapering at the stern was also required particularly under the counter but, again, the quality of the lime planking took much of the pain from this task. The natural run of the planking, which coincided with the line of the decks, indirectly helped when it came to cutting the gun-ports. However, several stealers were required, particularly at the stern.

I think that it is worth mentioning at this point that it is immaterial how many, and where stealers come in the application of the first planking. The sole purpose of this first layer is to provide a sound basis for the second, thus the main essential is that it conforms to the required shape of the vessel and has no bumps or hollows. Planks must also be well glued, both to the frames and to each other, edge to edge. The lower and upper counter curves were then planked prior to rubbing down the whole hull.

Bearing in mind what was just said about the sound basis for the next planking, the rubbing down operation was worth spending time on to eliminate any imperfections. The amount of time obviously being totally

Fig. 9.9 The bulwark patterns and start of first planking. The routed panel feature on the patterns should be on the inside.

dependent on how well the planks have been laid. Provided that all of the ups and downs of the surface are removed, a super smooth finish is not necessary. In fact, it could be argued that it is better to have a slightly rough surface to provide a better key for the adhesive used for the second planking. Sanding creates a lot of dust so the use of a mask was most advisable. Even so, I minimised the finer dust by initially using a scraper to get rid of the bulk of the waste. I also took care to re-mark the levels of the two lower gun decks.

Marking and cutting the gun-ports

The template was cut from the relevant drawing sheet and offered up to each side of the hull, aligning it relative to the pre-cut ports in the upper bulwarks. This needed doing with great care, because the slightest error in that local alignment area gets exaggerated as reference is made towards the bows. The finished first planking and the marked out gun-ports can be seen in **Fig.9.10**.

There were four specific things to watch for to get the gun-ports in their right places.

1. Watch the deck levels. I was glad that I marked their positions as I did the first planking, since they now enabled me to ensure that the sills of each port were at a constant distance above the deck.

2. Some of the ports on the upper gun deck came very close to bulkheads, so it was essential to make sure that their lateral position did not cause them to foul.

3. Several of the ports on the upper deck were for guns that fired through the shroud lanyards so another

Fig. 9.10 Gun ports marked on to the finished first planking.

positional check was advisable.

4. The dimensions of the ports as drawn on the template were not always consistent, so a Plasti-Card template was cut and used as a stencil for marking them out on the side of the hull. The sizes required were taken from the finished sizes of the pre-cut gun-port lids; they were 17 x 15mm for the lower deck ports and 15 x 13mm for the upper deck. These sizes allowed for the 1mm thickness on each face for lining the ports. A pair of small plug gauges was made from scrap material to ultimately help getting all ports to their correct sizes,

also a step gauge to ensure that the sill height above the upper gun deck was the same throughout.

Opening out each aperture was done by first drilling a small hole in each corner, then using a miniature keyhole saw to remove the centre portion. At this stage I worked to the inside of my marked lines, leaving about 0,25mm for finishing and final gauging. When I came to cut the ports for the upper gun deck, it became much easier to see what I was doing by removing the temporarily fixed poop and main decks. It was now that the coating of diluted PVA on the inner planking paid off and no splitting

Fig. 9.11 Gun ports cut.

Fig. 9.12 Temporarily pinned stern fascia permits proper alignment of quarter gallery details.

was experienced at all as drill and cutter broke through from the outside.

The hull with the gun-ports cut is shown in **Fig.9.11**.

The gun-ports that were not to be fitted with lids were then lined. This was not a difficult task since the sills all sat neatly against inner and outer planking, and thus had adequate support. However, the sills for the remaining ports, not to be inserted until after completion of the second planking, would have no such support. Having to be recessed to a depth of 1mm, the only fixing area available was that afforded by the 1,5mm thickness of the first planking. I reckoned that this was going to cause problems and so I decided to install some 4 x 2mm strip pieces behind the first planking so increasing the fixing area to 3,5mm wide. I did this before starting the second planking so that this additional support could be sized when the total gun-port apertures were cut to finished dimensions. The application of these12mm long pieces was fiddly, but worth doing to avoid an even more difficult task later on.

The main wale position was marked and, in fact, I put the first of the outer planks in place once I was satisfied that the position was correct. This plank, together with some of the lined gun-ports can be seen in **Fig.9.12**.

The forward bulkhead fascia assembly

This straightforward sub-assembly featured the two round houses that were vertically planked around pre-cut patterns and the addition of two sets of door furniture, **(Fig.9.17)**. The main thing to remember here was to paint the roundhouse capping pieces before assembly.

The quarter galleries

As pointed out in the instruction manual, this stage of construction needs a lot of care and patience. As much as the procedures were as straightforward as I had seen in a kit, I cannot emphasise enough how important it was to get everything right at that juncture if tricky corrective adjustments were to be avoided at a later, and very inconvenient stage of construction.

Having planked and fixed the stern gallery deck in place, the large stern fascia was pinned in place to be used as a guide to correctly position the quarter gallery patterns. All edges of each of these parts needed to be bevelled: the back edges to match the angle of the stern fascia, the long straight edges to match the angle of the hull side and the curved edges to recognise the correct seating for the various quarter gallery fascias. The angle on these latter edges was the most troublesome to achieve. This was because it varied as it moved forward round the curve in order that the ends of the fascias fitted snugly against the side of the hull at their forward end and against the stern fascia at the rear.

Once the lowest pattern was in place, it was found helpful to hold the relevant gallery fascia in place and mark the position of its top corners on to the hull side and stern fascia. Thus, when shaping and fitting the next pattern you have a visual guide to getting its position correct. I also found it advisable to work on alternate sides as I progressed upwards to the higher levels, thus ensuring that both the port and starboard levels were the same.

The quarter gallery lower patterns (34), two per side, were best glued together before attempting to shape

Fig. 9.13 Second planking with upper gun decks fittings in place. Note cleats on inner faces of bulkheads.

them. In order to get the shape right, I first angled the rear edge to match the inside of the main stern fascia, then the inner edge that seats against the hull side. Once a snug fit had been attained, I held it in place and marked round the shape of the bottom edge of the quarter gallery fascia. On its under-face, I traced the shape of the lower finishing castings (455 & 457). This provided lines to which the profile of the patterns could be cut. When satisfactorily shaped they were put away with the castings for later assembly. The fascias were temporarily pinned in place until they were required for glazing, again see **Fig.9.12**.

The second planking

Having already put in place the first plank each side relative to the top of the main wale, these obviously provided an ideal positional gauge for those planks above and below. Since it became very apparent that it would be useful to have the hull bottom up, or at least on its side, when planking its lower areas, I decided to plank above the main wale line first in order to give some additional strength to the tops of the bulwarks. All of this planking was applied with thick cyanoacrylate to avoid pinholes. Apart from those planks immediately above the line of the main wale and up to the level of the beak deck, which needed a slight taper at the front end, no further tapering was necessary.

For those planks below my "master" plank the situation was different. Careful tapering was required both fore and aft, particular attention being paid to

those that came up at an angle under the stern counter. These strips I also applied with thick cyanoacrylate. Once I had planked all those areas above the waterline, I changed to white PVA adhesive and, having used a plank nipper to induce the bends, pushed in a few pins at salient points. Getting the bends near enough correct made it unnecessary to pin at every bulkhead. However, it was most essential to get the whole plank securely stuck down to avoid any springing when rubbing down later on.

Finishing the surfaces after completing the planking was quite a lengthy business, even though my planks had been laid tight and flat. To make the best impression on the wood I used scrapers, a rectangular one, obviously with straight edges, and a curved one with a selection of various radii. These removed material at a fair rate without damaging the surface. In one or two places where it was difficult to gain access with these, I used my selection of PermaGrit abrasive tools.

Even though I had taken great care when planking, I still found a couple of sprung planks. These soon became apparent because the scraper pushed them down rather than scraped them! The easiest solution, other than doing the job right in the first place, is to trickle some thin cyanoacrylate along both edges of the plank and push it in for a few seconds. It gets round the problem but this is not something that you want to do too often.

Reducing grades of abrasive paper were then used to rub down the entire surface prior to sizing and lining the gun-ports. Fine filler was rubbed in before using the final grade. This filled in any small gaps between planks

Fig. 9.14 A selection of 9 pounder and 18 pounder carraige guns.

and particularly corrected the edges of those planks where the square edge had not held. This is, unfortunately, always a noticeable problem with small sections of walnut where the edges tend to flake away during cutting.

The wales

The key to success here was really one of accurate positioning. The top of the main wale had already been defined by the line of the initial second plank and it just had to be remembered that the upper wale and the slotted strip rails all ran parallel to the main wale.

Strips 1 x 3mm were used to make up the wales each stuck on with thick cyanoacrylate. The manual suggests that seven strips should be used for the main wale giving a nominal width of 21mm. A check on the strip widths showed that, although within tolerance, they were slightly greater than 3mm. Thus, taking the curve of the hull into account and the resultant slight gap between the strips, the combination of seven widths actually produced a wale width of nearly 24mm; therefore six strips were found to give the desired result. The upper wale, made up of only three strips, did not have a sufficiently accumulative effect to be a problem.

The slotted strips were all edge sanded and the slots cleaned out before sticking on to the side of the hull. To ensure that they were all parallel to the upper wales, (apart from the uppermost stern strip), I cut spacers from scrap 2mm ply, thus not only was I able to maintain correct parallelism but also keep the levels on both sides of the hull identical, **(Fig.9.13).**

All relevant gun-port openings were then cut into the wales as required before fitting the sills.

The gun-port sills

This was a task not to be rushed and one where success was largely dependent on how accurate the ports were cut earlier on. Because I had used a home-made plug gauge to get them all the same size, I was able to confidently set the stop on my plank cutter to cut all of the side linings from 10 x 1mm strip to the same length, this being just a "squeeze" fit into the sides of the gun-port apertures. The front edges of these pieces had to be set in 1mm from the outer face of the second planking; therefore it was necessary to angle those front edges to match the face of the planking before gluing the parts in place. Having increased the fixing area when I cut the ports, I was now able to use PVA adhesive to give me some adjustment time to ensure that both sides were set in to the same depth. I lined the vertical sides of all the gun-ports before cutting and fitting the top and bottom sills. Again, these pieces were cut to a tight fit and their front edges carefully fitted in line with the sides. It was important to get this match right or else be faced with a delicate titivating job with a scalpel later on!

The sills and the inside surface of those bulwarks so far planked were then painted red, again see **Fig.9.13**. Three coats were required to give a reasonable coverage, but it was necessary to keep an eye on the build up of paint in the corners of the recessed gun-ports. When the paint was thoroughly dry, I used a sharp blade to

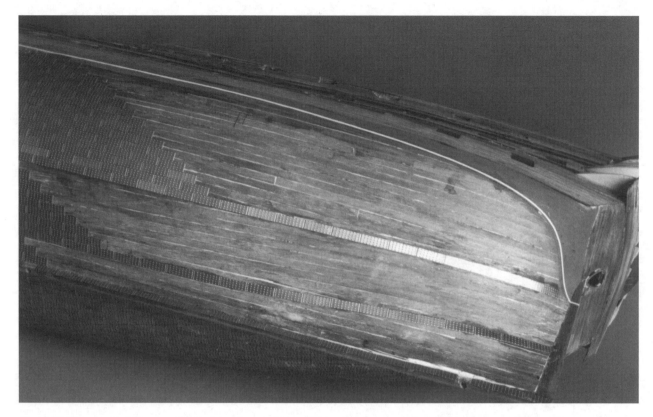

Fig. 9.15 The start of the copper plating. The position of the waterline and gore lines were established first.

gently scrape any excess paint from the outer hull surface.

Fitting out the upper gun deck

The gratings were assembled in the conventional kit manner using cross-halved slotted strips. These were put together dry then brushed with dilute PVA and left to set before framing. It was a pleasant change to find strips that didn't taper or come in varying thickness. After being cut to the sizes of the apertures in the deck, they were framed with walnut strip noting the different size of material for the coamings on each of the two decks.

The ladder sides, already shaped and slotted, were cut from the routed sheet. The top and bottom steps were then glued in place and left to dry before sliding in the remainder. It was noted that when the sides were removed from the ply sheet, the pieces adopted a pronounced curve. This problem was simply overcome when fitting the intermediate steps by putting a small elastic band around the ladder until the glue had dried. However, the ply sides did not inspire much enthusiasm and they would be better made in solid close-grained timber.

One task that needed to be attended to, not in the instructions or indicated on the drawings related to the hatchway just forward of the capstan position. One of the beams supporting the deck had to be cut away in order to fit the ladder.

The fitted out deck is shown in **Fig.9.13.**

The gun carriages

The 9-pounder and 18-pounder carriage guns were each made up of 23 parts (if you count the pins and eyebolts). Every part was provided either in pre-cut timber, turned brass or photo-etched brass. The drawings and instructions were quite clear as to the sequence and method of assembly and were followed exactly for an excellent job. Painting should be carried out at the suggested juncture to avoid a fiddly task later on. It was also noted that the quoin was better fixed to the bed before tapering. Considerable thought obviously went into the design of these guns and the results were most satisfying, **(Fig.9.14).**

One additional point that I found worthy of mention concerned the axles. On those parts for the 18-pounder units, the small tabs for holding them within the overall sheet of material were either at the top or the bottom of the wheel mounting spigots. It was absolutely essential to carefully trim the tab residue from the spigots in order that the push fit of the wheels onto the axles was retained, remembering that square axles fitted into round holes!

Coppering the hull

Thick cyanoacrylate was used throughout to stick the plates in place. A quick wipe over with a soft cloth, to remove any seepage of adhesive after fixing each plate, was essential to ensure that adjacent plates fitted snugly. Equally important was to make sure that the plates lay perfectly flat on the surface of the second planking.

The instruction manual advised that the best way to cut the plates was to use a craft knife with the plate laid on a hard, flat surface. This was good advice, but even better was the use of a self-healing cutting mat. What should be avoided is the use of scissors, since the shearing action involved tends to curl the copper.

The layout of the coppering needed to be thought about before getting carried away with the exciting task of sticking on 2500 little copper plates! The line of the plates does not follow that of the planking and, if you merely start at the keel and work your way up, there is a danger that the curves involved would become too severe as the waterline was approached. I was not able to find any definitive ruling on the establishment of coppering patterns, but it seemed that gore lines needed to be introduced to prevent the shape of the copper plate pattern becoming too complex. The most significant gore line, I suppose, is the waterline itself. A gore line is where the pattern of plating changes and, at the waterline, it can be seen that the plates curve upwards towards, and terminate at, that straight edge that defines the waterline. A similar situation was introduced at a point lower down towards the keel. I plated three rows on the hull adjacent to the keel then moved up, pyramid fashion, for twelve rows to a point midway along the length of the hull. At this juncture I took a strip of the spare planking timber and, using its natural run, found that it coincided with the waterline at the stem and stern-post. This seemed to be an ideal situation and I marked the hull with a pencil along the line of the strip. Thus, the thirteenth row of copper plates was then carefully laid along that line to define the gore line. Having got that line established, it appeared that one lower change in pattern would be necessary. I decided that the fourth row up from the keel should also be laid in the same manner as the thirteenth, allowing the wooden strip to take its natural course towards stem and stern.

Establishing a straight waterline by trimming the upper edges of plates as they were installed was not going to be easy. Remembering the reading that I had done on the subject, I recalled that it was not unusual to fit a 3in batten along the top edge of the plates at the waterline. Reducing strips of 0,5mm thick timber to the required width was never going to be very successful, but a search through my scrap drawer revealed a few 1 x 0,5mm plastic strips that I decided to use instead. These were stuck around the hull at waterline level. I considered that this innovation would look better than masking and the use of copper paint as suggested in the instruction manual. The initial pattern of plating showing the waterline and gore lines can be seen in **Fig.9.15**.

Plating then resumed on the lower half of the hull working up to each of the gore lines using stealers fore and aft as required. The plates were trimmed at the end of each row to match the underside of the gore line plates and also at the junction with the stem and sternpost. I avoided small awkward shaped pieces at the very end by making them almost a full plate, then cutting the penultimate plate shorter to reinstate the "bricklaying" pattern.

Having satisfactorily plated the bottom of the hull, a similar procedure was adopted to cover the space between the upper gore line and the waterline, again trimming the end plates in each row to conform to the waterline.

I experimented with several ways of ageing the copper plates but none of them looked right for the job in hand. In the end, rather than leaving them bright and gleaming as they came out of the packet, I decided to spray the entire plated surface with matt varnish. The result certainly took away some of the artificial looking shine.

The rudder

Having cleaned up and tapered the rudder blade, the first task was the copper plating, not forgetting that the back edge should also be covered. I positioned the plates so that I wasn't left with very short pieces at either of the ends, which were not easy to place accurately and had the habit of becoming unstuck when attempting to finally trim them to the edge of the rudder.

The pintles and gudgeons were fitted next and, contrary to the procedure advised in the manual, I glued both together before assembling them to the rudder, making sure that there was room for the gudgeon straps to pass between the assembly and the rudder. I knew that the rudder wouldn't turn on its hinges, but I seldom make moving parts on my models. What can move, will inevitably get moved and ultimately get broken! The ship's wheel is another prime example.

The pintle straps were added using thick cyanoacrylate and the holes drilled for the relevant pins. The latter were cut short to a length not exceeding half the thickness of the rudder blade and the drill size

Fig. 9.16 The rudder.

Fig. 9.17 The front fascia and round houses.

selected such as to provide a gentle push fit. The same size of drill was also used to drill the holes for the two "spectacle" eyebolts to which the restraining chains would be fitted later. The rudder is shown in **Fig.9.16**.

The counter and the inside of the hole through which the rudder head was to pass were then painted before attempting to fix the rudder in place. Holes were drilled in the sternpost to the *actual* spacing on the assembled rudder, starting at the correct distance up from the keel. The pintle straps were added to the rudder blade before fixing the whole to the back end of the hull. The gudgeon straps were then put in place in the same manner as the pintle straps, although except for the uppermost straps, it was not necessary to shorten the pins.

The bow cheeks and head rail assembly

Overall, the job was made about as simple as possible by careful design work and accurate pre-cutting. Nevertheless, it was necessary to do a sequence of dry runs and avoid the temptation to fix everything on to the hull in one go. It was also found helpful to paint parts before assembly with at least two coats. Painting afterwards would have been a bit fiddly and certainly more difficult to achieve straight lines where yellow meets black. It was also worth bearing in mind the key features in the bow area that acted as guides to getting positions right. The gammoning slot through the prow, the level of the roundhouse deck and the top edge of the main wale all helped to ensure good alignments and fits were achieved.

The upper bow cheeks were fitted first and each needed chamfering on their curved rear edge to attain a nice snug fit against the hull. I found it helpful to use the bow hair brackets to judge the correct position of the cheeks, since the undersides of these brackets passed just above the gammoning slot. This established where the forward end of the bow cheeks should be placed.

The hawse planks were added, followed by the lower bow cheeks, which also needed to be chamfered to fit the contour of the hull. Having positioned the hawse bolsters, the hawse planks and hull were drilled, cleaned up and fitted, **(Fig.9.17)**.

A dry run of fitting the three "V" shaped frames allowed slight adjustments to be made so that the deck grating could be assembled correctly, noting that the frames projected slightly each side of the grating to provide a support for the main bow rails. It was also important not to forget to file the slots in the two forward frames so that the cast metal rails would sit at the correct angle.

A little bit of trial and error was required to get the curves and end angles right on the cast rails. I found that starting at the hull end and working forward to the prow was a relatively straightforward procedure to adopt. I avoided the temptation to trim the ends with side cutters and found that a new blade in my craft knife produced a much more acceptable and less distorted end to the rail. Having once got them fixed, the main bow rails were put in place and the edges of the "V" frames capped to trap the cast rails in place, **(Fig.9.18)**.

This was work that needed patience and good light to achieve a satisfactory result.

Having said that, the procedures were as good as any I had come across in a kit for this potentially difficult area of assembly.

Fig. 9.18 The head rails in place and first painting completed.

Framing and glazing

I tackled this part of the project slightly ahead of the recommended procedure given in the manual. The main reason for doing so was that although I had made a reasonable job of temporarily fitting the quarter gallery fascias, it was obvious that some filling was going to be needed where they met the sides of the hull and I wanted to get that sorted before painting.

Because of the accuracy of the CNC routing, this potentially difficult job was relatively easy. There were a few things that I would recommend that help even further, some are a little bit obvious, others perhaps less so. Do paint the brass frames while still on the sheet, preferably by spraying, and certainly give the ply fascias at least two coats before any assembly work is attempted. Laying the relevant fascia, face up, on to the acetate glazing sheet and tracing the aperture shapes with a sharp darning needle easily marked out the correct shapes. This obviously had to be done before fitting the frames.

The brass frames were separated from the sheet one at a time taking care to identify which aperture it was intended for. The routed recesses were accurately cut but, remembering that the router was a tool with a diameter, the corners were not sharp.

So, having removed the frame from the sheet, I cut the smallest of chamfers on each of its corners. Now, I do mean small. If you don't have to look twice to see if you've cut them, you have probably made them too big! The frames then pressed into their respective recesses without any trouble or distortion.

The glazing pieces were then cut, again one at a time, and offered up for size behind the frames. The

merest speck of thick cyanoacrylate was applied to the back of the frames at the junction of just two of the glazing bars and the clear glazing dropped into place.

The bulkhead fascia columns were not fitted at this time but left until after assembly of the fascias when the columns could be made to seat tightly down on to the deck.

Painting the hull

First, a word about the actual paint. Whatever brand you use, make sure it is thoroughly mixed. The two main colours used on this model, yellow and black are particularly in need of a good stir. If improperly mixed, the poor covering ability of the yellow will immediately be apparent and the coarser and heavier pigment of the black will most likely lead to variations in the degree of matt finish achieved.

Concurrent with painting the hull, I also painted an area of scrap ply with black and yellow, again rubbing down between the four coats applied. The point of doing this was to try various masking tapes to get the joining lines straight. What I didn't want to happen, of course, was for the last finishing coat of paint to be ripped off when I removed the tape. The product that I found to work best was Henkel's Duck One-Touch tape bought in my local Woolworth store. This was gently pressed on, later carefully peeled off, *not leaving it on any longer than it took the paint to dry*. The latter condition being especially important in order to achieve the best results.

Having filled as many of the visible blemishes and sanded the various surfaces smooth, I applied the first coat of yellow, noting that the decorative strip at the top of the upper yellow band was also yellow. No masking tape was used at this stage since any encroachment of

129

Fig. 9.19 The back end with quarter gallery framed and glazed.

the yellow into the areas later to be painted black didn't really matter. When the first coat was dry, further minor areas of filling were seen to be necessary and these were done before proceeding with the second coat. I applied four coats in total leaving each to dry for twenty-four hours before lightly rubbing down and painting the next.

The yellow was left for at least seventy-two hours to thoroughly harden off before applying masking tape

to control the edges of the black area. The tape was removed after the first black coat; one coat on the edges of the wales was adequate to maintain the line. Thus, subsequent coats of black were applied only to the broad faces of the wales. The glazing of the quarter gallery fascias and the initial painting is shown in **Fig.9.19**. The glazed, upper gallery fascia can be seen in **Fig.9.20** and the finished stern plate with poop deck screen bulkheads in **Fig.9.21**.

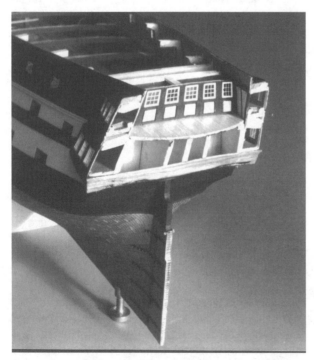

Fig. 9.20 Srern view showing the glazed upper gallery bulkhead.

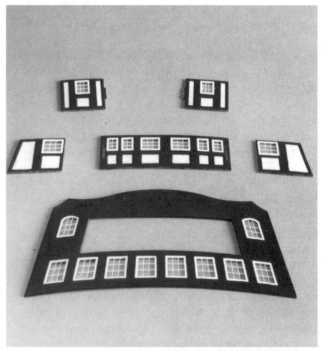

Fig. 9.21 The poop deck screen bulkheads framed and glazed together with the stern fascia.

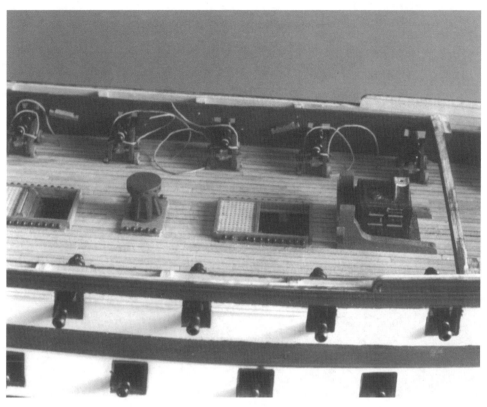

Fig. 9.22 Guns mounted and ready for basic rigging.

Installing the main gun battery

Having completed the basic paint job, the dummy gun barrels were fitted to the main gun deck and the carriage guns mounted on the upper gun deck. The dummy barrels presented no problems, although it was essential to ensure that they were all pushed completely into their respective mounting blocks. One tends to notice if an odd barrel projects more than its neighbours do. The carriage guns were also straightforward enough to fit although it had to be remembered that once the top deck was in place any loose ordnance could not be got at to re-install. To help avoid that problem, I placed a sheet of fine sandpaper face up on my bench and, taking each carriage assembly in turn, dragged its four wheels

for about 10cm across the surface of the abrasive paper. This produced a small flat on each wheel, almost imperceptible from the side, which greatly increased the sticking area between wheels and deck.

Fig.9.22 shows the carriage guns installed and ready for rigging.

Fitting the top deck

It was decision time again. Was it easier to glue the false deck in place then plank it afterwards, or should I plank it first then fit it in place? I decided to adopt the latter procedure because I reckoned that it would be simpler to sand the deck smooth on the bench rather than on the ship. However, it had to be recognised that dropping the slots in the deck over the rear bulkheads would be

Fig. 9.23 The upper deck beamed and planked. Note the two small separated sections to facilitate easier fitting.

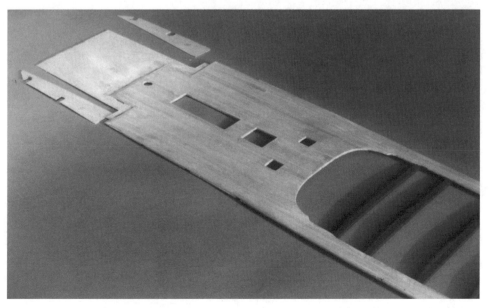

Fig. 9.24 Forecastle timberheads and cat-heads.

more difficult after planking. I therefore removed the rear port and starboard portions of the false deck so that it could be slid into place from forward, (Fig.9.23). The portions removed did not have to be planked since they were behind the bulwark screens, but would have to be dropped into place later so that the rearward gun carriages had something to sit on. The planked deck was pinned into place, the pins removed after the glue had set and the tiny holes filled.

Having got the deck in place the glazed fascias were assembled together with the intermediate brass pillars, the latter being positioned tight down against the surface of the deck and their height being adjusted at the top. It was important that they did not protrude above the top edges of the fascias so as to impede the subsequent seating of the poop deck.

The capping rails

These were further parts that benefited from painting before assembly. Following the recommended procedure in the instruction manual, I fitted those across the width and along the sides on the forecastle deck first and, having got the lower rails in position, I used PVA to glue the timberheads in place. Doing one rail at a time allowed

Fig. 9.25 Barricade rails.

Fig. 9.26 The shot garlands, ladders and ship's wheel in position.

me to use the upper rail (unglued) to hold the timberheads in place while they set in position. After a few hours it was removed and, using a set of 2mm spacers cut from scrap strip, it was then replaced and glued in its final position, **(Fig.9.24)**. Having fixed the side rails in the same manner, the rails to the main and quarterdeck were added. The poop deck rails were left until after fitting the deck. All rails so far assembled were then given another coat of paint carefully avoiding getting too near the extreme edges so as not to spoil the hard line between adjacent parts.

Deck fittings

The fitting out of the deck was not difficult but there were one or two things that I would suggest to make life a bit easier. First, all parts that would be subject to a rigging load must be pinned (dowelled) to the deck or bulwarks as suggested in the instructions. Later failure of these joints would be totally catastrophic and, in addition to pinning them it should also be remembered to scrape any paint or varnish away from the mating areas. Sticking parts to paint doesn't work too well even when using cyanoacrylate.

The barricade rails comprised three pieces separated by square and turned pillars. The upper rail comes ready drilled with eleven holes and I believe that this should be made the centre rail. I used this to position the square pillars and, having glued them on assembled this sub-unit to the base rail that I had already glued to the deck. I used this sequence to better accommodate the deck camber. Having allowed all the glue so far used to thoroughly set, I then put the turned pillars in place, *making sure that the hole through the decks for the main mast had been blocked off with tissue paper first,* since

I didn't want to lose any of the pillars into the depths of the hull. Finally, the top rail was fixed in place, **(Fig.9.25)**.

The ship's wheel went together easily but I added a further detail for greater authenticity. I drilled two holes in the deck, (one each side of the centre drum), the starboard hole to the fore and the port towards the stern. Thread was then wound around the drum, the ends passing down through the holes in the deck to simulate the steering system.

Eyebolts fitted to the deck were best put into position around the base of the foremast before putting the adjacent bitts in place.

Bitts, cleats, gratings and the belfry were all put into place to complete the fitting out of the top deck, **(Fig.9.26)**.

Fitting the poop deck

I fitted the false deck in place before planking on this occasion since I suspected that if I planked first, the size and shape, particularly with the skylight aperture, would lend itself to distortion as the adhesive dried.

The skylight was assembled and glazed, the eyebolts, cleats and bitts all fixed before adding and painting the capping rails either side, **(Fig.9.27)**.

Finishing the stern

All cast parts were thoroughly washed in water with a dash of washing-up liquid to remove any surface contamination prior to painting.

This stage of the construction has the potential to lead to crisis if extreme care is not taken to get the positions of the various rails and decorative features correct. One of the major problems is how to hold the model for best accessibility. The way that I adopted was

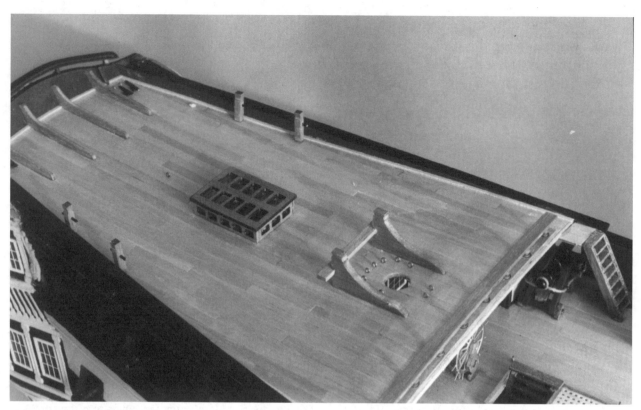

Fig. 9.27 The poop deck fitted out.

to sit on a fairly high stool, rest the prow of the model on the floor and support the copper plated undersides between my knees. This presented the stern on a convenient working plane and permitted the positions of the decorations to be eyeballed or measured accordingly. A folded towel was placed on the floor to prevent damage to the prow and stop the model slipping. Careful preparation was the order of the day and all cast parts were trimmed and painted and, together with the glue pot, placed where they could easily be reached without having to keep moving the model from its working position, the main danger being dislodging the lower gun barrels.

Fig. 9.28 The decorated stern fascia.

Having got the main stern fascia in place the tafferel pieces were added. At this point I realised that something was not quite right. The two cast figures that stood outboard of the upper windows would have to be fixed on to two different surfaces, obviously not very practical. I therefore continued the surface of the tafferel down the outer sides of the window frames to the level of the horizontal decorative strip below and let the inserted piece overlap the outer edges of the stern plate. These supporting pieces were later trimmed around the outer sides of the cast figures.

The cast decorative strips had, in some places, to be butt jointed to cover the length required. It was important to note that the section of these strips was such as to make it necessary to recognise that there was a top and a bottom to them. I did not realise this at first and it was only when I butted the ends of two pieces together incorrectly that it became apparent.

The gallery balustrade went on much more easily that I had anticipated and the positioning of most of the upper decorative castings was straightforward. However, I did find it necessary to make one or two "technical adjustments" here and there because, although I had taken a lot of care to get my basic levels right during the early stages of construction, the odd half millimetre error can make things difficult. Nevertheless, I was pleased with the final result, (Fig.9.28).

I found that at this stage it was a good idea to finish painting the back end using the same holding technique for doing the decoration. My main reason for this was because the next stage involved the fitting of the catheads and later, the figurehead, both of which would be at risk during the aforesaid holding method.

The lantern assemblies made up well, **(Fig.9.29)**, the only tricky was achieving the right proportions and curves on the wire supports. Gentle bending of the brass-etched lantern proper brought the meeting faces together perfectly and the fit around the spigots on the cast tops and bottoms required no additional support while the glue dried. However, before putting the top on, I decided to glaze the inside of each lantern. At this size, you don't have to think in terms of glazing each facet of the hexagonal shape separately, but merely roll a piece of clear plastic into the shape of a truncated cone and drop it inside the lantern body. I first cut a ring of sheet plastic 30mm inside radius with an outer radius of 37mm. From this I cut a segment through about 25 degrees and rolled it gently to form the truncated cone. This needed a little adjustment but the sizes quoted provide a good basic start. The lanterns were put to one side and not fitted until the model was virtually finished – prime candidates for being knocked off!

The hull side fittings

The fitting of the catheads is not always as easy as it might at first seem. On this occasion, I tried a somewhat different tactic. Having cut the two 5mm square catheads, I first drilled the holes at one end for reaving the anchor tackle then, ensuring that the angles on the associated brackets did, in fact, match my outer planking. I glued these on to the catheads not forgetting that one right hand and one left hand unit were required. When thoroughly set, I used my MiniCraft sander to face the inner end of the cathead and the inner edges of the brackets as one surface, thus ensuring one

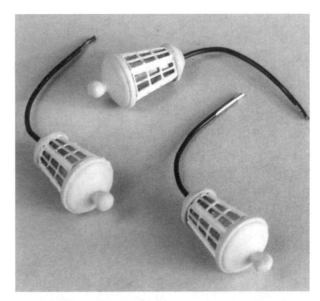

Fig. 9.29 The finished lanterns.

continuous angular face to sit against the hull. The decorative strip on the hull needed to be cut away where necessary to permit the whole cathead assembly to be pinned and glued in place. I found this far better than trying to cut notches in the back edges of the brackets. The cast decorative strip that fitted between the lower head rail and the underside of the supporting cathead bracket was then shaped and fitted.

The side fenders and chess trees were then fitted, **(Fig.9.30)**, these merely needed to be slotted on their rear edge to house the hull trim and wales. Being cut from ply it was necessary to make sure that the exposed front edges were well finished and then rubbed down between coats of paint.

Fig. 9.30 A view amidships showing rigged gun ports, side fenders and chess-trees.

Fig. 9.31 Companionway rails and hammock cranes.

Before proceeding further, I had a check on the alignment of the holes for stepping the masts, using lengths of appropriate sized dowel. It was considered easier to make any minor adjustments for rake and perpendicularity at this stage of the construction while there were no vulnerable bits sticking out - like gun port lids!

Gun-port lids

I particularly liked the pre-formed lids routed around three sides of the lower edge to simulate the two layers of opposing planks used to effectively seal the gun port openings. The etched brass hinges were cut from the sheet and glued to the upper surface of the lids, the

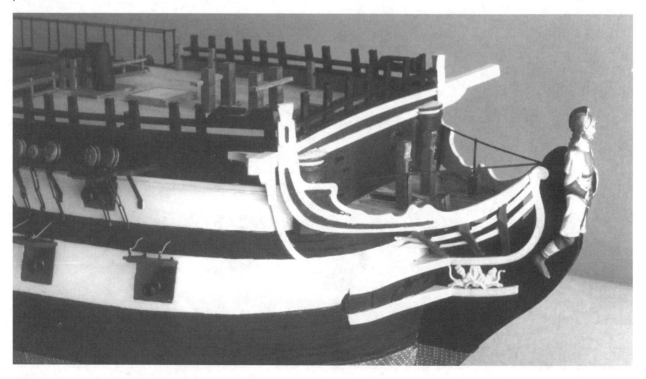

Fig. 9.32 The figurehead and bow timberheads.

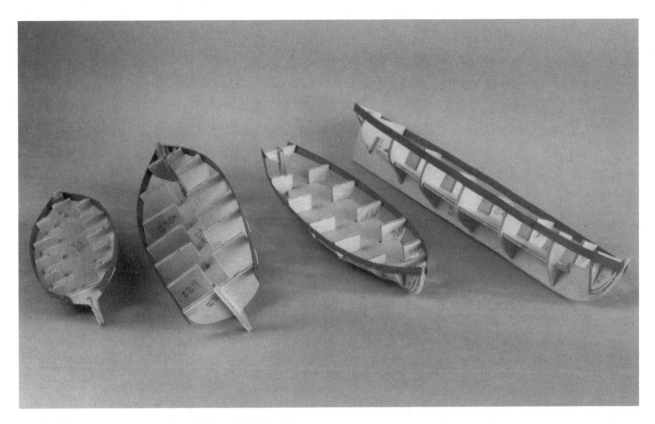

Fig. 9.33 The initial construction of the ship's boats.

holes drilled and the eyebolts added. Having taken the construction of all the lids to this stage, I painted the undersides red and put them to one side to dry before coating the top surface matt black.

The assembly of the lids involved drilling two holes above each port in the hull for the hinge extensions and gently scraping the paint away in a line between them to provide a more effective glued joint. The holes for each lid were done individually, using the actual positions of the extensions to centre-pop the hull. Inevitably, the paintwork needed touching in at one or two places, particularly on the hinges, but pre-painting maintained a sharp line between black and yellow where applicable.

After gluing all the lids in place, further holes were drilled in the hull for the port tackle. Again see **Fig.9.30**, which shows the mounted gun-port lids.

The hammock cranes were then fitted and rigged following the advice in the manual to ensure that the correct selection was made, particularly for those on the poop deck sides, **(Fig.9.31)**.

The figurehead needed some attention in order to attain a nice fit on the prow. It was then painted and fitted without the spear, which would be attached towards the end of the building and rigging process. This stage of the proceedings is shown in **Fig.9.32**.

The channels

The joint between the hull and the inside edge of the channels and chairs needed to be strong, so it was particularly important to ensure that the contour of the back edges were true. The hull was scraped clean

of paint in the contact area and pins were used to further strengthen the joint. The position of the pins was relatively unimportant and these were put into the channels first. I chose a drill that provided a fairly tight push fit without swelling the thickness of the channel ply and used cyanoacrylate to secure the pins in place. These were then cut off to leave about 3mm to go into the hull. The position of the pins was then transferred to the hull and holes were drilled using the same size drill as before.

A further essential before putting the channels on to the hull was to thoroughly clean out the slots that were to take the deadeyes and etched brass straps.

A set of brackets was prepared for each channel. Having bent the first one to the shape required, the remainder were bent to the same approximate shape and the set then nestled together and gently squeezed to make them all similar. These were then cyanoacrylate glued to the underside of the channel and, when set, holes were drilled in the hull to take the fixing pins at their lower end. Again, I selected a drill that provided a light push fit, not wanting to do any heavy work amongst the protruding gun barrels of the lower decks.

The unique design of the deadeye straps, shaped to prevent them pulling out of the channels under tension, worked well. Nevertheless, a touch of epoxy adhesive was considered worthwhile; just enough to assist in the holding of the strap without preventing the deadeye from being rotationally adjusted, if necessary, later on. There was a knack to easily inserting the straps into the channel slots. The merest smear of adhesive was put

Fig. 9.34 The boats ready for final sanding.

into the slot; the "spikey" bits of the strap were then fed into the right hand back corner of the slot and the entire assembly gently twisted into position. For left handed modellers, the left hand back corner would probably be the better choice.

An edging strip was then added to each channel assembly and the required painting done to complete the task.

I was not quite so happy with the chain-plate link system. The instruction manual quite correctly stated that the links should follow the angle of the shrouds and the drawings indicated that all the chain-plate preventer links for the 7mm deadeyes sit within the width of the upper wale. This meant that the link system had to be longer at the aft end of each channel than at the forward end and, by inference, that one of the links at each position should vary in length, the favoured variable being part 276.

In practical terms this meant that these parts needed to be stretched a bit at the back end and the system left a bit slack at the forward end of each channel.

For the two smaller sizes of deadeyes, there was no such adjustment required and these were set up first for maximum accessibility when mounting the 7mm deadeyes. It was necessary to keep an eye on the part numbers to be used and where to use them.

The boats

The construction of the ship's boats was probably the biggest challenge of the entire project. Fortunately, the basic framework was made up of accurately pre-cut parts

and having once got that initial stage of the construction done, **(Fig.9.33)**, the next step was to bevel the edges to provide best and proper seating for the first planking. I found that sharp scalpels and needle files did the trick, nothing being done that required too much pressure to overcome the fragility of the framework. I would suggest that if your experience in making models of small, open boats is limited then the 26ft launch is the friendliest design of the four to start with, having lines that are not too complex for planking with 3mm wide strips.

The first planking was a bit of a pain and I have to confess to using some words that didn't appear in my copy of Admiral W. H. Smyth's *Sailor's Word Book*. The main difficulty was that above the floor level, the planking was best not stuck to the edges of the frames, these having to be removed later. I fixed the top plank first using cyanoacrylate to stick the plank at each end and to the first or last frame that was not to be removed. The following planks, all of which needed to be tapered, were first glued at the front end and, working towards the stern, were glued edgewise to the adjacent plank above (between the frames). The plank was left overlapping the stern transom to be trimmed after all planks had been put on and the shell lightly rubbed down.

The second planking was much easier although it was, of course, still necessary to taper and use cyanoacrylate. This adhesive should be sparingly applied. Strip that is only 0,5mm thick will absorb medium or thin grade cyanoacrylate, so it was quite possible to overdo the quantity and finish up with the boat stuck to the fingers! The run of the planks was relatively unimportant

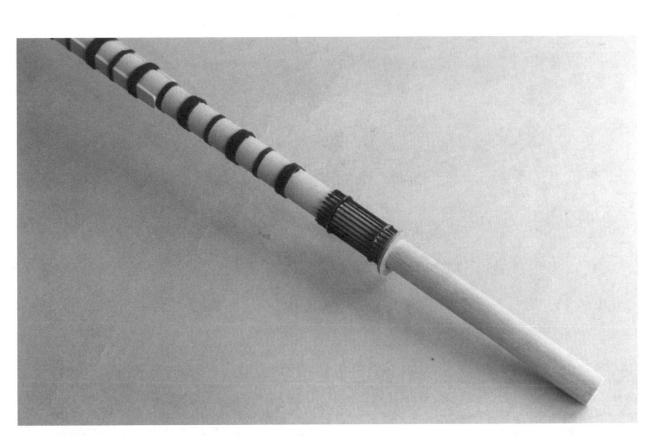

Fig. 9.36 The mast bands, wooldings and boarding pikes.

since the boats were to be painted. It was far more desirable to get them all lying as flat as possible and with minimal gaps between them. Tapering was again necessary to achieve this and some minor filling was required prior to the final sanding and finishing, **(Fig.9.34)**.

The gunwales and ribs were to be constructed from 3mm wide strip split down the middle to make widths of 1.5mm. Even soaking the material and then using a sharp scalpel, this was not found to be easy and, having eventually succeeded, there was a matter of bending the strips across their width for the gunwales. Having put the ribs in first, I made a start at the front end of each boat and carefully worked back towards the stern. I worked in successive sections about 10mm long at a time, applying cyanoacrylate with a worn scalpel blade to get the adhesive between the top edges of the boat shell and the underside of the strip. This worked fairly well but I felt that a different material might have made life easier and avoided the inevitable splitting problems. In fact, Evergreen Strip Stryrene of the appropriate section and size would fill the bill nicely. It would hold a hard, sharp edge and would readily bend but, of course, it isn't wood.

The strips for the benches and thwarts were sanded and painted before cutting to length and fitting into the boat shells in order to save some awkward re-touching later. I also fitted an eyebolt fore and aft to finish off the upper construction, which would be used for the hoisting and lowering of the boats.

Several coats of white paint were applied to the

outside surfaces of the hulls to attain the finish required, **(Fig.9.35)**. No mention was made in the manual, or on the drawings, of the black band around the gunwales of each boat. It needed to be about 3mm wide and was a fiddly masking and painting job. However, there is an easier solution! The local motorists' centre stocked 3mm wide self-adhesive trim tape, ("better known as "go faster stripes"). This was very thin and moulded around the compound curves of the boat hulls without creasing. A band of gloss varnish applied round the top of each boat provided a suitable base for the tape and after a couple of hours for the tape to settle in, each boat was sprayed with a coat of matt varnish.

The boat chocks were fitted to the beams on the main hull, but the boats themselves were put to one side until later in the rigging process, mainly to leave maximum access to the rigging at the foot of the main mast.

The masts

All mast fittings were pre-cut, leaving just the actual masts to be shaped and tapered as necessary. Care was taken to make and assemble the various pieces strictly in accordance with the instructions so as not to finish up with a part over that couldn't be assembled! The instructions for making and assembling the masts and bowsprit were extremely good and when used in conjunction with the drawings excellent results were achieved.

Mast tapering was carried out in the conventional manner by first planing the taper to an octagonal section

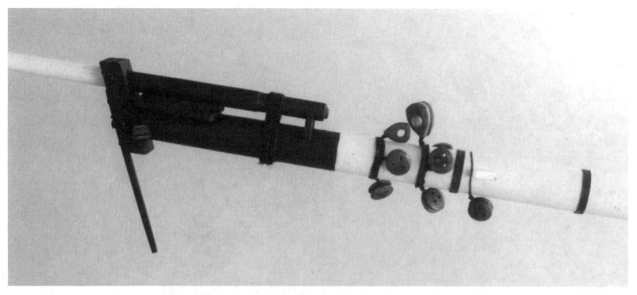

Fig. 9.37 The bowsprit rigged with dolphin striker, hearts and deadeyes.

then sanding to a circular section with reducing grades of abrasive paper. It was helpful to have a small lathe to do this work, but an electric drill on a stand or held in the vice would have proved adequate. Constant reference to the size and spacing of dry assembled trestletrees and crosstrees helped to ensure that the tops area was accurately made. Mast bands and wooldings were put in place after painting the lower masts, **(Fig.9.36)**.

With regard to the tops themselves, it was noticed that once the actual top had been removed from the pre-cut sheet, there was a tendency for it to slightly warp. To counteract this, I made up the trestletrees and crosstrees and glued them to the underside of the tops and clamped them up until the glue had thoroughly cured. Some time was spent ensuring that the battens were correctly spaced around the platform, one slightly out of balance would stand out like a sore thumb. White PVA was used to glue these to the platform so that there was some adjustment time to get everything right but, with only 1,5mm wide strips to work with, it was inevitable that there was some seepage of adhesive on to the surface of the platform. This was immediately removed by a piece of scrap strip shaped to have a chisel point. All holes were then drilled and eyebolts fitted.

The 1mm diameter holes were drilled around the front edge of the tops to take the crowsfeet to be installed later during the rigging process. The number of holes in the tops, should be twice the number of holes in the relevant euphroe blocks (Parts 271-2-3) in order that the threading sequence is correctly maintained, so it was important to strictly adhere to the numbers indicated on the drawings.

I think that a couple of points concerning the boarding pike rings are in order. It is an unfortunate fact of life that the diameter of dowel rod is produced with quite a large manufacturing tolerance. Thus when considering etched brass parts that come in the shape of a ring there is likely to be the need to expand the inside diameter of the ring or place a packing band around the mast to tack up the slack, according to where within the tolerance the dowel has been produced. The second point that needed watching was the size of the holes around the rings that house the boarding pikes. If the brass parts have been painted "on the sheet" then it will almost certainly be necessary to clean them out. At the same time it was thought wise to check that the pikes did actually go through the holes; getting the rings assembled on to the mast then finding that the pikes couldn't be racked up would have been a problem not easily solved. The upper ring was put in place first. The lower ring needed to be positioned such that the pikes would all be upright before permanently gluing it in place, **(Fig.9.36)**.

The drawings and rigging diagrams were studied closely to identify any and all rigging blocks best assembled before stepping the masts. With a model of this size it was inevitable that somewhere in the rigging process a block had to be threaded or tied in place at a height that would be neither a " sitting down" or a "standing up" job. Any that could be applied in a comfortable position on the bench in advance were well worth doing. A check was made as to the diameter of the thread that was to pass through these blocks, in particular the mainmast stays, to ensure that the holes through the blocks were of suitable size. **Figs.9.37** and **9.38** show the bowsprit and foremast rigged prior to assembly.

The yards and spars

The drawings showed all the relevant dimensions, positions and sizes of all rigging blocks and the set-up of the footropes. Tapering was done using the same method adopted for tapering the masts having first filed or planed the basic dowel to the octagonal section that is required at the centre portion of the yard. The instructions are quite adequate for this stage of the construction, but I would emphasise a couple or so points that are important. Painting should be done before fitting the stun-sail booms. Footropes, blocks and pendants should be put in place before assembling the yards or spars to the masts. It should also be noted that the brace pendants on the crossjack should be rigged forward rather than aft.

When assembling the stun-sail booms, it was ensured that the blocks for the leech lines and buntlines all laid forward of the booms.

The suggestion to pin the yards to the masts is a sound move. However, depending on how much space you have in your workroom, you may find it more convenient and certainly less hazardous, not to fit the yards to the masts until the shrouds and ratlines have been rigged. I say this because, as will be realised by this stage of the proceedings, the model is both long and heavy and, repeatedly turning it round on the bench in order to rig the shrouds, alternately port then starboard, is an arduous business even without the yards in place. I have an old computer trolley on castors to which I clamp my models thus making life a bit easier but, if you don't have an "island" bench that you can freely move around yourself, or have a bench width that will accommodate a turntable to swing a 1300mm length, it is a problem that needs some thought.

General Notes on the rigging

Looking at pictures of the finished model, it had to be admitted that the rigging appeared somewhat daunting but, as is often the case, it was really a matter of quantity rather than complexity. There are features not too frequently found on model boats such as the breast stays, Burton pendants, buntlines and leech lines, all of which add to the apparent maze. However, on the plus side, with a model of this size, accessibility was good and the recommended sequences of setting up the rigging ensured that there were no real problems. The more experienced model maker will no doubt have set ideas as to the best procedure to adopt and, certainly, one gets the best results with the way with which one is most comfortable. Nonetheless, the sequence in the manual works very well.

Writing a manual with instructions for rigging is not easy and, getting everything on the drawings in a logical manner, even less so. The main problem is the fact that it is very difficult to get every associated bit of information on one sheet. Unless you have a fair knowledge of rigging this type of vessel, it is inevitable that there will be some hopping around from drawings to manual to ensure that correct cordage sizes are used, the correct passage of each part of the rigging is recognised and that nothing gets missed. In this kit, a successful effort has been made to keep this to a minimum. I only found one or two adverse comments to make about the rigging instructions and my ongoing comments are, therefore, more concerned with points supplementary to the manual and

drawings, rather than being critical of them.

As I mentioned in the previous section I stepped the three masts without the yards. There are a few things to watch for here. First, and probably the most obvious, is to double check that all three masts are still in line and perpendicular to the deck with the correct rake angles before applying the glue; also that the bowsprit had adopted its correct alignment. Having made this check earlier in the construction of the hull, there should not be a problem. If there is some minor adjustment required for whatever reason, try to do it now. *Pulling things into line by tensioning up the shrouds and stays will not work!*

Some of the rigging is fixed to the channels using etched brass hooks. Although the hooks can be removed from the sheet very cleanly leaving only the smallest residue of the joining tabs, it is essential to clean up the business end of the hooks with a small file. The hooks only just go through the eyebolts provided.

Finally, before making a start with the rigging, I did manage to remember to remove rings and watch. A simple precaution, but one that can save a lot of grief as the quantity of rigging increases.

The shrouds

When tying on the shrouds, I made sure that the lashing was pulled up tight to the masthead and that the lashing on each sequential pair, gradually moved from the front part of the square sectioned masthead towards the stern. It would be wrong to have all the lashings vertically one above the other!

The 1.3mm thread used for the main and foremast shrouds had considerable elasticity. The 15mm separation between the deadeyes quoted in the manual for making the deadeye jig was therefore increased so that adequate tension could be applied to attain 15mm as a final separation distance. I would suggest that a bit of trial and error be used in case the elasticity factor varies in the thread manufacture. The smaller diameter thread for the mizzen and upper shrouds did not have the same degree of stretch and no adjustment to the suggested jig length was necessary. In all cases it was desirable to get sufficient tension, so that when tying on the ratlines, it was not so easy to pull the shrouds out of shape.

When using the wire jig, it will be found that the deadeye will probably rotate within the shroud lashing or the deadeye straps. This did not cause a problem, the orientation just had to be corrected before rigging the lanyards and any slight variation, that resulted in the initial separation distance, was taken up when tensioning the lanyards. It was noted on the drawings that the lanyards were rigged to suit cable laid rope (left hand twist) instead of shroud laid rope that was more frequently used until 1805. Don't look for cable laid material in a kit though, it is almost exclusively manufactured with a right hand twist and, if you want to be accurate to that degree, then it's a case of laying your own.

Fig. 9.38 The underside of the foretop with blocks in place.

Ratlines

Apart from the sheer tedium of tying on the large number of ratlines, the use of natural thread blackened by brushing on Indian ink can be a bit hazardous. In addition to covering the back of the shrouds with paper while brushing on the ink, I would suggest that the deck also be gently covered with soft toilet tissues. These are easily removed and do not snag on deck fittings etc. DO NOT use cloth or woven material of any sort. The use of a soft brush, as against a stiff bristly one, for applying the Indian ink will also help avoid splatter.

In general, black thread is indeed stiffer than the natural variety but, a visit to your local haberdasher may yield a supply of Gutermann CA02776 black machine thread, which doesn't have the offending stiffness and comes in 100 metre reels. It also "holds the knot" well. Having a diameter of 0.17mm, at 1:64 scale, it relates to 1.35in rope, which is just smaller than the 1.5in rope used for ratlines. (0.25mm diameter thread converts to 2in rope, remembering that rope was measured around its circumference).

The allowance of 15mm of ratline at each end of the shroud to aid trimming was a sound suggestion but should be treated as a minimum. For the first end it was easy to judge the right amount but, it was barely long enough to manipulate the last clove hitch comfortably. Knots take a surprisingly long length of thread, so the length of thread for the first (bottom) ratline was cut over length and used as a basis to gauge the amount to be used for the remainder.

A piece of white paper placed between the shrouds

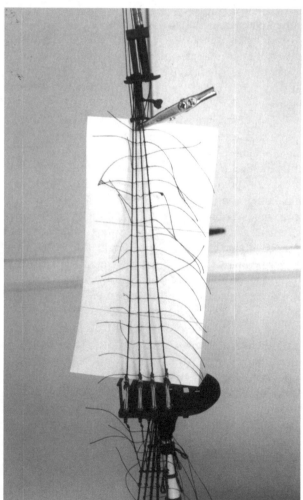

Fig. 9.39 Ratlines being applied to the fore top-mast shrouds.

Fig. 9.41 The crowsfeet to the foremast. Note also the snaking between the fore and preventer stays.

and the relevant mast helped the eyes focus better on the fine black thread in use, **(Fig.9.39)**. The paper was clipped at the top only to allow the fingers to get between the shrouds and the paper to assist in tensioning up the knots without distorting the shrouds.

It was reckoned that, at this stage, it was a good time to fit the shroud cleats. A touch of cyanoacrylate to make the initial positioning was found adequate prior to doing the two lashings. As castings, they have to be painted and this was done after fixing – CAREFULLY! Shroud cleats were normally fitted just above the upper

deadeyes at the lower end of the shrouds although, in the case of the lower shrouds, the drawings did not make this clear. Cleats were fitted to all foremast and mizzen shrouds as well as the foremost of the upper shrouds, **(Fig.9.40)**.

The mizzen gaff and boom

No problems were experienced in the fitting or rigging of these two spars. The initial running rigging to these two spars was best done at this stage in order that their correct relative attitude to the mizzen was achieved.

Fig. 9.42 Bowsprit shrouds and bobstays. Note the sheet block toggled to the clew garnet block.

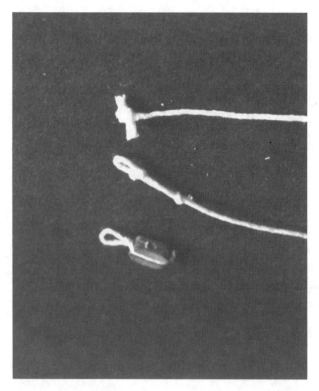

Fig. 9.43 Details of toggled and looped ends together with a looped block

Stays

These were set up without trouble and, at this scale, I was able to get a fair amount of tension on the cordage. This helped enormously in avoiding pulling things out of line when rigging crowsfeet, snaking and other stay-mounted tackle.

In order to get the best accessibility, I did the snaking immediately after rigging the relevant stays and their preventers. I cut a length of the correct thread for the snaking and seized it to the preventer just below the mouse then, to keep light tension on it, threaded it through the stay collars down below. A pair of dividers was used to maintain constant spacing of the seizing at each kink of the snaking to stay and preventer. After all the seizings had been done, the snaking was gently pulled up to produce the final tension without pulling the two stays together, or at least not too much!

The crowsfeet were rigged next, (**Fig.9.41**). The stay tackle and euphroe blocks were assembled on the bench and tied on to the stays before rigging the crowsfeet proper. Because of the tension in the stays, these could be pulled up fairly tight without distorting the run of the stays.

The remaining fore and aft stays were then fitted together with the bobstays, shrouds and martingale to the bowsprit, (**Fig.9.42**).

The breast backstays, standing backstays and shifting backstays were then put up. It is not often that one sees breast backstays fitted to a model and, in fact, not all vessels carried them. It says something for the research that went into this model that *Jotika* identified them

and included them in the kit design.

The stays to the topgallant and royal masts required only light tension in order not to pull anything out of line and concluded the application of the standing rigging.

The running rigging

Study of the manual and drawings at the commencement of each section was a great help to make sure that the process went without trouble. Every line that passed through a block was stiffened on its leading end to aid threading and further help was gained by trimming the end after the cyanoacrylate had dried, not straight across the thread, but at an angle roughly the same as the angle of twist.

Mounting the yards

The yards were now attached to the masts and the trusses, parrels and halyards rigged to the deck via block and tackle at the bottom of the relevant masts or channels. Again, to maintain accessibility, I mounted the yards one at a time starting with the spritsail yard then the foreyard, main yard and crossjack.

It was found easier to rig the truss loops to the lower yards before assembly, ensuring that the eyes of the loops were large enough to facilitate easy threading of the falls noting that the truss on the crossjack was rigged only on the port side. A similar consideration was given to the loops for rigging the slings on the three lower yards. In fact, I found that it was easier to rig the slings to the loops before assembling the lower yards to the masts and bringing the ends of the sling together across the top of the relevant cap. Not technically correct, I know, but it is a technical adjustment (cheating) that is very difficult to spot!

The topsail yards were then put up followed by the topgallant yards, the same rigging procedures being adopted as for the lower yards.

The halyards and lifts

These were quite straightforward procedures. The main thing to watch was the downward run of each line ensuring that it had a straight passage through rigging previously put up on its way to being belayed.

The spritsail yard rigging

I have to say that I found the manual a little confusing in its description of the sheet set-up and its relationship with the clew garnet and block. When I realised that there should be a second block toggled to the one shown on the drawing, (again see **Fig.9.42**), the matter became clear. A toggled end, a looped end to take the toggle and a looped block can be seen in **Fig.9.43**. I am given to understand that *Jotika* have now modified the paperwork as necessary.

The first instance of sagging lines was encountered at this stage. Getting a realistic looking curve to a sagging line has always been a bit of a problem and again, many

Fig. 9.44 The boats rigged in position. The bottom ends of the stay tackle have been hooked to eyes in one of the boats.

modellers will have their own favourite method. The method recommended in the manual of using dilute PVA is adequate and one that I have used many times in the past.

However, an alternative method, which I have also found to be very effective, is to cut the thread basically to length and soak it in water. Then, laying it on the ironing board, pass a hot iron down its length. This takes all the kinks and natural twist out of the thread. It can then be rigged without the use of dilute adhesive but still attaining the curve required without deviation from the true line in both planes.

The clues, sheets and tacks

These were relatively straightforward to rig provided that one or two features were not forgotten. The clue lines to the fore and main masts were left hanging below their respective yards for the later rigging of the relevant sheets and tacks.

All clue blocks were rigged with loops for the toggle attachment of sheets, again see **Fig.9.43**.

The topgallant clue line does not pass through a clue block, but is toggled directly to its sheet.

Mounting the boats

These were now placed on their chocks and lashed into place before cutting off accessibility by adding the lower sheets and tacks. Once they had all been mounted I rigged the stay tackle, using the eyebolts on the centre-most boat to attach the hooks. This avoided leaving the tackle hanging limply with that weightless artificial appearance, **(Fig.9.44)**.

The yard braces

The topsail and topgallant yard braces were rigged first, before the fore and mainmast sheets and tacks. The fore and mainmast braces were rigged last. This reversal of the sequence in applying this last section of rigging is again solely for the purposes of accessibility.

The anchors

It was necessary to make four anchors. The shank and head of each anchor came as an integral casting with virtually no flash to clean off. They were then washed in warm water with a dash of washing-up liquid to make sure that they were absolutely clean prior to painting black. The two halves of the stocks were glued together and given a couple of coats of shellac with a gentle sanding between coats. The hoops were simulated with black cartridge paper cut into 2mm wide strips. Bending 1.5mm brass wire around 8mm diameter dowel formed the anchor rings. To stop them from moving through the shank of the anchor and exposing the joint in the ring, a simple hitch of thread was made on the ring each side of the shank and super-glued. This avoided all sorts of problems when doing the puddening.

The anchors were then rigged to the ship with only the foremost anchors having a hawse rope.

Finishing off

The last repetitive job of the project was to make coils of rope to be positioned at the various belaying points.

Fig. 9.45 Rope hanks and coils around the base of the foremast. Make sure that the right size of thread is used

The size of the coils wouldn't be far from proper proportions at 10mm or 12mm diameter, but it is equally important to make sure that the thread size is the same as the line that has been belayed at that particular point. According to rigging concerned, some will hang on belaying pins and others will lie flat on deck, **(Fig.9.45)**.

Adding the spear completed the figurehead, **(Fig.9.46)**, and it then only remained to have a good look round the model to remove any bits of trimmed rigging or other detritus that had accumulated over the many weeks of model making.

Only when I had satisfied myself that all deck work had been done did I rig the sheets and tacks to the hanging clue blocks on the fore and main masts.

Fig. 9.46 "Agamemnon" now has his spear to finish off the model.

Conclusions

Without any doubt, this was one of the best kits I have had the pleasure of building. The subject was well chosen and the research, together with the design of the kit, was excellent. High quality materials and drawings were supported by a superb standard of pre-cutting. The use of three-axis routing to cut the parts permitted many joints to be provided ready made and to a high degree of accuracy and, of course, not a burnt edge in sight. Cast parts were crisp and clean with virtually no flash. The use of photo-etched brass for chain plates and deadeye straps was a novel innovation that took a bit of getting used to, but the results were most satisfying.

Problems? Yes, one or two mainly concerned with the ship's boats. The grain of 3mm wide timber is, by definition, very coarse for its section and as such does not lend itself to easy use. Cutting it lengthways to 1.5mm width for the internal ribs and gunwale construction resulted in some pieces having to be made several times. However, patience, persistence and solitude won the day and I would have to agree that even my results looked better than would have been provided by an obviously plastic shell.

As a kit for the more experienced model maker, it was an absolute gem, albeit a formidable project. However, serious consideration must be given to the problems of working space and manoeuvrability. You must be able to either get around the model or readily move it, remembering that it is 1300MM long and, once all the spars are in place, 480mm wide

Value for money? Looking round the market place and comparing it with other kits of similar size in the same price range, most definitely, yes. If you are one of those kit builders who, in the past, have moaned about accuracy and lack of research and all round quality, then this should satisfy all your demands. However, if you judge a kit by how many layers of bubble packed, gleaming ornamental castings you see when you open the box, then you might think it a bit expensive. My own opinion is that this kit sets a new benchmark in the market place and is one that really does have the potential for a "museum" quality result.

Display Case

A model of this size and complex detail deserves to be displayed in a relatively airtight environment to avoid the accumulation of dust, the removal of which is an almost impossible job, not to mention the risk of damage while making the attempt.

A suitable case will require the use of 5mm thick toughened glass; in fact, this would be a legal requirement if the model were to be displayed in a public place

CHAPTER 10

The English Carronade

The Carron Iron Company based near Falkirk in Scotland developed the concept of the shorter and lighter gun during the latter half of the eighteenth century. The design evolved over a number of years and eventually resulted in a gun that that could fire a shot that was something like four times as heavy as that projected by a long carriage gun of similar weight.

Designed as a gun having short range, the barrel was considerably shorter than that of a long gun of the same calibre. The thickness of the metal was also smaller due to the fact that a smaller charge was needed to retain effectiveness over a short range. These two features, together with less mass of metal around the chamber where the charge was ignited, resulted in the great weight reduction. The accuracy was also improved by boring the gun from solid. This enabled the windage to be reduced; that is, the difference in diameter between bore and shot essential to prevent the shot jamming in the barrel with disastrous results.

The first carronades were produced in 1778 and were initially used to arm the Carron Company's own ships. There was still some opposition to the Company's products in official naval circles following the earlier failure of Carron guns, bursting on proof. It was not until 1779 that the first carronade establishment was seen.

The effect of the carronade in use was devastating. They were normally mounted on the upper decks and, firing case or grapeshot, the scene on the enemy decks would be absolute carnage.

In order that the carronade be used to maximum effectiveness, special carriages were necessary. These comprised two main parts and the upper part, known as the bed, housed the gun and contained features that permitted the barrel to be elevated or depressed. The lower part, or slide, permitted the bed to recoil and allowed the gun to be traversed by means of a pivot at its forward end. This pivot was, in some cases inside the bulwarks, providing better protection for the firing crew although restricting the degree of traverse. When mounted outside the hull, the pivot afforded a wider angle of traverse and, perhaps more importantly, allowed the muzzle to project through any adjacent rigging, thus reducing the chance of blast damage to the rigging upon discharge. The position of the pivot was said to be to according to the "inner principal" or "outer principle" respectively.

The earlier mounting of the barrel on to the bed followed the conventional system for carriage guns, i.e. trunnions and cap-squares. Later development led to the introduction of the ring beneath the barrel by means of which elevation and depression could be attained, the adjustment being carried out either by a quoin or a screw passing vertically through the cascable.

Mantua's kit for an English Carronade is at 1:17 scale and mounted on a base 189mm square, with a section of bulwarks. The design appears to have been taken from that of the two carronades mounted on the forecastle of H.M.S. "Victory". Thus we have a 68-pounder, mounted according to the inner principle, with under-barrel ring and quoin adjustment for elevation.

The kit

All major wooden parts are provided in pre-cut ply. Ready mitred corners for the base unit corner pieces help to provide a nice foundation for the unit. The barrel is well cast with a minimum of flash together with the two similarly cast fixing brackets. A fittings pack, rigging thread, strip wood of various sections and a brass nameplate complete the package. The quality of all items was good, but it was necessary to study the instructions carefully before doing any cutting - there was only just enough of the various pieces. The multi-lingual, one sheet combination of drawing, instructions and parts list was clear enough and no difficulty was experienced in following the assembly procedures. The set of parts can be seen in **Fig.10.1**.

Building the base

The first task was to simulate the deck planking. The instructions suggest that the base piece be lined with a

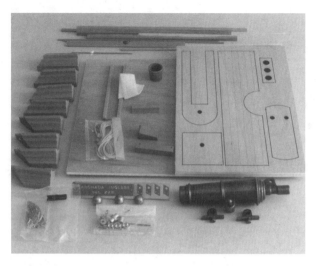

Fig. 10.1 The kit of parts

soft pencil, but I chose to score the base with a fairly sharp scriber. This was better done before assembling the mitred corner pieces. The scriber method calls for one cautionary comment. Use a steel rule and select the direction of grain that guides the scriber in towards the edge of the rule. The indentations were then lined with the soft pencil and the surface immediately sealed with matt or satin varnish. If you use the pencil method to simply draw the lines on to the surface of the wood, then I strongly recommend that the surface be sprayed with varnish, since a brush would almost certainly remove, or smear, the soft lead pencil lines. The corners were then added and the edges of the base covered with the strip material provided, see **Fig.10.2**.

The pre-cut bulwark was lined in a similar fashion to the base to simulate the planking and the four stanchions added. The fixing positions were carefully marked out so that the outside pieces were not fixed in exactly the same position as the inner pieces. Holes were drilled with a diameter that was just a tad smaller than the fixing pins so that the latter, having been cut short, could be gently pushed home with just a touch of cyanoacrylate. It was noted that, at four positions, the pins were replaced by eyebolts.

The rails and their supports were, perhaps, those items that needed the greatest of care and attention. The secret of success in this part of the assembly was to get all of the six support pieces exactly the same length, and with square and flat end faces. I was fortunate enough to have a small 12v sander and, having cut all six slightly over-length, I then faced up one end on each. Then, taking the shortest, I finished it to size by sanding the opposite end, and then matched the remaining five to it. The assembled and completed bulwark piece is shown in **Fig.10.3**.

Building the slide

The slide was built up around pre-cut ply pieces which first had to have the edges well sanded to remove the discoloration left from the cutting process. The numerical sequence was followed successfully in assembling all the parts, but it was noted that the centre of the forked section No.11 had to be filled with a length of channel section, not clearly shown on the drawings, to form the track for the slide. Two pieces of tee section were then inserted, one to act as a stop and the other, longer part to become part of the recoil slide. This latter piece was subsequently trapped in the track by two retaining strips No.14. It was important, since I wanted the bed to actually slide, that the longer tee piece be gently sanded to ensure that it would move easily once the retaining strips had been glued in place.

The brass channel and the traversing rollers were then fixed to the underside of the slide. **Fig.10.4** shows the slide assembly parts.

Assembling the bed and barrel

The barrel was first cleaned up to remove the minimal flash lines left from the casting process, the painted satin black together with the two cast fixing brackets.

The wooden parts for the bed, shown in **Fig.10.5** were then assembled taking care to position the wedge shaped quoin so that the barrel was at the required elevation should you want it anything other than level as shown on the drawings.

It was convenient at this stage to stain and varnish all wooden parts before further assembly. Once this coating had thoroughly dried, the brass brackets on the side of the bed were drilled and mounted and the eyebolts fitted into the side of the slide unit, see **Fig.10.6**.

The barrel was temporarily mounted on to the bed, see **Fig.10.7** in order to determine exactly where the bed should be attached to the slide. The sliding tee piece in the slide assembly was pushed right forward, then with the bed and barrel laid on top and the muzzle of the barrel protruding through the bulwarks by the correct amount, the position of the bed on the slide was carefully marked. The barrel and its brackets were then removed and the bed and slide units separated. The top surface of the tee piece was then coated with glue, taking care not to get any on to the track, and the bed and slide re-united in the previously marked position. When the adhesive had completely cured, the barrel was permanently assembled and it could be demonstrated that the bed would correctly slide back under recoil.

Auxiliary parts

The bucket, cannon ball rack with three balls, and swab completed the outstanding constructional details. The prefabricated bucket needed drilling and a rope handle to be threaded in position, all clearly shown on the drawings. The cannon ball rack was a pre-cut part that just needed cleaning up and the three balls were painted before gluing in place on the rack. The temporary assembly of these parts to the base unit can be seen in **Fig.10.8**.

The strip of material provided for the head of the swab was fixed to one end of the dowel shaft with glue

Fig. 11.2 The assembled base unit.

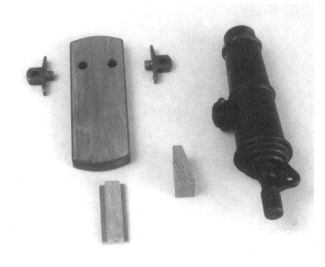

Fig. 11.5 The barrel and bed pieces.

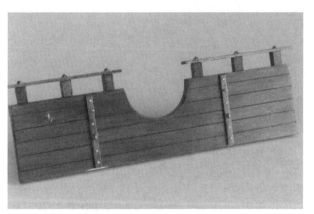

Fig. 11.3 The completed bulwark.

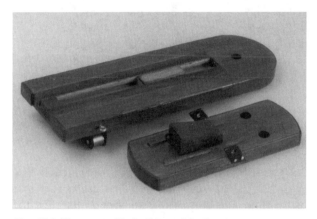

Fig. 11.6 The assembled slide and bed.

Fig. 11.4 The parts for the slide. Note that the piece on the right is a sub-assembly of two individual parts.

Fig. 11.7 The temporary mounting of the barrel to the bed.

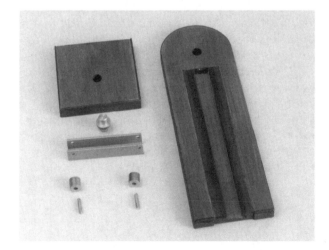

then, having completely coated the under surface of the material with adhesive, the strip was tightly bound round the shaft. Once the glue had set, the shaft was cut to length and varnished.

The various parts were then brought together as shown in **Fig.10.9** ready for the final rigging operation.

The rigging

There was not too much to do in the way of rigging. The single breeching rope, the gun tackle both sides and the training tackle at the back that controlled and held the traverse position. The tricky bit was laying the coils in some sort of decent shape. I had previously soaked

Fig. 11.8 The base unit ready for the final mounting of the slide, bed and barrel.

the thread in very dilute PVA primarily to lay down any hairs that often stick up and catch the dust. This, in turn, stiffened the thread and subsequently allowed it to be formed relatively easy into the required shape.

This also facilitated the rigging of the breeching rope that, with the gun fully run out, hangs slackly each side of the unit. The brass wire hooks which attached the rope to the inside of the bulwarks were provided roughly formed, but needed to be tidied up and slightly re-shaped before lashing them to each end of the rope. It was noted that only one hook was to be fitted before passing the free end of the rope through the cascable!

Finishing off

It only remained to permanently hang the bucket and place the swab in position to finish the construction of the model.

The brass nameplate provided was cut out and the front surface painted black to highlight the engraved lettering. When dry and rubbed down with a piece of fine wet and dry abrasive paper, the finished plate was fixed to the base to complete the project. The finished model can be seen in **Figs.10.10** and **10.11**.

Conclusions

This is the ideal kit for someone who wants to do something a bit different or needs a fill-in job between major projects. It had everything needed, except adhesives and finishing media, to complete a well-detailed model. Referring to a portfolio of plans of H.M.S. "Victory" as in 1805 by Basil Lavis, the model appeared to be historically accurate and a true replica of the 68-pounders that were mounted on the forecastle of that vessel. My only criticism was the size of thread for the breeching rope, which I thought should have been somewhat thicker.

The selection of material was such that some staining was needed to represent reasonably realistic surface colours. I also reckoned that a covering of veneer, or strips of 0.5mm thick material, would have enhanced the exposed edges of the ply parts.

Overall, I found this to be a very enjoyable project and extremely good value for money.

Fig. 11.9 The unit ready for rigging.

CHAPTER 11

H.M. Barque "Endeavour"

Made famous particularly by the first voyage of Captain James Cook, "Endeavour" was originally the "Earl of Pembroke", a collier purchased at Whitby by the Royal Navy in 1768. It was bought specifically to take a group of astronomers to the south Pacific to witness the transit of the planet Venus across the face of the Sun in June 1769. The Royal Society's choice to command the ship was Alexander Dalrymple, the eminent hydrographer and cartographer, but the Admiralty, who selected James Cook for the command, known by them to also be an excellent surveyor and mapmaker, vetoed this proposal. The voyage was to last until July 1771 during which time much of the Pacific area was accurately mapped for the first time.

"Endeavour" was sold to the whaling trade and re-named "La Liberte" in 1790 and eventually condemned as un-seaworthy at Newport, Rhode Island.

This model of the "Endeavour", one of those in Caldercraft's Heritage Series, is made to a scale of 1:64 and measures 725mm long, 590mm high and 279mm wide.

The kit

This kit follows the same high standard of design and material quality found in the other models in Caldercraft's "Heritage" and "Nelson's Navy" series. Where it has been possible to pre-cut parts, this has been done by CNC routing to extreme accuracy, creating all necessary slots and cross halving joints in the process. Five sheets of walnut and a similar number of other sheets have been produced in this manner. Together with a sheet of photo-etched brass parts, all necessary strip and dowel and nine different reels of rigging thread, the package should permit the construction of a really high class model. There are eight sheets of well-detailed drawings, an instruction manual and complete parts list.

Research across the whole product range is of the highest standard as is the thought that has gone into the overall kit design. It is important to remember the latter when tempted to stray from the instruction manual or the recommended sequence of doing things.

Tools required

A very basic tool kit is all that is needed for this kit such is the content of pre-cut parts. I list below those items recommended in the kit manual:

Craft knife
Needle files
Razor saw
David plane
Pin chuck or small electric drill (preferred)
Drills 0,7mm to 2mm diameter
Selection of abrasive papers and sanding block
Paintbrushes
Pliers/wire cutters
Tweezers
Dividers or compass
"Crocodile" clips
Consumables
Masking tape
White PVA adhesive
Medium grade cyanoacrylate
White spirit
Paints and Finishes
Dark wood dye
Dark wood filler
Black Indian ink
Matt polyurethane varnish
Black paint (Humbrol 85)
Red paint (Humbrol 60)
Ochre paint (Humbrol 74)
Blue paint (Humbrol 25)
White paint (Humbrol 34)
Brown paint

Note that the white paint was used primarily for the undersides of the hull although, as stated in the manual, this was used for publicising the prototype and, for historical accuracy, should be brown.

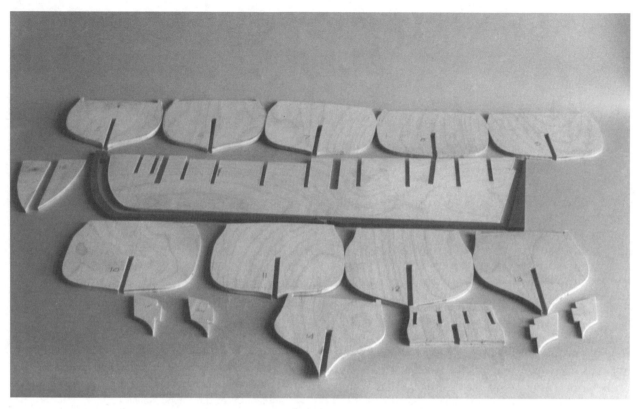

Fig. 11.1 Hull carcase parts. Parts were numbered before removal from the sheet.

Hull construction

This followed the conventional kit format of false keel and bulkheads and all parts were numbered in the sheet before removal, **(Fig. 11.1)**. I passed a piece of the 5mm ply down the slots in the false keel and found them to be the correct size. The slots in the bulkheads needed to be slightly widened and it was seen that the routing had left pads in the slots for such adjustment. A dry run of the complete assembly was done to ensure squareness and straightness; joints that are too tight can introduce a bend to the false keel.

The edges of the bow and stern-most bulkheads were roughly chamfered together with the plank termination pieces before gluing the whole assembly together.

The three false decks were then added, fixing with both pins and glue and the assembly left overnight for the glue to thoroughly cure before finishing off the bevelling of the edges of the bulkheads. I left the fitting of the keel and prow pieces until after this chamfering operation in order to avoid possibly damaging the pre-cut walnut parts, **(Fig. 11.2)**.

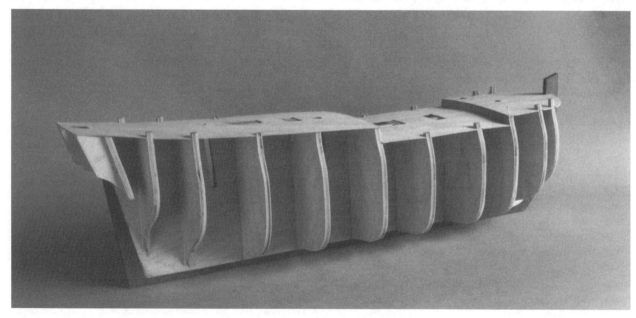

Fig. 11.2 Hull carcase complete and ready for planking.

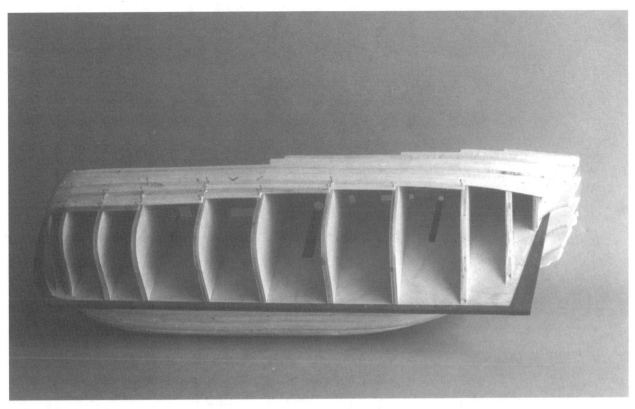

Fig. 11.3 The first planking. Note the lower planking in two pieces.

First planking

The first planking was laid using 5 x 1,5mm lime strips. Although the vessel was of moderately simple lines, there were severe bends at both bow and stern, which can make for a few difficulties in the planking process. The actual bending was straightforward enough, soaking or the use of a plank nipper sorted that out easily enough.

The main problem in such cases always comes when trying to get the overall length of a plank correct while, at the same time, getting the tapers and the curves at each end right as well. Not forgetting that the plank has to lay flat against the edges of the bulkheads. From the deck level down to the bottom of the last bulkhead (No.15), the planking overlapped the rear end so that the problem did not occur. Below that level, planks needed to be curved and/or tapered at both ends. In such instances I have always found that it makes life a lot easier if you make the plank in two pieces. The bow piece was made and fixed first, the "inner" end of the plank cut to sit halfway across, say, bulkhead No.13, **(Fig.11.3)**. The stern length was then tapered and bent

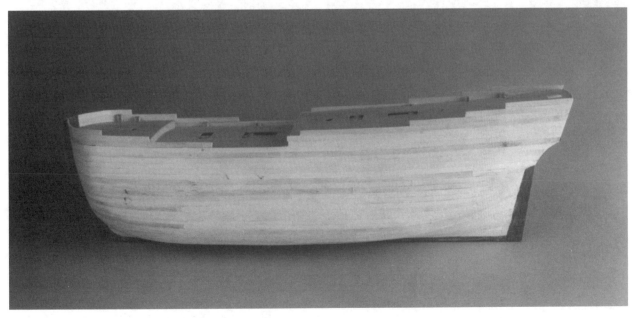

Fig. 12.4 The first planking sealed and rubbed down.

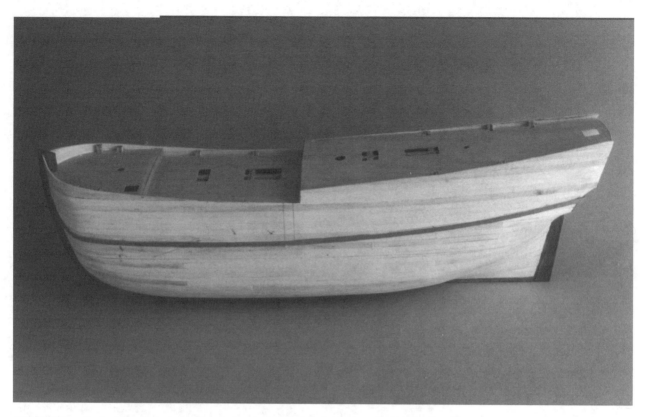

Fig. 11.5 The first of the outer planking in line with the top of the main wale.

as required and its length trimmed to butt up against the end of the bow piece. The next bow piece was similarly prepared but the butt joint made on bulkhead No.12 and so on to No.8 until six duplex planks had been laid. The process was then repeated, this time starting at No.11.

This procedure does not eliminate the need for stealers and the laying of the planks flat against the edges of the bulwarks is still a prime requirement. However, it should be remembered that the cosmetic pattern of

the first planking is not of great concern provided that a sound, unblemished surface free of lumps and bumps is attained.

The stern fascia was temporarily pinned in place in order to establish the correct curve to which the walnut planking below had to be set. Having done that, I removed the fascia prior to starting the second planking, which would overlap, then be trimmed back to the outer seating for the fascia. This would make life a lot easier when finally rubbing down the second planked surface.

Fig. 11.6 The second planking complete.

Fig. 11.7 The main wale in place. Note the pre-painted top and bottom planks and first coat painting of the upper hull.

Rubbing down is always a messy and dusty business and using a mask was essential to avoid breathing it all in. I normally use one with an exhalation valve in order that I don't constantly steam up my spectacles. Having roughly sanded all over, I applied sealer/filler to the required surface before finishing, **(Fig.11.4)**.

Second planking

The first plank that was laid was on that line defined by the top of the main wale. It was important to achieve accurate alignment port to starboard, thus careful measurement and quite a bit of eyeballing was necessary, **(Fig.11.5)**.

Apart from the first plank, as with the first planking, the majority of strips were put on in two pieces but this time I had to choose more carefully where I made the butt joints. Above the line of the main wale, choosing the position of either of the two side fenders, which would, in the final analysis, cover the joint, easily solved the problem. Neat joints for those exposed butts between the bottom of the wale and the waterline were essential. Below the waterline, which is ultimately a painted surface, the position was relatively unimportant.

Before planking that area below the initial plank, I pared away the first planking immediately in front of the sternpost to a depth of about 0,5mm. This made it easier to attain a neat and tidy joint.

I soaked the ends of all planks rather than use a nipper to achieve the bends. This decision was largely dictated by the severity of the curves at the bow and below the transom plate. I normally put the end of all the planks into a vase of water a couple of hours prior to starting the planking operation then, as I cut the plank into two lengths, the dry piece gets put back to soak for use later on.

Cyanoacrylate was used throughout this procedure, which meant that I had to be sure that the strip was accurately cut to shape before I applied the adhesive, then move with alacrity and precision if the strip was still damp. The key to success here was to make certain that the hull was well propped up on the bench so that it couldn't move about while I was putting the strip on.

The completely planked hull was then roughly rubbed down before sealing and filling prior to finishing with fine grade abrasive papers, **(Fig.11.6)**.

The main male and upper side rail

I deliberately left the planking of the inner surfaces of the bulwarks until after I had completed the deck planking; it always seems easier that way to attain a nice clean line between deck and bulwark.

The main wale had to be painted black so, to avoid hand trembling attempts not to get paint onto the surface of the hull, I pre-painted the top and bottom strips of the five pieces that go to make up the wale.

The top strip was laid directly on to the first of the second planking strip, which had been previously positioned with great care. The other four strips were then assembled tight up against the underside of the first, making sure that the bottom piece was the other pre-painted strip. All of the lengths were un-tapered and stuck down with cyanoacrylate. The wale was then filled and rubbed down ready for painting, although only the face needed such attention, the pre-painting taking care of the top and bottom edges.

The upper rail was put on in a similar manner, parallel to the top edge of the main wale. However, again bearing in mind the trembling hand syndrome, I drew a pencil line to represent the top edge of the upper rail and then painted the side of the upper hull blue before

159

Fig. 11.8 The rudder assembly.

actually sticking the rail in place, **(Fig.11.7)**.

Deck planking

One thing that became immediately apparent was the fact that one edge of the tanganyika strips was not well cut, probably having something to do with the relationship of the direction of cut with the direction of grain. Whatever the reason, if you are a modeller that likes to simulate nice straight lines of caulking, then every strip needed to be straightened up.

The first piece was laid along the centreline of each of the three decks and the deck planked working out from that central guiding strip to the margins of the deck. Each deck aperture was left open by at least one strip in order to get a scalpel in later to trim the aperture to size.

After sanding to the desired finish, the inner surfaces of the bulwarks were then planked with pre-sanded strips, ensuring that the bottom plank was firmly down on to the deck. The inside of the transom plate also had to be vertically planked using the same 4 x 1mm material. These planks, together with the decks were then sealed with a couple of coats of matt varnish.

The rudder

It was decision time. Whether to make the rudder moveable or fixed? On the basis that once the tiller was rigged it wouldn't move anyway, I decided to firmly fix it in place. This also made the assembly of the hinge parts that much easier. I fixed the pintles and their straps to the rudder first, then securely glued the gudgeons on to the pintles, ensuring that the spigots on the gudgeons were in line and square and had left enough gap between them and the rudder edge to slide the gudgeon straps through. The spacing between the spigots was measured and the relevant positions drilled into the edge of the rudderpost. Once the rudder had been assembled to the post and the glue had thoroughly set, the gudgeon straps were put in place, **(Fig.11.8)**.

The tiller was made up, dry fitted, and put to one side for later permanent assembly.

Bulwark capping rails

The forward and aft lower capping rails were cut out and offered up to the hull to check for position and correct seating. It was noted that the aft end of the forward rail should be in line with the forward end of the aft rail for later alignment of the upper capping rails. It was also noticed that there was one square hole missing from the forward end of each of the aft rails 107 and 108 (for housing parts 67) and this was drilled and filed prior to assembly to the hull. The shaped and the single timber posts 66 and 67 needed little adjustment to correctly fit them in place; neither did the timberheads 68.

The forward upper capping rail was located on top of the relevant posts, checking that it aligned with the lower aft capping rail, then glued in place. The quarterdeck upper rails were dry fitted to establish the height of the short stern rail, the latter being permanently fitted first. The 3 x 2mm posts needed to have angled ends so that the relative surfaces of the three rails concerned matched up. This, coupled with getting the length of the posts correct required a lot of trial and error to get an acceptable result. When adhesive had thoroughly cured, all rails were painted matt black. Adding the fore knightheads completed this section of the project, **(Fig.11.9)**.

160

Fig. 11.9 The rails and timberheads in place.

Hull fittings

The first part of this section of the project was to clean and prime the photo-etched brass sheet. The individual parts were then painted with two coats of the appropriate colour. I knew that when I cut the parts from the sheet, I would expose a small area of brass, but this would easily be touched in the final stages of construction. What I did not want to do was to attempt to paint pieces in their entirety after assembly and risk spreading paint into places where it should not be. Thus, a spray of grey primer followed a wash of the sheet in a mild solution of washing-up liquid. The individual parts were brush painted with the relevant colour.

The various sizes of port lids (not forgetting the two for the stern chasers), were cut from the appropriate strip and assembled with brass hinges prior to putting them into place on the side of the hull. Although such assembly is arguably better left until after fixing the channels and chain plates. The side fenders and chess-trees were then positioned. In the latter case it involved either cutting a notch in the back edge of the part to sit over the upper side rail on the hull, or, cutting a gap in the rail to take the chess-tree. I found it easier to cut notches for all these parts but this was purely a personal choice.

The channels were then prepared by drilling holes into the back edge and fitting two pins into each to strengthen the joint to the hull. I cut the heads off small brass pins and pushed the cut ends into the channel edge, fixing with a touch of cyanoacrylate. This left the pointed end of the pins to be used as scribers to permit accurate marking for drilling on the side of the hull. *It was important to recognise that the channels have a fore and an aft aspect due to the spacing of the slots for the deadeyes in order not to assemble them the wrong way round.*

As far as the assembly of the chain plates is concerned, the procedure largely depends on how fumble-free your fingers are and the standard of your eyesight. My own choice was to insert the deadeye into the strap first then hang on the links below. The strap was then inserted into its slot in the edge of the channel and fixed with a dab of epoxy adhesive. Bearing in mind that the design of the straps is such as to lock their tongues into the slots, the use of epoxy may seem a bit "belt and braces". If however, the lower deadeyes *should* pull out when tightening up the lanyards, it would be something of a disaster. After all slots had been filled, the 1,5mm square sectioned capping strip was glued in place. To pin the links to the hull, I chose a drill diameter that would allow me to push home the pins rather than have to tap them in. A small dab of cyanoacrylate prevented them from ever coming out.

The castings for the stern decoration were cleaned up and painted. These fitted extremely well and needed no attention to get them sitting correctly. The lantern was also very straightforward to make although, along with the four stern window covers, I chose not to assemble them to the hull at this time due to their vulnerability during the ongoing construction.

An interesting point for discussion arose when I came to insert the window frames both in the stern and the

161

Fig. 11.10 The forwrd hull fittings.

quarter-badges. Should they, or should they not be glazed? The kit does not mention glazing, nor does it contain glazing material. However, one has to ask why there are hinged covers to the four stern windows and, is it because the windows are not glazed? Try as I might, I could not find any definitive answer to the question and discussion with knowledgeable colleagues revealed about a 50/50 difference of opinion. My gut feeling pushed me into the "glaze 'em" camp, and that is what I did, although I can't help feeling that there will be yet more "experts" to join the discussion. The completion of the hull fitting stage can be seen in **Figs. 11.10** and **11.11**.

Deck fittings

Before getting too deeply involved in the construction of all these interesting little self-contained projects, I decided to paint the 30 cleats. This could have been a fiddly job but past experience has led me to evolve a rather neat and efficient way of doing it. I measured the spigot end of the cleat and selected a drill size that permitted a gentle push fit. I then took a piece of scrap wood and drilled thirty holes into which I pushed all of the cleats. They were then painted and when dry were removed one at a time as required on the model. One

Fig. 11.11 The fittings aft and the stern decoration completed.

Fig. 11.12 The mid-ship deck fittings.

huge plus point was the fact that the spigots and joint faces were paint free and ready to accept the adhesive without further attention.

The windlass was a particularly interesting feature to make. I have to admit that I was a little sceptical about the construction process before I started. The design of the barrel assemblies was most unusual, if not unique, in that each facet of the octagonal barrels was a separate pre-cut and drilled part, glued to octagonal discs mounted on a central shaft. In fact, the process was extremely well thought out and produced an excellent result. The only thing I had to watch was to ensure that the radial orientation of the octagonal discs on the shaft was the same for all sections of the barrel. The windlass assembly is shown in **Fig.11.12**. The capstan, binnacle and ship's wheel assemblies are shown in **Fig.11.13**.

The accuracy of the pre-cutting came into its own

Fig. 11.13 The rigging to the tiller and wheel assembly.

Fig. 11.14 Deck fittings at the fore end.

during the construction of the many sub-assemblies in this section of the project and, when everything was finally fixed on deck, the model took on quite an impressive appearance, see **Figs.11.14** and **11.15**. One point that was clearly shown on the drawings was the dowelling of some parts to the deck. This was not something to be missed and essential for taking the stress and strain of the rigging to be applied later.

The small carriage guns were readily made, as were the eight swivels round the after deck, although the latter were not fixed to their respective posts

until the very end of the entire project.

The ship's boats

This stage was probably the biggest challenge of the whole project. Each boat had to be double planked and, unlike boats on some other vessels, these were not painted, so accurate tapering was the order of the day if unsightly gaps were not to be left.

The first constructional stage was to make the carcase for each boat from the pre-cut 1,5mm ply pieces. It was essential to ensure that the bulkheads were

Fig. 11.15 Deck fittings looking aft.

Fig. 12.16 The pinnace and longboat stowed amidships.

correctly numbered before removal from the sheet and then assembled to the false keel in the right sequence. Once this sub-assembly had been completed, the edges of the bulkheads were faired up to provide proper seating for the planking. It was important to get this stage right or you could finish up with a distorted boat. It also had to be remembered that the planks above the boat's floor level could only be glued to the fore and aft-most bulkheads. Having got the first (top) plank in place, I found that having the second and subsequent planks fixed at each end, a small dab of cyanoacrylate at one or two points along the longitudinal joints was useful in holding the construction fairly rigid.

The drawings and the instructions were closely studied once again at this stage and it thus became apparent that the instruction to commence planking at the top was only pertinent to three of the four boats. The skiff was shown on the drawings to be clinker built and therefore the second planking would start at the bottom in order to recognise the overlapping planks.

The second planking was simpler in application although it was still necessary to taper and use cyanoacrylate. Previous experience reminded me that using cyanoacrylate on 0,5mm material could be tricky in that it may soak through, particularly if the wood is wet. You could finish up with the boat stuck to your fingers!

One of the difficult aspects was the need to shape the end of each plank to match with the face of the false keel, particularly at the bow end. I decided to taper the edges of the keel at these points and plank initially to a sharp edge. I then filed a 1,5mm flat around the keel and stem to accept 1,5mm square walnut strip

stuck on afterwards to simulate the exposed part of the stem-post and keel. This provided a nice crisp edge to the feature and also matched the shade of wood used for the planking.

This part of the project was assessed in the manual to take about two weeks of evenings to complete. I reckoned that I spent about fifty hours making the four boats, mostly during daylight hours. Working in artificial light only may have extended that time.

The two boats are shown mounted on the beams in **Fig.11.16**.

The anchors

Not much was said about the anchors in the kit and I have always felt that they are items that maybe need a little more attention than they sometimes get.

A sequence of assembly that I have always found to give a good result is to paint the casting matt black then, while the paint is drying, make the two part wooden stocks. The parts were first glued together then finished all round after the glue had set, making sure that the square hole was suitably cleaned out to accept the anchor. The iron bands, simulated by 2mm wide strips of black cartridge paper were then added. Because of the angled underside faces of the stock, it is not possible to properly add the bands using one continuous strip of paper. For a perfect result, I did the undersides first followed by the remaining three sides in one strip, trimming ends with a scalpel between the two applications. The stock was then added to the anchor.

I made the anchor rings from 1mm diameter brass wire wound around a piece of 6mm diameter dowel. Each ring should ideally be puddened, or served all round. I

Fig. 11.17 Anchors, yawl and skiff ready for later assembly.

cut a 250mm length of 0,5mm natural thread and stiffened one end with cyanoacrylate to a length of about 20mm. The other end I threaded through the hole in the top of the anchor to leave about 10mm protruding, then sprung the brass ring into place such that the join in the ring was buried inside the casting; the whole being secured with a touch of cyanoacrylate.

The ring was now served all round, using the stiffened end of the thread as a bodkin. When tied off and trimmed, I had quite a respectable set of anchor assemblies that were then put to one side to be mounted to the hull later in the project. The four anchors together with the yawl and skiff can be seen in **Fig.11.17.**

The bowsprit

Both ends of the bowsprit needed to be tapered taking the lengths of the tapers from the drawing sheet 3. Considerable care was exercised to fit the cap at the fore end and to attain the correct angle and orientation of the seating at the butt end. The bowsprit fairlead was drilled with the seven required holes and fitted together with the jibboom saddle to the top of the bowsprit. The cleats were cut from 1,5mm square strip as directed and glued in place with cyanoacrylate then, when thoroughly cured tapered with a scalpel.

The jibboom was cut to length and tapered then lashed to the bowsprit. This sub-assembly was then stained and the cap and doubling painted matt black.

Having fitted the bowsprit to the hull, it was necessary to apply the gammoning. 0,5mm thread was used for this and a gammoning ring (239), attached to an eyebolt, was fixed to the stem post and rigged as shown on the drawing. These items are shown in **Fig.11.18.**

The masts

The drawings and the manual, when read together, give a very good insight into the making of the masts. However, from a personal point of view, I found it easier to make the tops assemblies complete with back rails, crosstrees and trestle-trees and furnished with eyelets before locating them on the masts proper, (**Figs.11.19** and **11.20**). It allowed a far firmer base on to which to construct the back rails and it was certainly easier to drill the holes for the eyelets that had to be inserted into the under-surface of the crosstrees. The lower deadeyes and their straps were fitted to the tops again using a small touch of epoxy. Remembering that the futtock shrouds were *hooked* to the straps, I made sure at this stage that the ends of the straps were trimmed fairly close to the holes in order that the hooks would be well fitted.

All tops and doublings were to be painted black with the main portions of the masts stained. I found that it was best to do the staining first then, when thoroughly dry, do the black paintwork followed by the addition of the 2mm wide bands, wooldings and cleats. Using that sequence avoids any stray adhesive sealing the wood and not allowing the stain to properly cover.

All rigging blocks were tied on before stepping the masts into the hull. The two small blocks at the bottom of the poles on the fore and main topgallant masts were found to be redundant since the topgallant sails were set flying and, therefore, lifts were not rigged. The three masts can be seen in place in **Fig.11.21.**

A point worth stressing relates to the blocks on the underside of the main and fore tops. It was important to make sure that they were well secured since, should

Fig. 11.18 The fitted bowsprit. Note the triangular gammoning ring on the stem.

Fig. 11.19 The upper surface of the fore top, battened and eye-bolted with holes drilled for the crowsfeet.

Fig. 11.20 The underside of the fore top showing the eye-bolts in the cross-trees.

The yards

These were basically made by planing to an octagonal section, taking the edges off with a file to get to a circular section then finishing off by spinning and sanding. In the case of the foreyard and main yard, the octagonal section was first planed parallel over the entire length of the yard. The length of the parallel centre portion was marked and the outer portions tapered to octagonal then circular sections.

The other yards were tapered leaving a short, central, parallel portion for seating the sling cleats. The latter, together with the yardarm cleats were glued in place and left for 24 hours before shaping in situ with a scalpel. The holes for the wire footrope stirrups were marked and drilled and the stunsail boom rings drilled and fitted. It should be noted that the crossjack should also be drilled vertically at each end for the later rigging of the clews, see sheet 8 for the relevant position. The mizzen topsail yard was fitted with brace pendants having 3mm single blocks as shown on drawing sheet 8 rather than the detail on sheet 4. All yards were then painted matt black.

All blocks were then tied in place together with the footropes. A 1mm diameter wire peg was fitted centrally to the back of each of each spar to facilitate the later mounting of the yards to the masts. Finally, the stunsail booms were put in place, **(Fig.11.22)**.

I chose not to assemble the yards to the masts at this time. This is a purely personal choice based on a greater accessibility problem during the application of the standing rigging, particularly tying on the ratlines and their subsequent inking.

The standing rigging

The lower shrouds were put up first followed by the relevant catharpins and futtock shrouds. The upper shrouds were then fitted, **(Fig.11.23)**. I questioned the fact that the lower mizzen shrouds unusually interfered with the deck rails but was advised by *Caldercraft* that this was in fact correct.

At this stage, the temptation is always to leave the

Fig. 11.21 Ready to start rigging. Now was a good time to make sure that no blocks had been missed.

they become detached during the rigging process, they would be almost impossible to replace.

The three topmasts and two topgallant masts were duplicated as spares to lie on top of the gallows at deck level. These were to support the skiff and the yawl.

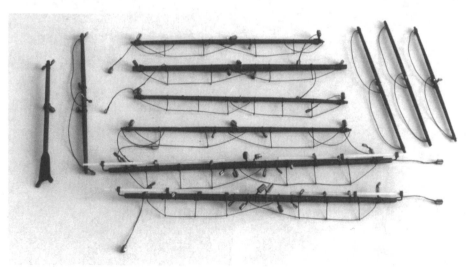

Fig. 11.22 The yards blocked up and the foot ropes fitted.

Fig. 11.23 Mainmast upper and lower shrouds rigged.

monotonous job of tying on ratlines until later. However, they have only to be done once and tying them at this juncture had the advantage of best access for fingers and hands before further rigging got in the way. *Caldercraft* has an unusual approach to the application of ratlines, inasmuch as the recommended method is to use natural thread and then paint with Indian ink to blacken them afterwards. I have to confess that I was not particularly thrilled with this idea at first but soon found that the process actually worked very well. All the knots were brushed with dilute PVA using a soft round brush before trimming. The quality of the 0,10mm diameter thread provided in the kit was ideal for the job, holding the knots well. In fact, everything worked so well that I estimate that I saved at least thirty percent of the time that I would have usually taken, and the finished job looked better, (Fig.11.24). A good covering of toilet tissue to protect the deck and fittings when applying the Indian ink was used. I found this to be preferable to cloth or similar woven material in that there was no possibility of snagging on deck fittings when removing after the ink job. The ink was *gently* painted on to avoid unwanted splashes and, although it penetrated the thread fairly well, it was still necessary to do both the inboard and outboard surfaces. It was fairly inevitable that, after the protective covering had been removed, a few isolated places would come to light that had been missed. These were put to rights using a black marker pen.

Before going any further, I decided to add the shroud cleats. These were fitted to the inside of each of the lower shrouds to the fore and main masts, just above the upper deadeyes. These are metal parts and therefore need to be painted. On balance it was found easier to paint them after assembly, although a little care was required. The groove in each cleat was cleaned up using a needle file before sticking it to the shroud with cyanoacrylate. They also had to be tied in two places, and this was done by tying two extra "ratlines" one at the top level and one at the bottom of each row of cleats, cutting the intermediate thread away afterwards. This was far quicker and neater than tying each cleat individually. The cleats to the fore mast can be seen in **Fig.11.26**.

The fore and aft stays were added next followed by the breast backstays. The topmast and topgallant backstays were not put up until the rigging had almost been completed in order to avoid accessibility problems.

I am advised that the lower end of the main preventer stay should be rigged using two closed hearts and not by use of 5mm deadeyes. The photographs of my model show the incorrect use of deadeyes; my error being discovered after it was too late to easily make a correction. The forestay and its preventer (fore top to bowsprit) should be rigged using 1,3mm black thread, information missing from the relevant drawing.

The running rigging

As mentioned previously, I chose not to assemble the yards to the masts until I came to do the running rigging. I chose this procedure because of the accessibility factor. I have found that starting this stage of the rigging by fitting first the crossjack, then the gaff and mizzen topsail yard, (Fig.11.25), keeps the maximum amount of space available in which to move fingers, forceps and cutters. In the main, it conforms to the basic proposition that you work from the middle outwards and from the bottom upwards. If there are a couple of yards on the

Fig. 11.24 The ratlines before colouring.

Fig. 11.25 The crossjack and gaff rigging.

bowsprit as on "Endeavour", **(Fig.11.26)**, then I find that working from aft forward is more convenient. This overcomes the vulnerability of those front-end yards when moving the model about on the bench; hence my choice to work on the mizzen first.

The running rigging on "Endeavour" is not too complicated and the drawings indicated belaying points quite well, but there is a lot of it, **(Fig.11.27)**, and you need to constantly be careful to attain the true unimpeded run of each line as it is added. On the fore and main masts, the clews to the lower yards were not

initially rigged, but left until later.

Having got the running rigging done to all three masts and bowsprit, the spare spars were lashed to the gallows and the third and fourth boats put in place, **(Fig.12.28)**. The tackle hanging below the mainstay was then rigged before moving on to complete the rigging of the topmast and topgallant backstays. The braces were then added followed by the lower yard clews, tacks and sheets.

Coils and hanks of rope were made and either hung or positioned at relevant places throughout the vessel before finally rigging the anchors and mounting the ten

Fig. 11.26 Rigging to the bowsprit. The lower end of the mainstay and its preventer can also be seen. Hearts and lanyard to the bowsprit with deadeyes and lanyard to the rear of the foremast.

Fig. 11.27 There is a lot of rigging but it is not as complicated as it first appears.

Fig. 11.29 Flagstaff and lantern in position. Note also the swivel guns.

swivel guns. Finally, the flagstaff and lantern were added to the stern, **(Fig.11.29)**.

Conclusions

The design concept behind the production of this kit was excellent and up to the standard expected with the "Nelson's Navy" and "Heritage" series from JoTiKa.

The quality of the timber in all its forms was of extremely good standard and the accuracy of all of the pre-cut parts was faultless. The rigging threads were good to work with and all blocks and deadeyes were well drilled, needing no work done on them to clear holes. The provision of photo-etched parts added a clean-cut look to many areas.

Designed for the intermediate and above constructor, "Endeavour" makes up into an extremely nice model and provides several hundreds of hours of enjoyable model making.

Fig. 11.28 Spare spars on the gallows with yawl and skiff lashed in place.

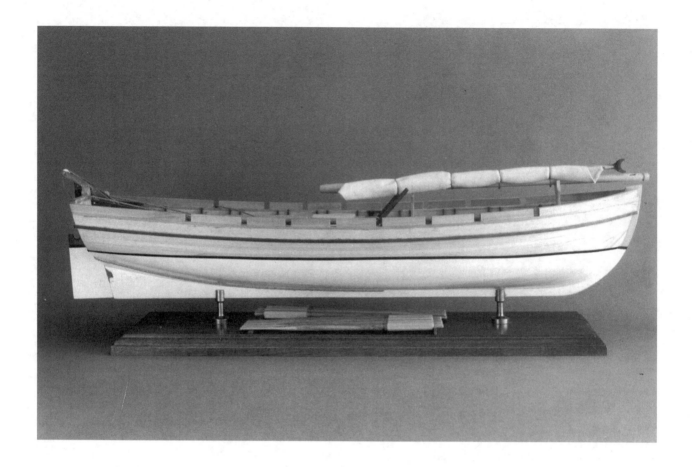

CHAPTER 12

H.M.S. "Victory's" Launch

This is another in the series of successful kits by Panart featuring open boats. The ship's boat made a vital contribution to the efficient running of any man of war, carrying out duties as diverse as inter-ship communication, transport of personnel and water replenishment. The launch was the largest of "Victory's" boats and was fitted out specifically to handle anchorage duties, having a windlass amidships and davit at the stern. The finished model is 620mm long at a scale of 1:16. The craft is totally fitted out and as much work goes into the interior detail as that for the construction of the main shell.

The model may be presented in sailing or stowing rig.

The Kit

The box contained good quality timber in various woods and most essential shaped parts were laser-cut. The drawings were very good in terms of the way in which the construction procedures were illustrated although the notes were all in Italian. There was an instruction leaflet in English although the translation from the Italian left a little to be desired. The fittings pack was to the usual Panart high standard.

Tools and materials

A craft knife
Razor saw
Light hammer
A selection of small drills
12Volt drill, lathe and disc sander
Various grades of abrasive paper
Matt white paint and varnish
PVA adhesive
Thick grade of cyanoacrylate
Small "crocodile" clips.

Fig. 12.1 The bulkheads and Platform No.9 screwed together.

Fig. 12.2 3mm holes drilled in the platform and false keel to dry assemble the core structure.

Making the shell

Study the drawings and instruction leaflet to familiarise yourself with the construction and assembly procedures before picking up your tools. It is imperative that the fundamental principles of building the shell around a removable core are fully understood and that both temporary and permanent joints are identified. The bulkheads No.s 1 through 7 should NOT be glued to the false keel at this stage or it will not be possible to remove the core after planking. The lower parts of the bulkheads are now provided as separate items. The problem then arose as to how to assemble the removable parts to the keel and securely hold them in a stable manner while the planking was carried out.

Having shaped the edges of bulkheads No.1 and 8 and the edges of two pieces No.13, I held the false keel in the vice and dry assembled all the bulkheads and part No.9, ensuring everything was a nice snug fit. Part No.9 was then fixed to each of the bulkheads No.1 thru'7, (**Fig.12.1**). Pins or screws can be used for this temporary fixing although I chose to use the latter for later ease of taking everything apart once the planking had been finished. This fixing should be done while the bottom slots in the bulkheads are still located in the false keel. To secure the bulkhead/ centre platform sub-assembly to the false keel, I drilled three pairs of 3mm diameter holes in part No.9 and one hole beneath each pair through the false keel inside the line of the planking, (**Fig.12.2**). I then threaded lengths of soft wire through each trio of holes and tightened up with a twist on the upper surface of No.9, (**Fig.12.3**). A length of strong thread with a

tourniquet would serve equally as well. Bulkhead No.8 was then permanently glued in place at the stern, and pieces No.13 were glued to the sides of the prow, gluing only on that surface below the line of the partial separation, (**Fig.12.4**). The assembly was then stable and sufficiently rigid to start the planking, but also very easy to dissemble at the conclusion of the planking process, without the risk of damage to the inside of the shell.

The first planking was probably the most difficult of all the construction procedures involved, the main problem being that while the planks had to be glued to each other, edge to edge throughout their entire length, they could only be permanently fixed to the frame core at the stem and stern. The edges of each bulkhead were waxed to prevent any adhesion with excess glue. Each plank was pinned to each frame and to the filler piece No.13 at the stem. White PVA was used for the edge-to-edge work and thick cyanoacrylate for sticking each plank to the stem. It was important to remember that the inside of the planking would be a visible finished surface, so it was worth taking time to ensure that the planks were well mated. This was largely accomplished by accurate tapering particularly at the front end, pre-soaking where required, and the judicious use of small "crocodile" clips. Excess glue was wiped off with a damp cloth, both inside and outside as the planking proceeded.

Having allowed at least 24 hours for the adhesive to thoroughly cure, the outside surfaces of the planking were then sanded to a smooth finish, (**Fig.12.5**). Any

Fig. 12.3 The retaining wire twisted up on the upper surface of the platform.

Fig. 12.4 The core structure ready for planking.

Fig. 12.5 The first planking in place and sanded.

Fig. 12.6 The second planking and floor supports installed.

slight gaps were best left until after the second planking, when they could be filled from the inside of the shell.

The second planking was not difficult. However, a decision had to be made as to the best adhesive to use. This was not so much a technical question as to one that suits the modeller best. Without special planking clamps, PVA is not very practical; cyanoacrylate is acceptable but a bit on the expensive side, so I plumped for a thixotropic contact adhesive. A bit of procedural discipline was necessary so that the task did not become too messy and, of course the planks have to be fairly accurately tapered and bent before application. Nonetheless, this part of the construction worked out very well.

The side faces of the stem and keel were then faced with 0,6mm veneer making sure that the grain ran in the direction shown on the drawing. This results in quite a few pieces 50mm wide but makes it easier to accommodate the curves, particularly around the stem area. I used cyanoacrylate to avoid the problems of clamping that would have been necessary had I used PVA, the instant adhesion also overcoming the potential difficulties of warping of such thin material.

Having trimmed the edges of the veneer, it was now time to remove the inner shell framework. The three loops of soft wire were cut through and the framework gently eased out of the shell. The two bow support pieces No.13 were then carefully broken away to the level of the former pre-cutting. This operation needed to be done with a degree of delicacy so that the joint between the planking and the stem was not disturbed.

The inside surfaces of the shell were then cleaned

up, the inner stem and sternpost sides and edges veneered and the rear bulkhead (transom) faced inside and out.

Fitting the floor supports concluded the making of the basic shell ready for trimming and ribbing and fitting the floor, (Fig.12.6).

Completing the shell

The floor pieces were fitted and faced as required. The 2x10mm strips specified for edging the gunwales were listed as walnut. However, in my box the strips were in lime or similar white wood. This made the bending somewhat easier but it did mean that if the colour of the timber was to have the same contrast with the second planking that was shown on the box art, then the strips would need to be stained. The inner and outer pieces were dry fitted to ensure a snug fit fore and aft and then held in place while the PVA glue set thoroughly. The top capping strips, also 2x8mm, were shown on the drawings to be segmented in seven pieces, six of them being short and arranged near the bows. This did not turn out to be very practical and I found it was necessary to spread the segmentation further down the length of the boat, mainly because 2x8mm stock will not bend across its edge, a requirement if the pattern on the drawing was to be followed. The length of each piece will be largely dependent on how well the planking conforms to the curves subtended by the top corners of the bulkheads. The inner edges were then trimmed to match the concave face of the inner pieces and the convex outer edges cut to match the outer gunwale strips. Care was needed to accurately measure and joint

Fig. 12.7 The gunwale edging and floor framework in place.

Fig. 12.8 The gunwales proper needed some coercion to attain the bends at the front end as did the ribs.

Fig. 12.9 The floor frame needed slotting to permit the gratings to seat properly.

Fig. 12.10 Eyelet blocks and davit fulcrum block in position. Note that the foremost eyelet block visible in the photograph subsequently had to be moved aft to its correct place.

up the several top pieces, there is only just enough material to do the job. The model at this stage is shown in **Fig.12.7**.

Similar circumstances existed with the gunwale edging; there was no spare to allow for any errors or breakages. The 8 x 4mm strip was not easy to bend and needed both heat and moisture to attain the correct curve around the bows. I bent the first three sections coming back from the stem-post in one piece, cutting

them into separate parts afterwards. The remaining sections were cut straight from the strip and glued into place using a 6mm wide spacer at each rowing position ensuring that the port and starboard placing was identical. There were two key points get these positions correct: the rear edge of the bow decking and the centreline of the holes down through the hull amidships. Getting those marked in first helped get all the others in the right place. Once the gunwales were complete,

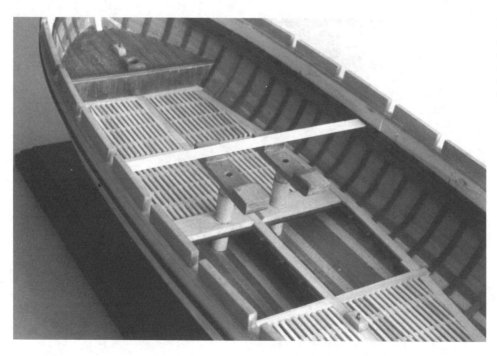

Fig. 12.11 The two hawser tubes and thwart supports dry fitted. To establish their correct height use scar strip seated on top of the side stringers.

Fig. 12.12 The thwarts cut and shaped ready for assembly. Note that the sixth item down from the top should also have been fitted with belaying pins.

the capping strip across the top edge of the transom was glued in position and the ribs fitted, **(Fig.12.8)**. The latter needed the services of a heated bending tool to prevent breaking or splitting the timber provided.

The whole model was then cleaned up prior to finishing all surfaces so far produced before carrying on with the fitting out process. I chose to use shellac based sanding sealer, which provided an acceptable colour for the upper works and innards, as well as a sound base for the painted undersides. I marked the waterline position, masked off the upper parts of the shell and sprayed the undersides with matt white paint. One or two areas needed a little filler after the first coat before applying a further two coats.

Fitting out the inside

The floor panels and gratings were made up next and these were straightforward enough although careful measurement was needed to ensure that minimum wastage of the 2mm square strip was attained - there was only just enough. In theory, there should be strip to spare, but there were some 140 individual pieces to cut and so, it was desirable not to leave more than 1mm at each end for trimming.

Fig. 12.13 The thwarts in position.

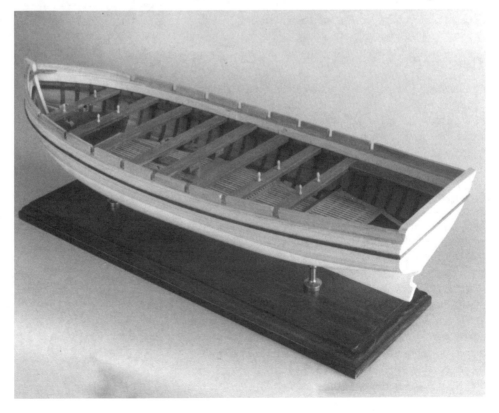

Fig. 12.14 The knees were a pain to make as per kit instructions. Sharp tools and not too much pressure were essential to success.

Neither the drawings nor the instructions were really clear when it came to fitting the removable panels flush into the floor framework. Making the panels was straightforward enough, but it was necessary to make cut-outs in the inner edges of the floor framework to take the ends of the combed strips and thus allow the panels to seat flush down. These cut-outs can be seen in **Fig.12.9.**

The eyelet blocks and davit fulcrum block were made and glued in place noting that the position of the forward of the two eyelet blocks that sat centrally on the lower floor, as shown in its correct position on sheet 2 of the drawings. These features are shown in **Fig. 12.10.**

The stand

At this stage I decided that it was a convenient time to mount the model.

Unfortunately, the kit does not include parts for a stand, so rather than see it propped against a bowl of fruit on the sideboard, I invested in a pair of pedestals and mounted my model on a plain baseboard.

Continuing the fitting out

The two hawser tubes were fitted next ensuring that when topped off by the two 60mm long thwart supports, the top surfaces of those supports were level with the tops of the side stringers on the inside of the shell, **(Fig.12.11).** This was achieved by adjusting the length of the bottom portions of the tubes that seat on the inside bottom of the shell. To get this sub-assembly in its correct position relative to the thwarts, the 4mm diameter holes in the longitudinal parts of the thwart supports should be drilled 27,5mm from the fore end and NOT in the middle.

The thwarts were cut to basic length then angled in two planes to fit snugly against the inside of the shell. The brass mast butt strap, the housings for the mast supports on the two relevant thwarts and the holes for the various belaying pins, were added before fixing the thwarts in place, **(Fig.12.12).** It went without saying that

Fig. 12.14 The rudder in position.

Fig. 12.16 The davit and guide rail assembly.

they all had to be square across the centreline of the boat and thus parallel to each other. Having securely fixed the first one accurately, the others were positioned by measurement *not* by eye; there were too many curves around to confuse the eye! See **Fig.12.13**.

The secret of successfully making the thwart knees undoubtedly lies in the use of sharp tools. I used a razor saw to cut the basic triangular shapes and a 12mm diameter Perma-Grit, round file to introduce the concave edges. The "vertical" edges needed to be angled in two planes to match internal lines of the boat. The direction of the grain was kept horizontal throughout. Because of the somewhat low strength of the triangular pieces, I found that it was best to cut and file in the front curve after the knee had been glued in place. The whole lower and back edge was that way better supported to take the thrust of the scalpel and file. The knees can be seen in place in **Fig.12.14**.

The rudder

The pre-cut rudder blade requires only to be cleaned up and the aperture cut for the upper pintle and strap, the lower pintle being housed in the stem post. The bit that needs some care is the positioning of the eyes, or gudgeons, such that when the rudder is rigged, its bottom edge is coincident with the bottom of the keel. I worked on the basis that the upper eye was to be fixed into the trim across the upper transom and calculated everything else from that point.

The davit and guide unit

The davit sides and the guide rails were made and drilled in pairs to ensure accurate alignment of spacers and brass pins. However, having done a dry run before drilling, I considered it wise to leave the drilling of the holes for the locking pin in davit and rails until after initial installation. The fulcrum block, previously fixed to the

floor of the boat, was used to determine the length of the davit spacing dowels. The pin and pulley were then assembled and the unit pinned to the fulcrum block, checking freedom of movement back and forth.

The guide rail spacing block, that was to be fixed to the inside of the transom was made using the overall width of the davit to gauge its length. This piece was then pinned between the ends of the two rails and offered up to the davit assembly. Once the position of the block on the transom had been established, the position of the locking pinholes through the rails and davit could be marked and drilled. The whole unit was then pinned and glued in place and the retaining blocks on the top edge of the transom added. **Figs.12.15** and **12.16** show the completed davit assembly and the rudder in position.

The mast and spar

Both of these items were simple enough to make. The mast tapering was done by the conventional method of filing the section to an octagonal shape, then spinning to attain the circular tapered section. In the mast, holes were drilled and filed out to house the brass pulleys and really, there wasn't much more to do. The gaff was handled in the same way; followed by the fitting of the gaff jaws, see **Fig.12.17**.

The ancillary equipment

The three tubs were probably the most fiddly to make. A good core structure was essential, making sure that the upper and lower discs were properly centralised. The first stave was super glued in place to provide a firm start and, as suggested on the drawings, a tapered stave was introduced every so often round the tub. I worked on all three tubs at the same time, fitting about a dozen staves to each in turn. This gave the PVA adhesive time

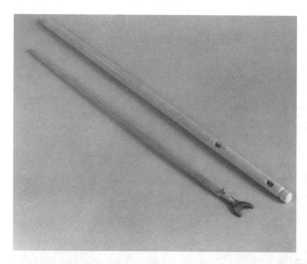

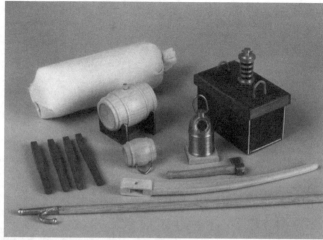

Figs. 12.17, 18 and 19 The mast and gaff, three tubs and ancilliary equipment.

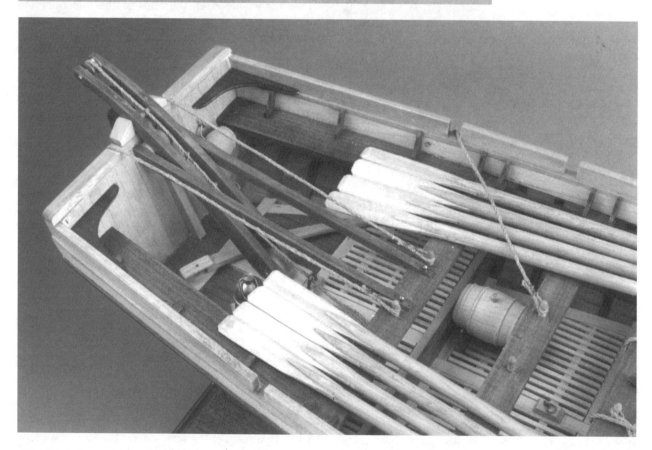

Fig. 12.21   Equipment stowage at the stern end.

Fig. 12.20 Oar construction.

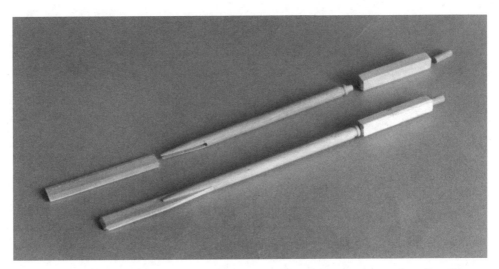

to make its initial grab and avoided the risk of pushing the earlier fitted staves out of place. When all staves had been fitted to the three tubs, I gave them a thorough soaking with diluted PVA and left them overnight to dry before rubbing down and fitting the bindings, (**Fig.12.18**).

The barrels, compass, lantern and tool chest presented no difficulties, the drawings adequately describing the construction process. I would make one comment about the axe however, do remember to shape the handle, rather than leaving it as a straight piece of dowel!

I felt that the making of the sail bag was improved when, having the basic cylindrical shape made and the bottom end closed, the bag was stuffed fairly hard with cotton wool and a drawstring stitched around the neck. This allowed the tying to be done easily and tidily and a more satisfying shape to the bag achieved. However, one question comes to mind. If the sail is to be deployed, or shown furled to the un-stepped mast, should not the bag be left empty? Probably, yes, but I decided to carry a spare sail for the sake of completing the kit! All these items are to be seen in **Fig.12.19**.

There were sixteen oars to make and it was found easier to shape the section of the blades before cutting the individual pieces to length. Similarly, the corners of the square sectioned material for the inboard end were planed off in the length before separation. The shanks of the oars were slotted by first drilling a 2mm diameter hole across the dowel 25mm from one end, then by sawing and filing until I had a 2mm wide slot. A 4mm diameter spigot and groove were turned on the other end using a 12-volt lathe. A miniature 12-volt disc sander was used to taper the slotted end before inserting the blade portion. The blades were finish shaped after assembly to the shanks and before proceeding further. The inboard stocks were then cut to length and drilled at each end with 4mm diameter holes to take the shanks and handles. This sub-assembly was finished prior to fitting to the blade/shank assembly. A completed oar is shown in **Fig.12.20**.

Final assembly

It now became decision time - how to display the model. There were several choices to be made, each largely a personal preference rather than one of authenticity or historical accuracy. The first decision to be made concerns the mast, spar and sail. They can be lashed up and laid in the boat as depicted on the box-art or, the mast can be stepped and rigged.

The ancillary equipment was stowed in positions shown on the drawings and all lightly glued in place. If things can move, they will inevitably get moved by inquisitive fingers and eventually broken or lost. The stowage of equipment used is shown in **Figs.12.21** and **12.22**.

Oars were another problem. They tended to clutter up the boat if merely laid on top of the thwarts bearing in mind that there are sixteen of them. However, since I had chosen to make a stand and pedestal mounting for the model, I felt that this was a place where the oars could be displayed to advantage. This can be seen in **Fig.12.23**.

Two tubs were layered with a coil of rope, ensuring that there was enough free end to go round the windlass and around the rear of the boat to be belayed as indicated. The third tub was similarly coiled up for the grapnel and positioned at the fore end as seen in the colour section.

Conclusions

There is no doubt about it, like the other open boat kits from the Panart stable that I have reviewed over the years, the kit for the "Victory" launch can be made up into an extremely nice model. Having said that, those modellers not too well versed in the ways of wood may have to visit the store for some additional timber if things don't go according to plan. There is only just enough in the kit to do the job right first time. The strip wood for the gratings and the timber for the thwart knees are particular cases in point. The drawings are good in as much as they pictorially show what has to be done and, where necessary, the sequence of working. This is just as well since the English instructions were poor and don't do justice to an otherwise quite good kit.

For the experienced model maker, this kit can result in an exhibition standard model and one that could be entered into major competition with some degree of confidence.

CHAPTER 13

A Summary of Practical Notes

This final chapter brings together the techniques used in the making of model period ships. Many of them have appeared in the same, or similar, form earlier in this book where they have been recommended in the construction of specific models. I have chosen to summarise them, together with other useful procedures, in this section for use in a more general sense by kit builders and scratch builders alike.

Again, I would stress that these are methods that I use and find successful. They are not purported to be the best, or the only, way of doing things. Indeed some situations call for a variation on the main theme, which is why you may find subtle differences between what is written in this chapter and what has been read in earlier sections of this book. I have no doubt that many readers will have their own preferred methods, which will be different to mine. Nonetheless, for newcomers to the hobby, I put my preferences forward for consideration in the knowledge that they work and should make reasonable starting points for the less experienced model-maker to build on.

Deck planking

There are several methods by which decking can be laid or simulated and, the system to adopt is really dependant on the physical size of the model, your own patience and to how much trouble you wish to go to in order to achieve the desired result.

In the simplest form, the deck may be lined out by drawing the plank widths and butts onto the base material, which should have been well sealed and lightly rubbed down. There are not many, if any kits today, that call for this procedure, but if it is the method you are faced with, then the Edding pen is probably the best option. Available in a variety of widths, it draws a line of constant thickness and is ideal for the job. However, the secret of success is in the sealing of the base surface, at least two coats of sealer being the order of the day because, should the ink penetrate through to the wood, it will spread into the grain and blotch.

Another method, found mainly in very basic and simple kits, is to score the lines with a scriber and then run a soft pencil into the grooves so produced. A word of warning about the use of the scriber; if the grain of the material runs away from the edge of the straight-edge, it will almost certainly take the point of the scriber with it with most horrendous results. Thus, always watch the direction the scriber is drawn.

The most usual deck laying procedure is the application of full-length wooden strips to a ply false deck, **(Fig.13.1)**. This is neither technically accurate, nor aesthetically pleasing and there are several ways in which the appearance of such a deck can be enhanced by simulating the caulking. The choice is largely dependent on the scale of the model and your individual preference.

One method is to lay thread between the edges of the planks as each plank is stuck in place. This may be

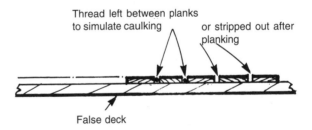

Thread left between planks to simulate caulking
or stripped out after planking
False deck

Fig. 13.1

left in place for a pronounced and definite line or stripped out after the glue has dried to leave a softer line caused by the shadow across the gap. If the former method is adopted, the diameter of the thread must be less than the thickness of the planking so that later sanding does not produce a furring up effect.

The simplest form of caulking is to use a black marker pen on one or both edges of the planking strip before gluing in place. Try this on a short length first to establish which provides the required density of line, one or two blackened edges, and to ensure also that the ink does not run into the grain of the timber. Unfortunately, the production of strip wood less than 1mm thickness may

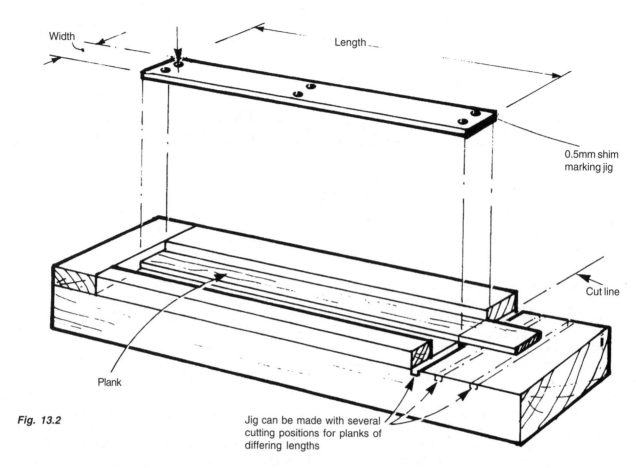

Width

Length

0.5mm shim
marking jig

Cut line

Plank

Fig. 13.2

Jig can be made with several
cutting positions for planks of
differing lengths

involve a guillotined edge which can be somewhat uneven and which may need some attention.

At the end of the day, merely cutting the strips to scale length and laying them in the appropriate pattern may provide the acceptable result you are looking for without recourse to simulating the caulking.

As to the laying of the planks, choosing the right adhesive is important. The quality and thickness of the timber play a part in the selection. PVA tends to warp thin sections before it finally cures thus making the later rubbing down operation difficult. Contact adhesive works well but, at smaller scales, is a bit messy. Probably the best is cyanoacrylate, or super-glue. You need to be precise in the initial locating of the plank because of the instant grab effect and care needs to be exercised to avoid sticking your fingers to the deck. Having said that, it does a good job and makes for easier finishing.

If the deck is going to be enhanced by cutting planks to scale length, then it is essential that all the lengths are identical. A small cutting jig is one way of ensuring this and something very simple as shown in **Fig.13.2** is ideal. For greater detail, a template made up from brass shim will help to mark or drill plank-fixing holes. Actually cutting the planks can be more accurately done with a fine razor saw rather than a craft knife. However, if you can cut square with the knife, the push effect tends to turn over the end edge of the plank, which helps delineate the butts on deck without artificial marking.

Deck planking in most kits is fairly straightforward in that any margin planks are ignored and the planks go right out to the inside of the bulwarks. If margin planks are to

be included as part of an enhancement process, they should be laid first, **(Fig.13.3)**. A master plank laid centrally down the centreline of the deck is the basis for alignment of all others so attention should be paid to get it seated straight and true. The deck is then laid from the centre out to the edges and, if using individual planks, remembering to stagger them so that the butts line up every third or fourth row. This will depend upon whether the drawings depict a three butt or four butt shift system.

To include a margin plank, there are certain rules to follow. The ends of the planks should never come to a sharp point, sharpness being when the length of a tapered end is more than twice the width of the plank. In those cases the end of the plank has to be joggled into the margin plank by making the butt end never less than half the plank width, again see **Fig.13.3**.

Once the deck has been laid, it only remains to sand the whole area smooth. Bearing in mind the handling the model is still to have, it is a good idea to give it a couple of coats of varnish or sealer to protect it from the inevitable finger marks.

Hull planking

The planking of a model ship is a feature that discourages many would-be modellers from embarking upon this fascinating branch of model making. Yes, it can be long-winded and sometimes tedious, but the satisfaction of a job well done is very much worth the effort. Patience is an essential quality with which most modellers are

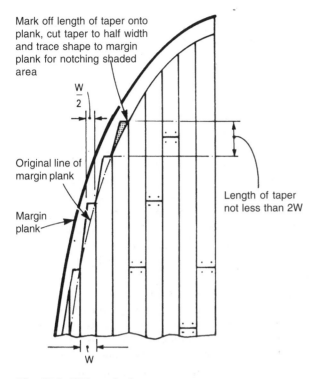

Mark off length of taper onto plank, cut taper to half width and trace shape to margin plank for notching shaded area

$\frac{W}{2}$

Original line of margin plank

Margin plank

Length of taper not less than 2W

W

Fig. 13.3. Fitting planks

necessarily endowed and planking a model ship should not unduly stress that capacity. An excellent result does not always stand out in the overall picture, but even the uninitiated will recognise a lousy planking job.

These notes are concerned with the type of construction used in most kits where frames or bulkheads are mounted onto a false keel and filler blocks or termination pieces are glued in place at stem and stern.

The first essential is to prepare the edges of the frames so that they follow the lines of the hull and permit the planks to lay across the full edge thickness of the frame, (**Fig. 13.4a** and **Fig. 13.4b**). PermaGrit abrasive tools are ideal for this operation, but a strip of say, 3mm ply, faced with coarse abrasive paper is a more than adequate substitute for the convex surfaces; a piece of 16 to 20mm dowel similarly faced is suitable for working on the concave areas around the stern. To minimise breakout, always aim the abrasive strip at the frame edges from which the most material has to be removed. Use one of the planking strips to constantly monitor progress until such time as it makes contact across the entire thickness of all the frames concerned, (**Fig. 13.4c**).

With regard to the planks themselves, few retain full width over their entire length. One or both ends will require to be tapered and, in some instances, one edge will require bevelling in order to attain a snug fit alongside its neighbour. If such bevelling is required, always bevel the opposite edge to which the taper is applied. All this is painstaking work and it is worth making as assessment of the planking operation before you start

to ascertain the overall situation. Most kits today specify double planking that is a base layer of say, lime strips, covered by a finishing and thinner layer of perhaps, walnut or mahogany. Some earlier, or more basic, kits may only involve single planking requiring a more precise approach where the accuracy of mating edges will be apparent on the finished model. Remember that the single planked hull is not the easy option, especially if the model is to remain in the natural wood condition. In addition to the tapering required for every planking job, edge bevelling of the thicker planks involved will definitely be necessary. If the hull is to be painted, however, you are somewhat 'let off the hook' since any imperfections can be filled before final rubbing down.

The double planked job is a far more amenable task. The first planking fundamentally provides a sound base

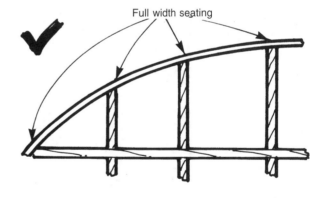

Inadequate seating

Plank

Frame

Keel

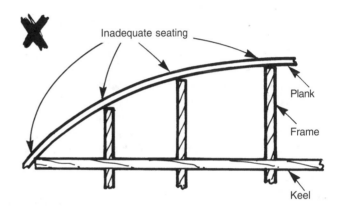

Full width seating

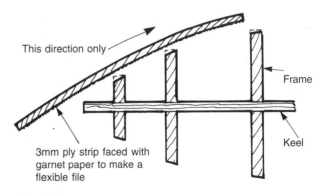

This direction only

Frame

Keel

3mm ply strip faced with garnet paper to make a flexible file

Fig. 13.4

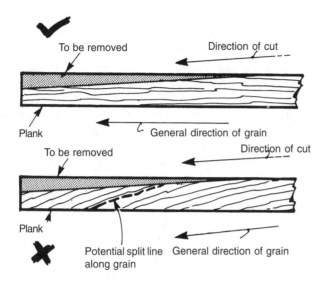

Fig. 13.5

for the second and, as such, can tolerate some degree of imperfection that can be corrected by the use of filler. I am not suggesting that you approach the task in a slapdash fashion but merely to be aware of what it is that is being done. The second planking needs to be more precise, but it is usually done in thinner material and edge bevelling will not be required. A good tapering

job will obviously provide a better cosmetic effect, especially for those models to be left in the natural wood. For the model that is to be painted, filler can be more widely used since it will not be seen in the final analysis. I would stress again that I am not advocating that filler is used as an excuse for poor woodwork, but it does form an acceptable medium and has its place.

The tapering of planks is probably best effected with a razor plane or a David plane. A craft knife may be adequate in some cases but control of the cut is less precise particularly if the grain of the material is not very friendly. A drill will be required to introduce holes at the pinning positions. Use a drill size just smaller then the pin itself in order that pins can be pushed into place with the fingers before knocking in with a light hammer. Pins should be left proud for easier removal, the use of the correct hole size allowing the timber to grip on to the shank of the pin.

Examine each plank carefully and put to one side any that have knots or a complex grain pattern. These can be useful for stealers or other parts later in the construction, but will either be very difficult to shape prior to fixing or will break when bending. Also watch which way the grain runs and, where possible, taper so that the plane does not "lift" the grain, **(Fig.13.5)**. In the case of walnut particularly and, to a lesser extent, mahogany, planing the "wrong way" can split a plank of

Fig. 13.6

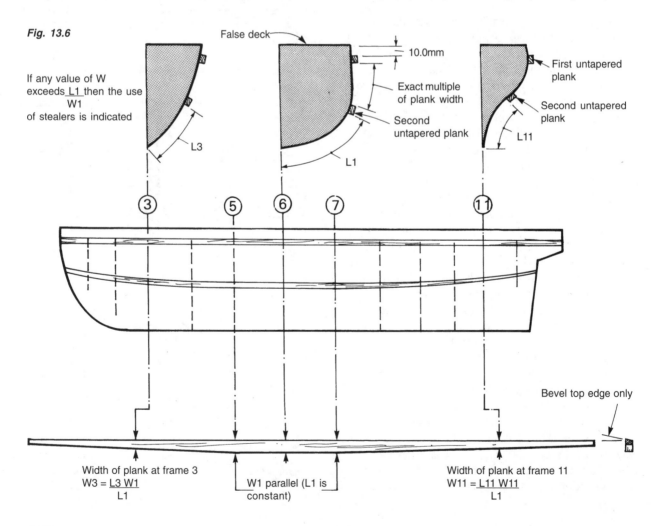

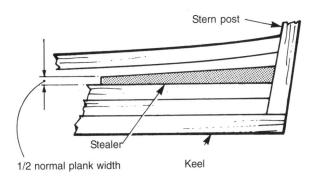

Stern post

Stealer

1/2 normal plank width   Keel

Fig. 13.7

the small sections normally used.

Most kits provide instructions as to where the first planks are to be laid on to the hull and how to progress to gradually complete the planking operation. If however, your kit does not include such advice then a good starting point is around deck level. An un-tapered strip applied with its top edge between 5mm and 10mm below the line of the deck will leave a convenient area for the later fixing of the bulwarks. A second plank, also without taper, is then placed with its top edge where the waterline intersects the stem and stern posts and allowed to take up its natural line along the hull. A dry run is advisable so that slight positional adjustment amidships can be made to make the distance up to the underside of the first plank a multiple of the plank width, see **Fig.13.6** to avoid any excessive gaps as planking proceeds. If at the stem, the distance from the underside of the upper plank is less than the distance amidships, then drop the lower plank a further width. When fixed, these two planks will form reasonable key locations for the rest of the planks.

Almost certainly, tapering will be required to some degree at the bows and probably the stern as well. The amount of tapering may be decided in one of two ways, the theoretical or the practical hands-on method.

The theoretical method relies on fairly accurate measurement and can be followed by reference to **Fig.13.6**. It will be apparent that the distance along the edge of the frames is different at each frame. In order to determine the width of planks at each frame (and hence the taper) it is necessary to measure and record the distance "L" at each frame. It is anticipated that "L" will be almost identical on two or three amidships frames and decrease frame by frame towards the bows. This may also be the case in the frames towards the stern, but in many cases "L" may increase, thus indicating the later use of stealers, see **Fig.13.7**. In theory, you might therefore expect that tapering the planks would be unnecessary. In fact, tapering is done for the convenience of fitting and fixing, and has to be done according to the contours involved.

At the stern end particularly, there will almost certainly be small triangular shaped areas that will need

to be filled with small pieces of planking strip. These pieces are called stealers and are shown in **Fig.13.7**. If your model is to be finished in natural wood where the planking lines can be seen, it is important that the stealers do not come down to a sharp point but have a definite width at the narrow end. If the model is to be painted or plated, or you are looking at first planking, then obviously a sharp point would be acceptable.

To get back to the tapering; take dimension "L" at the centre frames and divide this distance by the basic plank width. This will tell you how many planks it will take to cover that section. Now divide that figure into all the other values of "L" and the result will be the plank width at those particular frames where the value of "L" was measured. Transferring this information to the planks will define the degree of tapering required.

The practical method of tapering, and perhaps the one most model makers tend to use, involves placing a new plank tight up against the underside of the previously laid one and noting where the edges start to interfere as the new plank is gently bent into position. The interference point is where the taper should start. The top edge of the plank is then planed until the necessary degree of taper is achieved and the plank lays flat against the edges of the bulkheads or frames.

Bending planks need not be the difficult task that you might at first think and in most cases planks can be bent dry with a Plank Nipper without recourse to soaking or steaming. The Plank Nipper does have one limitation however, it leaves marks on the inside surface of the bend but is ideally suited for most hull plank bending. It should not take the average modeller too long to become proficient in the use of this tool. It is largely a case of adjusting the hand pressure according to the thickness of the wood involved and remembering that the closer the "nips," the tighter the bend produced.

Woods that have a greater reluctance to bend may be soaked for a while before use and a tall vase or similar shaped vessel filled with water kept on the bench will prove useful to hold several planks for pre-soaking the ends to be bent. There are electric benders on the market which are invaluable for the very tight bends occasionally necessary but the vast majority of kit-built models can be constructed quite readily using a Plank Nipper.

Fixing the first plank layer is normally achieved by pinning and gluing. Guide holes for the pins should be drilled through the planks to avoid splitting the wood and white PVA used as the adhesive. Pins should be left proud to facilitate ease of removal before rubbing down. If the model involves only one layer of planking then keeping the drilled fixing holes in line down the edges of the bulkheads will add to the cosmetic appearance of the finished job. Keeping the holes in line may be helped if the centre of the hole is marked and indented with the sharp point of a hard pencil. Centre "popping," if done properly will start the drill point in the right position and prevent run off. Make sure that planks are well glued, both to the bulkheads and edge to edge to each other.

Fixing the second layer of planking, usually of thinner material, is frequently done using adhesive alone. Thixotropic contact adhesive is fine provided that any pre-bending necessary is done properly and that the plank sits well onto the bulkheads in the "dry" state. Cyanoacrylate is probably the best medium and used with care will do a good job. Damp planks should be handled with extra care since the moisture will accelerate the grab time and also act as a wetting agent. Remember that the object of the exercise is to stick the planks to the model not to the fingers!

It now only remains to finish off and the first stage is removal of all the fixing pins. You will understand why if you have ever torn the pads of your fingers while sanding across the head of a partially removed pin! There are a few things worth remembering when starting this process which, if ignored, can spoil your model. The choice of grade of abrasive paper is less important when rubbing down first planking and a coarse grade can help remove a lot of material at a fairly fast rate. In fact, a less than perfect finish can provide a useful key for applying the second planking adhesive. However, a coarse grade can put deep marks into the surface which may be difficult to remove with the use of progressively finer grades during finishing, so care must be taken when rubbing down the second planking or any finished surface like decking. The same consideration should be given to the planking of single planked hulls.

Any gaps should be filled with filler before final rubbing down. There are a number of different suitable products on the market and a selection should be made according to whether the finished model is to be left in its natural wood state, or be painted, the colour of the filler being pertinent if the former condition applies.

Sanding sealers can be useful for finishing or preparing the surface for painting. There are two main types available, cellulose based and shellac based, the latter being particularly well suited to the natural finished look. When finally rubbed down it provides a hard, matt protected surface.

In all the finishing processes described above, the wearing of a protective facemask is recommended. The dust and fumes can cause havoc with your breathing. Prolonged use of cyanoacrylate is especially hazardous in that its effects are not always immediately apparent.

Any pinholes remaining from plank fixing will appear highlighted with filler and, if they were kept in line as suggested earlier, will now provide a nice authentic look of fixings to the hull.

Hull plating

Many naval vessels had copper-plated bottoms and some kits provide individual scale plates with which to cover the bottom surfaces of the model. When done well, the effect of plating certainly enhances the appearance of the model. I would refer the reader back to **Chapter 4**

and **Chapter 9** where the modelling process is described in detail. I refer to both chapters because the lines of the hull can vary the approach to adopt, particularly in the selection of gore line positions. One piece of advice I will repeat here however, is that with extended use of cyanoacrylate as the adhesive, a suitable respirator should be considered.

Masts and spars

Even in the top quality kits, masts and spars are rarely provided already turned and tapered and, in the vast majority of cases, all that is given is straight dowel rod of suitable diameter. However, it should be noted that some masts are not of round section throughout, but have square or octagonal sections at the head or butt ends where trestle-trees, tops, or crows nests are later assembled. Thus, dowel is not always as convenient a material as would at first appear.

Starting with a dowel rod or length of square sectioned timber, it is essential to ensure that the grain is long and straight with no knots or other obvious blemishes. If you have turning facilities, cut the length of dowel about 25mm longer than finished requirements. This short length is useful for holding and may be removed later. If you are going to taper the masts by hand, a shorter addition of 3mm at the smaller end will be adequate in order to accommodate the inevitable increase in taper where the file runs over the end.

Having chosen your material you are now faced with the tapering operation. Whether working from scratch or building from a kit, the plans should enable you to define the length, position and diameters of the tapered section. Such data should be marked on to the material. The first step is to carefully file four flats each opposed at 90° roughly tangential to the finished diameter and over the length of the taper required, **(Fig.13.8)**. Note that this sketch shows the circumstance where the taper is within the overall length of the mast, leaving material at either end for a different section. A straight taper throughout is much easier to handle, of course. Secondly, file four further flats in the same manner to produce an octagonal section. Obviously, one can continue by filing the eight corners off to produce a shape nearer to the circular section required, but except where larger diameters are involved, an octagonal section will reduce quite readily by sanding during the next stage of working.

The first piece of equipment that comes to mind for reducing the mast to circular section is the lathe. However, I have not found that to necessarily be the ideal tool for the task in hand and frequently use an electric drill held in a horizontal stand. The spare 25mm is held in the drill chuck and, using diminishing grades of abrasive paper, the mast is finished by hand. A few words of caution. It is inadvisable to use the continuous run button on the drill and safer to use the trigger only. Hold the abrasive paper between thumb and forefinger to provide both pressure and steadying action, see **Fig.13.9**. Make sure that the paper is folded correctly

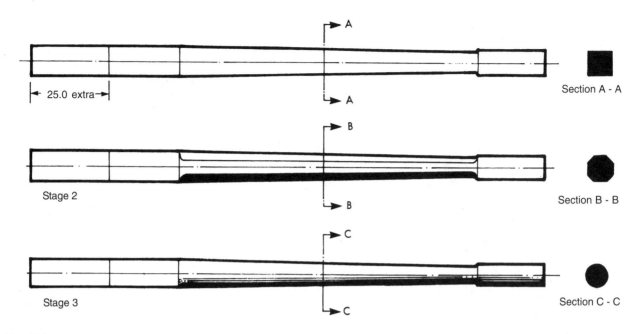

Fig. 13.8

relative to the direction of rotation in order to avoid "snatch" and don't squeeze too hard – it can get somewhat hot. Try to anticipate when, for any reason, you need to stop the drill and release the trigger before removing the working hand. This helps to retain good axial alignment between the mast and drill centre lines.

Extra care will be needed if the small end of the taper runs into the underside of a larger square section, both from the point of view of producing the shape required and preventing pulling the mast out of the chuck. Small outside callipers will be handy to check the diameters at various places along the taper of such a mast, whereas if the taper runs out to the end, a draughtsman's circle template makes an ideal ring gauge. They can be bought at most stationers and have the advantage of being useful in the marking out process as well – so quite a good investment.

The procedure so far described is for masts, bowsprits, booms, etc., where the taper runs in one direction only. Yards and spars, having to be tapered towards each end can be done in a similar manner but with one or two essential differences. First, you need about 10mm to 12mm spare lengths at each end **(Fig.13.10)**, and secondly, considerably more care is required due to the smaller diameters involved. In view of this, it is often a good move to either file or use a scalpel to gently scrape longitudinally to attain the section required, using the electric drill only for knocking off the last corners. Final sanding should be done longitudinally by hand.

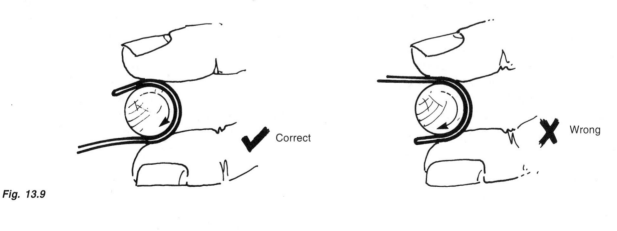

Fig. 13.9

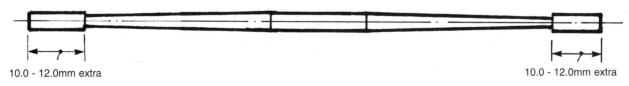

10.0 - 12.0mm extra   10.0 - 12.0mm extra

Fig. 13.10

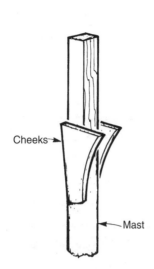

Fig. 13.11

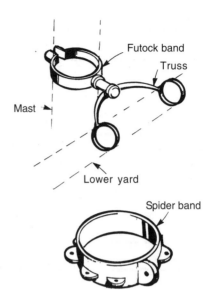

Fig. 13.12

Some of the lower yards may have an octagonal centre section. These features can be simulated by filing eight flats on to the dowel before tapering, remembering that the dowel diameter must reflect the size of the octagon measured across the corners, rather than across the flats. Alternatively, having filed on the flats the section may be built up by the addition of battens. A flat should also be filed centrally on the reverse face of the yard in order to accommodate a saddle, if fitted, **(Fig.13.13)**.

Having got your masts and spars tapered and turned, there are several things to be done before the various pieces can be assembled together. On masts, flats should be filed on those areas where the hounds, bibs, or supporting cheeks for trestletrees fit, **(Fig.13.11)**. There may also be several holes that are more easily drilled at this stage rather than after assembly. Holes for fitting eyebolts and sheave holes for passing some of the upper rigging come immediately to mind, but careful and continual study of the plans is worthwhile to ensure that all such features are taken care of. Such study will also reveal where things could be put on too soon which will prevent later assembly. Sequence of assembly is most important and, for instance things like trusses and spider

bands **(Fig.13.12)**, should be fitted to the lower masts before assembling cheeks, trestletrees and crosstrees. Woldings are also best wound on at this time.

Battens and saddles may be permanently fitted and left to thoroughly set before adding any stirrups or jack-stays **(Figs. 13.13 to 13.15)**. Note that the eyebolts for the jack-stays may not be coincident with the foot-rope stirrups but are shown as such in the sketches purely for convenience. Whilst there is some time to go before you commence rigging, again it is worth consulting the plans and look ahead to see what will be needed in the way of blocks for clews and buntlines etc. You should also consider fitting the brace pendants at this stage.

Now that as much work as possible has been done on the individual masts and spars, all pieces can be assembled together. It should be pointed out that depending on the scale of the model, it might be more expedient to assemble the lower masts to the hull and rig the shrouds before assembling the upper masts. The larger the scale, the more likely is this to be the case, but the convenience gained is entirely dependent on the actual model being built and your own preference of working procedures. There are no hard and fast rules.

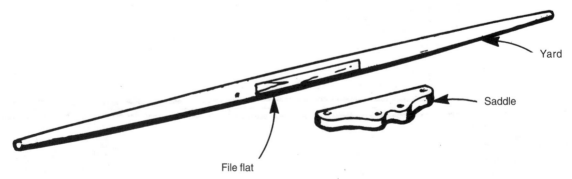

Fig. 13.13. Fitting Saddles

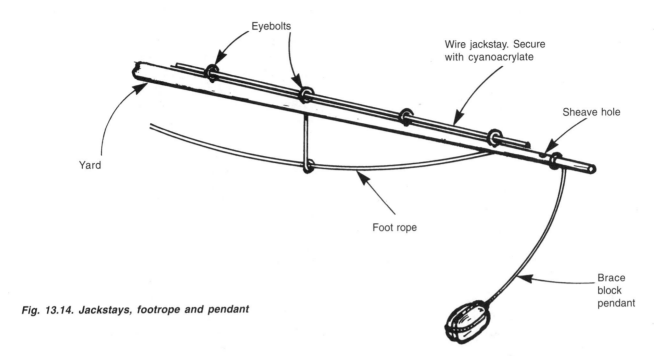

Fig. 13.14. Jackstays, footrope and pendant

Building the tops calls for considerable accuracy. The physical size of the parts involved could well be fairly small but, even so, an attempt should be made to properly joint the crosstrees to the trestletrees to give the best job and added strength. With the advent of routed or laser cut parts in period ship kits, these sort of features are, in most cases, already prepared for the modeller. However, if you do have to make your own joints, ensure that you slot these items in pairs to maintain correct spacing and squareness, **(Fig.13.16)**.

Tops may be planked as in **Fig.13.16**, or could be battened or grated. In all instances tops are best made up as a sub-assembly and fitted separately to the masts, but again, each case should be judged on its merits. Constantly monitor the plans and your progress to make sure that all the various rigging points, blocks and eyebolts are recognised and catered for before final assembly.

Rigging

Before starting to rig a model ship, it is well worth familiarising yourself with the fundamentals. Once you recognise what each part of the rigging does, it becomes clearer why particular lines are belayed where they are

and, what appears at first sight to be a total maze of rope-work becomes more comprehensible. The better books on the subject tend to be a little on the expensive side so a visit to the local library could well help. Three works are particularly recommended, *Plank On Frame Models* by Harold Underhill, *The Masting and Rigging Of English Ships Of War* by John Lees and *Rigging Period Ship Models* by Lennarth Petersson. When you have acquired the desired basics, the first things to look at are the rigging materials, cordage, blocks etc. Since the aim of this text is to be of assistance to the less experienced, I am going to assume that you have been supplied with these items in a kit or have bought them from one of the well known fittings lists. Either way, you are not going to lay your own rope or make your own blocks. Having said that, it is wrong to suppose that such provided or bought items are necessarily ready for immediate use.

Taking the cordage first, this usually comes in either natural or black, the former being for the running rigging and the latter for the standing rigging. Sizes vary from 0,1mm through to around 1,8mm diameter. The term "natural" covers a multitude of shades and can vary from

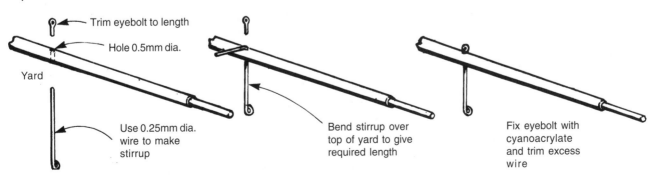

Fig. 13.15. Making footrope stirrups with wire

Fig. 13.16. Assembling tops

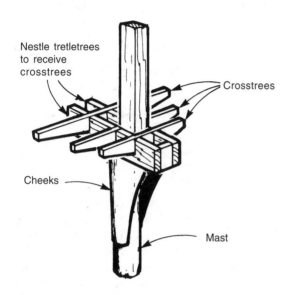

best solution is to dab all the knots with dilute PVA, which dries clear and fairly quickly allowing closely trimmed ends. PVA is also useful for laying down the surface of the thread. Pulling a cut length of thread between thumb and forefinger liberally coated with the adhesive, not only stabilises the cordage and stiffens it up, but also smoothes off all the little surface fibres which stick up and later provide 'hooks' for any dust to settle on.

As far as tools are concerned, I have found that a selection of tweezers is useful, a slim handled scalpel (with a few spare blades) and a couple of crochet hooks also come in handy. For trimming ends, nail clippers are good but the ideal tool is a pair of manicurist's cuticle clippers, both being better and safer than the scalpel, where one slip while in amongst the rigging can cause total disaster.

Looking at a completely rigged model, it may seem a difficult decision as to where to start the process. Obviously, different types of vessel present different content and complexity, particularly in the running rigging. However, there is a logical breakdown and allocation of sub-divisions of working, which help the model-maker avoid creating problems for himself, particularly those of access. The standing rigging is that part of the setup that holds the masts and bowsprit in their correct relationship with the hull and to each other. Secondly, the running rigging, which is the working part of the rigging and used for raising and lowering the yards

tan to almost white, too light to look right on a finished model. If this is found to be the case then the thread concerned should either be replaced or dyed. This should be done at the outset of the project so that plenty of time is available for adequate drying before use. The thread should be wound into hanks about 250mm long and hung to dry with weights to remove all of the give from the material and thus, its natural tendency to twist.

As far as blocks are concerned, **(Fig.13.17)**, the prime task is to clear out the holes and remove any "whiskers" left from the manufacturing process. It may seem a little long-winded, and even pointless, to re-drill holes already provided, but there are few things more frustrating than a length of thread that gets stuck halfway through a block. You can lay odds that such a block will have been rigged in the very place that denies access to the drill.

The other essential material that must not be overlooked is adhesive. Cyanoacrylate immediately comes to mind but it has to be remembered that there are serious disadvantages unless great care and discretion is used. It is possible to make the thread brittle to the point of being broken if unduly stressed and with some threads there appears to be a danger of deterioration over a length of time. It would not be a pleasant experience if, after a couple of years, your pride and joy were found with the rigging collapsed down to deck level. I'm exaggerating, of course, but be careful. The

Fig. 13.17.

Deadeyes - for rigging shrouds, backstays etc. Usually made from boxwood or walnut. Various sizes ranging from 2 - 10mm dia.

Single block

Blocks - mainly for running rigging. Various sizes, usually of boxwood or walnut

Double block

Belaying pins usually in boxwood, walnut or brass

Link type

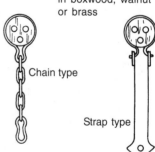

Chain type

Strap type

Chain plates - house lower deadeyes. Lower ends fixed to side of hull, upper ends locate in "channels". Usually plain or blackened brass.

Fig. 13.18

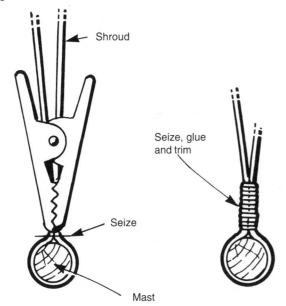

Fig. 13.20

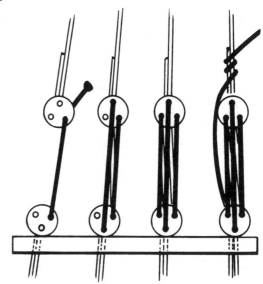

Sequence for rigging lanyards. Note relative positions for deadeyes

on the masts, adjusting their position relative to the centre line of the ship and for setting the attitude and shape of the sails. Each of these divisions should be handled separately.

The standing rigging starts with the gammoning. This lashes the lower end of the bowsprit to the stem of the ship, the rope passing over the bowsprit, down through a hole in the prow and back up the other side continuously for a number of times. The system is finally tightened up by a number of frapping turns between the underside of the bowsprit and the stem.

The shrouds are set up in pairs alternating from starboard to port, the first shroud starting at the foremost starboard deadeye, going up round the masthead and returning to the second starboard deadeye. A similar pair are set up next for the port side, followed by the shrouds for the third and fourth starboard deadeyes, and so on until all the deadeyes have been catered for. Each shroud pair should be secured at the masthead as they are first assembled. A simple method is to pinch the two sides of the thread together close to the mast with a small crocodile clip and seize them with

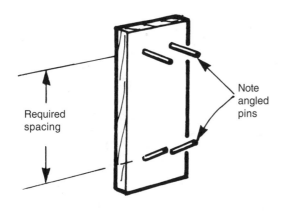

Fig. 13.19

thread between the mast and the end of the clip. The clip is then removed and the seizing completed over the doubled thread as shown in **Fig.13.18**.

The fitting of deadeyes to the lower ends of the shrouds needs a little care to ensure that when the lanyards are subsequently tightened up, the separating distances between the lower and upper deadeyes are roughly the same across the whole assembly. The lower deadeyes have, of course, by this time been assembled to the channels and chain-plates during the construction of the hull. To get the deadeye separation correct, I make a very simple jig from a small length of scrap planking and four short pins, **(Fig.13.19)**. One pair of pins locates into the lower deadeye while the other pair accepts the upper deadeye, keeping it in place while it is attached to the shroud. Holding the jig and loose upper deadeye in position with the forefinger and thumb of one hand, the end if the shroud is passed between finger and thumb, round the deadeye and back up to be gripped with a small crocodile clip and seized close to the deadeye. Check that the alignment of the deadeye holes is correct before brushing the seizing with dilute PVA.

Lanyards should be cut to length, a knot put in close to one end and cyanoacrylate adhesive used to stiffen the leading end into a built-in bodkin. A set sequence should be followed when rigging the lanyards as shown in **Fig.13.20**. This sketch shows the sequence used when the shrouds were made from shroud laid rope. The starting hole would be on the left-hand side as viewed if the shrouds were cable laid. Research done by the kit manufacturer should have defined the correct application for your model. I find it preferable to merely take up the slack initially, leaving the final tightening until both port and starboard shrouds have been rigged on a particular mast. This helps to make sure that the masts are not pulled out of line and that the separation

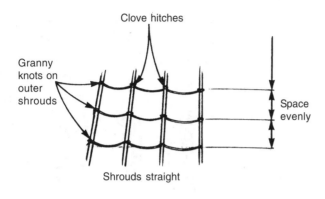

Clove hitches

Granny
knots on
outer
shrouds

Space
evenly

Shrouds straight

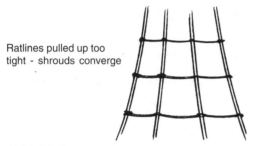

Ratlines pulled up too
tight - shrouds converge

Fig. 13.21. Ratlines

of the deadeyes can be reasonably constant throughout. The free ends of the lanyards can now be tied off to the shrouds above the upper deadeye. The number of holes through which the lanyards pass prevent them slipping

back through the deadeyes so that tension in the shrouds is not reliant on the final tying off.

We now come to the dreaded ratlines. A great number of model-makers, (including myself) have, at some time or another, spent hours trying to evolve an easy, but effective way, of getting around this chore. In spite of several inspired bouts of enthusiasm I, like the others, have learnt the hard way that the best way is the obvious way – tie them all on properly. Prior planning can avoid some of the monotony by breaking the task up between sessions of yard making and the construction of other ancillary parts. I normally use clove hitches for larger scale models and simple hitches for models below say 1:72 scale. Being right handed, I start at the extreme left-hand shroud of the group to be rattled down. Using fine nosed tweezers to thread and guide the free end, I work my way from left to right across the span of the shrouds. It is essential that the ratlines are not pulled up too tightly and that the shrouds remain straight as shown in **Fig.13.21**.

Some of the finer threads used for this task do seem to have a mind of their own and it is not always easy to attain that slight sagging look of the ratline between each shroud. It always helps to avoid tying the hitches against the natural twist of the thread but this only comes with considerable practice. However, all is not entirely lost. Try tying on a group of four or five ratlines then brush them over with dilute PVA. This will not only seal

Fig. 13.22. Sequence of initial rigging

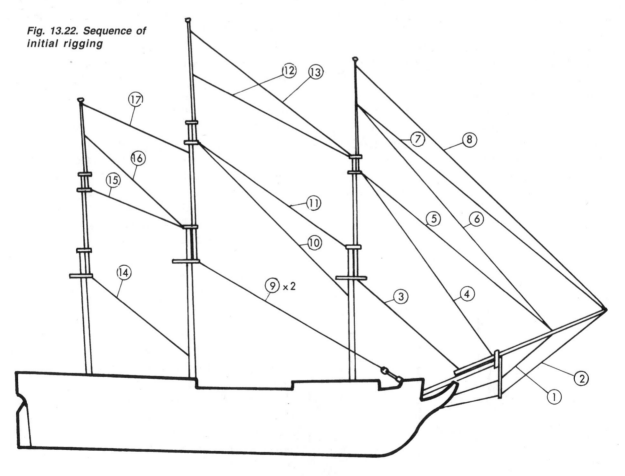

Fig. 13.23

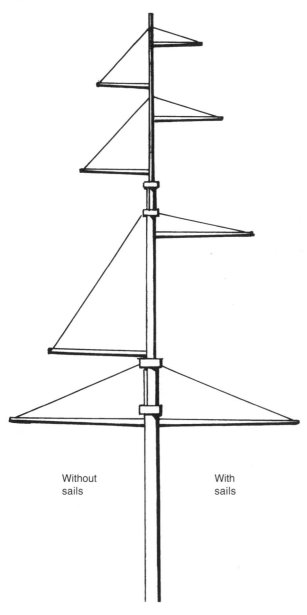

Without
sails

With
sails

means by which adjustments are made to the attitude of the yards and the trim of the sails, which brings us to the subject as to whether sails will be fitted or the spars left bare. It is really 'make your mind up time' at this stage and although this is not really the forum for such a discussion, your choice will affect both the content and the placement of the running rigging and the position of the yards on the masts, see **Fig.13.23**. When in port for any length of time, sails would be unbent (taken down), repaired as necessary and stowed. Some of the rigging would also be removed; others pulled out and conveniently hooked up. Without sails, the yards would normally be lowered down on to the caps and not hauled up in the operating position, again see **Fig.13.23**.

Before starting to rig it is wise to have a final look round to make sure that as many blocks as possible have been put in position on masts, yards and deck since it becomes increasingly awkward to tie on blocks as the rigging process develops. Where to start? In general, it is easier to begin with those lines that are tied off nearest the centre-line of the vessel and gradually work outwards. Combine this with working on the lower spars first and it will be easier to see the appropriate run for each line; obviously no line should interfere with the working of another. Having adopted the basic rule, *centre and lowest first*, it has to be said that there will inevitably be exceptions depending on the rig in hand. But, it is a good rule and exceptions can usually be conveniently and sensibly sorted out.

When it comes to belaying and tying off, most drawings provided in kits indicate the correct tying off positions or maybe even a formal belaying diagram. These positions were far from being haphazard and, on naval vessels at least, followed a standardised pattern that permitted a ready and more efficient interchange of crew between ships.

When tying off, a turn and a half around the belaying pin or bitt with the running end hitched and sealed with a spot of adhesive, is all that is needed, see **Fig.13.24**. Snip the end off close to the pin rail and add

the knots, but also stiffen the thread to the point where carefully stroking the ratlines with a small rod or cocktail stick, will help induce the required sag.

One final word about ratlines; they have to be done and it really doesn't help to put the task off until later in the rigging process, when additional rigging will inevitably get in the way of tweezers and fingers.

The standing rigging continues with the application of the stays and **Fig.13.22** shows a good sequence to adopt. However, I would add that some vessels have rigging that would suggest a different sequence but the better quality of kits available today would, in any case, indicate the best sequence in the associated instruction manual. Unless instructed otherwise, I normally rig the bowsprit shrouds and stays to the fore part of the vessel first in order to take the strain of the mainstay and fore stays, followed by the others in the sequence shown.

The running rigging, as mentioned before, is the

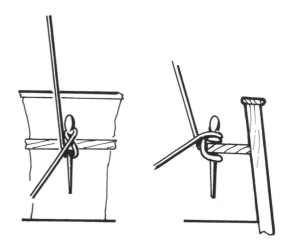

Fig. 13.24

Fig. 13.25

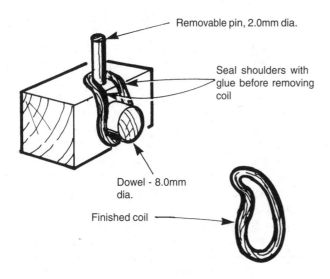

Removable pin, 2.0mm dia.

Seal shoulders with glue before removing coil

Dowel - 8.0mm dia.

Finished coil

a coil or hank of thread on to the pin to complete the job. If tying off to a bitt, take the running end down to the deck and cover the end with a coil of thread. In all cases hanks or coils should be made up using the same thread as used for the falls with which they are associated.

Making up coils of thread needs a little care or they may turn out looking somewhat artificial. In theory, they should contain sufficient length of rope to cater for the

task that the rigging demands, so that the free end doesn't disappear aloft when the line is unhitched! Unless the model in question is of very large scale, most modellers use some licence and make merely a neat acknowledgement of the coil. Flat coils lay on deck and are not too much of a problem to make; those that hang on to belaying pins need a different approach, the task being to make it look as if they hang naturally. I use a small jig made up using two different diameters of dowel according to the size of coil required. A typical jig is shown in **Fig.13.25**. Mine is made to make up a dozen coils at once, but obviously this number can be adjusted to suit your own convenience. The coils are removed by pulling out the smaller pin. Use the adhesive sparingly so as not to stick the coils to the jig.

Adhesives

The proper use of the correct adhesive can generate quite a bit of extra cost to that already expended on the kit. The technical advancement made in the world of adhesives during the past few years is quite staggering and has reached the point today, where there are very few materials that cannot be stuck together, or to each other. Having said that, selecting the right adhesive for the job in hand is important, both from a technical and a cost standpoint. For example, it would be most expensive to plank the hull of a large model using only superglue.

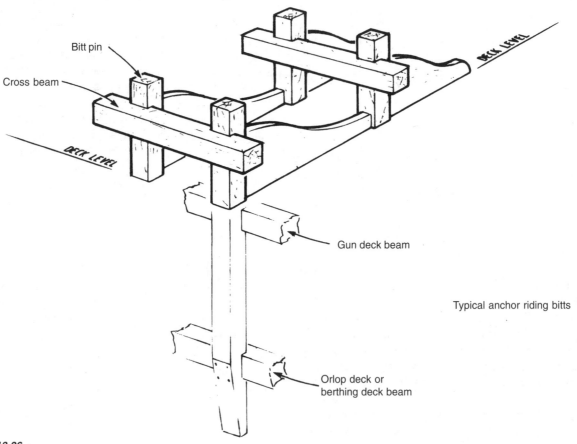

Bitt pin

Cross beam

DECK LEVEL

DECK LEVEL

Gun deck beam

Typical anchor riding bitts

Orlop deck or berthing deck beam

Fig. 13.26

Probably the most important aspect of joining materials together is preparation. This applies to any adhesive and, in general, the more 'high-tech' the glue, the higher the degree of cleanliness and surface preparation needed. The instructions found with the adhesive pack will usually tell you what is required to attain a good joint and frequently list those materials for which the adhesive is not suitable. Most poor, or failed, joints occur due to disregard of the instructions given.

Obviously, it is highly desirable to produce a good mechanical joint prior to sticking the subject parts together. The mating surfaces of a butt joint should be flat and mitred corners should come together without major gaps. Many adhesives have gap-filling properties, but proper fitting makes for a far more superior joint, both in strength and appearance.

Cleanliness is most important, the major contaminants being oils, grease, paint, varnish and finger-marks. Oils and greases are more easily removed from metal and plastic parts, but almost impossible from wood. Paint and varnish should be scraped away from the area to be stuck to reveal the base material. Clean hands are essential when working with wood, the natural oils produced at the fingertips are sufficient to contaminate a joint and even leave stains that are difficult to remove. Some woods produce their own oils. Teak is such a material and this can often make it difficult to stick.

As to the adhesives themselves, there are five that I keep to hand that are particularly useful in model boat building. I am not saying that after purchasing your kit you should go and buy all five, but I guess that after a few models you will accumulate them and, like me, will keep stocked up.

White PVA will probably be used more than any other and it is worth buying the largest size pack you can afford, it certainly comes cheaper that way. While it takes several hours to thoroughly cure or properly harden, it does have a fairly quick grab time. With planning, you don't necessarily find yourself having to wait for the glue to dry before proceeding with the next stage. One word of warning though; if you are planking a hull and intend to finish leaving the natural wood, make sure that you remove all excess glue from the surfaces and wipe off with a damp cloth. Failure to do this will result in a patchy finish, which cannot be overcome with stains or varnish. For best results, always pin or clamp all glued joints until the glue has set.

Contact adhesive is ideal for second planking or deck planking where the planking material is less than 1mm in thickness when PVA, because of its liquidity, tends to warp the strips as it dries. The secret of using a contact adhesive successfully is to make sure that both surfaces to be joined are completely but thinly coated and that sufficient time is allowed for the adhesive to become touch dry before bringing the parts together. The non-drip varieties are undoubtedly the best to use, less messy and do not string.

Two-part epoxy or acrylic bonders usually come in special dispensing packs, which enable the correct proportions to be mixed. These are ideal for fixing metal parts such as the decorative castings frequently found in period ship kits.

Cyanoacrylate or **superglue** has a wide range of uses. Available in grades, thick, medium and thin, it is particularly useful for small parts and certainly for speed of working, its grab capacity being a mere few seconds. However, it can be expensive for large jobs such as copper plating hulls and its continued use can affect the respiratory system if a suitable mask or respirator is not worn.

Clear glue is useful for sticking various plastics, wood, card etc. Normally it comes in a tube and can be difficult to apply in the sparing way necessary not to make a messy joint. Some 'string' very easily and this can be a disadvantage. It has a place in the overall scheme of things but needs care in application.

With all the adhesives mentioned, extended use can have nasty effects on your breathing. Cyanoacrylate and acrylic bonders are definite irritants and it is wise to wear an appropriate facemask or respirator.

Deck Fittings

This section is aimed more at the potential scratch builder rather than those who choose to use a kit, hopefully the latter being provided with researched designs and parts.

Significant among the fittings are those concerned with the handling of the anchor cable; the riding bitts, the capstan or the windlass. The riding bitts were massive timbers used to secure the cables while the ship was at anchor. Such was the force acting on the bitts that the vertical members extended to the beams of the deck below, see **Fig. 13.26**. The sizes of timber and proportions of these assemblies were governed, like so many other things in the 'man of war' by the number of guns carried. To give some idea of the sizes involved, for a 74-gun ship, the timbers were in the order of 500mm (20 inches) square. It is important for the model maker to be aware of the use of fittings in order that he can not only reproduce them at the correct size and scale, but to put them in the correct position for this purpose.

The windlass was a mechanical device used particularly on older and smaller vessels for hauling up the anchor cable. It consisted of a wooden barrel, usually octagonal in section and horizontally supported at each end by bearings housed in the bitts and associated cheeks. Earlier versions were turned by handspikes inserted in the barrel; hese were later discarded and the equipment turned by cranked handles at the extreme outside ends of the barrel spindle. For heavier use, offsetting the crank-spindle from the barrel centre-line, and transmitting the manual power via a pinion on the crank and a wheel on the barrel, enhanced the mechanical advantage. The barrels were ridged with eight whelps, which were also tapered. Thus, the cable not only moved along the barrel

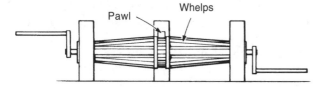

Fig. 13.28 Early windlass with cranked handles

Fig. 13.29 Pump brake windlass

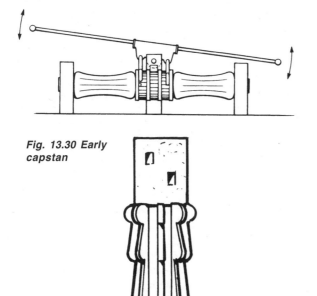

Fig. 13.30 Early capstan

Fig. 13.31 Later capstan

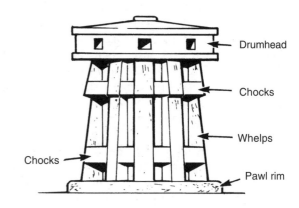

Drumhead

Chocks

Whelps

Chocks

Pawl rim

Fig. 13.32 Double tier capstan

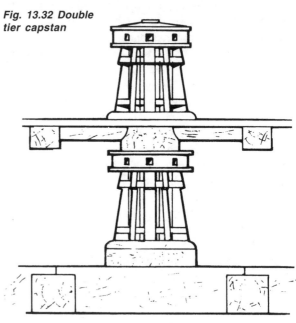

Fig. 13.33 Capstan bar

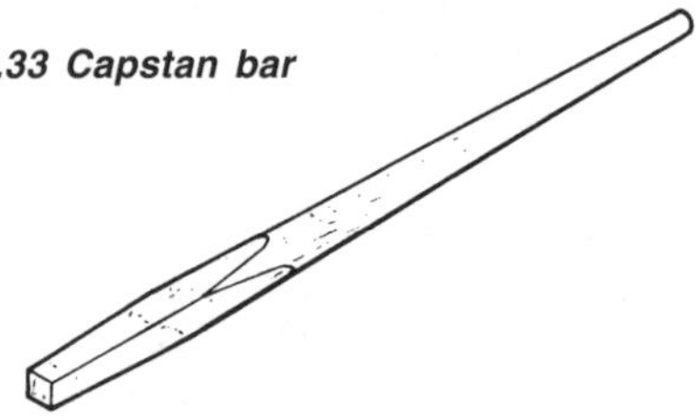

as it was turned on, reducing slip and increasing the effective diameter of the barrel. A ratchet device was fitted at the centre of the barrel to prevent the loss of manual control when the cable was under strain, **(Fig.13.28** and **13.29)**.

The capstan could almost be described as a vertical version of the windlass, **(Figs.13.30** and **13.31)**. By the end of the 17th century, the double capstan was not uncommon. This allowed two capstans, one on a deck immediately above the other, to share the same spindle, the advantage being that twice as much applied effort could be used to raise the anchor and the crew on one of the decks were not encumbered by any cable. A later innovation produced the double-tier capstan, which had a device that allowed the upper capstan to be disengaged from the lower thus permitting the capstan to be used for different tasks at the same time, **(Fig.13.32)**. The

model-maker should bear several points in mind. Obviously you always need to recognise scale and, one particularly good tip is to remember that the height of the capstan bars above the deck level should be about chest high on a scale man. A capstan is usually best fabricated rather than adapted from a solid turning. This allows the holes for the capstan bars to be correctly formed in square section. Finally, don't forget to make, and conveniently stow the capstan bars near to the capstan. They were normally of round section at the handling end and had a tapered square section at the heavy end to fit snugly into the capstan head, **(Fig.13.33)**.

Pumps were an essential part of every ship's equipment, to remove water from the bilges, to fight fires caused by enemy action or to supply water for washing the decks.

Fig. 13.34 Chain pumps

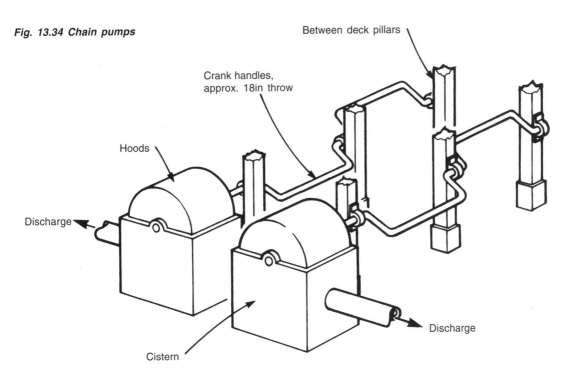

Between deck pillars

Crank handles, approx. 18in throw

Hoods

Discharge

Cistern

Discharge

The main chain pump was usually installed on the lower gun deck and is not always seen on a ship model. However, on a large 'man-of-war' this was a sizeable piece of gear employing some seven or eight men to operate it. The parts visible above deck level are the cisterns and the cranks **(Fig.13.34)**, although the pipes through which an endless chain pulled the buckets extended right down to the bottom of the ship. The pump well was at the deepest part of the ship, usually just aft of the main mast. The singular term 'pump' is something of a misnomer because it was usually a combination of two or four pumps on larger vessels.

In addition to the main chain pump, larger vessels would also have one or more elm tree pumps for the more domestic tasks, although on the smaller man-of-war it would also serve as a bilge pump. Its name derived from the fact that the main pump case was made from elm because of its natural ability to withstand long periods of exposure to salt water. Again, from the model standpoint, you only see the working head above deck level, although these pumps drew their supply directly through the bottom of the ship. In some cases the supply was taken from a cistern that could be flooded via pipes and valves leading from the cistern to the outside of the hull below the waterline. All very simple, but not very efficient. Plunger pumps improved the situation somewhat, in that being in pairs and operated by a rocker arm, the downward stroke on one was the upstroke on the other and thus, every stroke brought up water, **(Fig.13.36)**. Diaphragm pumps, **(Fig.13.37)**, introduced

Fig. 13.36 Plunger pump

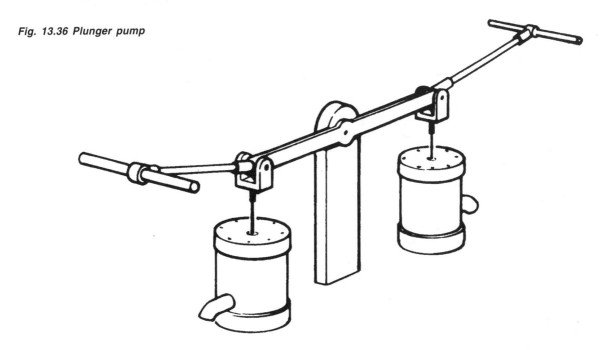

Fig. 13.38 Flywheel pump

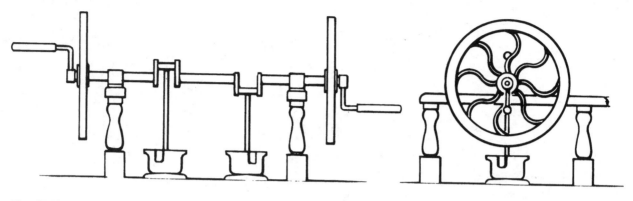

Fig. 13.39

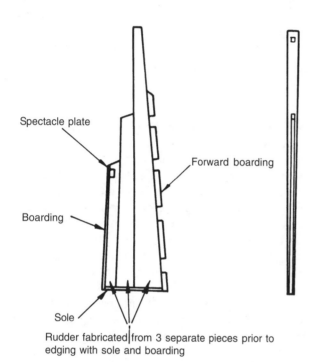

Spectacle plate

Forward boarding

Boarding

Sole

Rudder fabricated from 3 separate pieces prior to edging with sole and boarding

Fig. 13.40

Pin

Pintle

Use suitable adhesive or solder into pintle before assembly with rudder

Trim to suit width of rudder

Gudgeon

Fig. 13.41

Ensure pin enters gudgeon at all assemblies before trying to hang rudder

Modify to suit triangular section of stern post bearding

Fig. 13.42 Spectacle plate

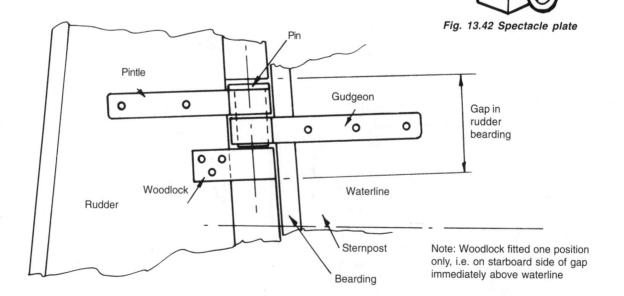

Pin

Pintle

Gudgeon

Gap in rudder bearding

Waterline

Woodlock

Rudder

Sternpost

Bearding

Note: Woodlock fitted one position only, i.e. on starboard side of gap immediately above waterline

later, were much more efficient, a much shorter stroke delivering a greater volume of water. On some larger ships these would be mounted in pairs with their plungers connected to a crank driven by two men each side. The motion was smoothed out by the action of flywheels on the ends of the shaft, (**Fig.13.38**).

The Rudder

An area where many kits fall down is in the construction and hanging of the rudder. There are several features which, if recognised, can be added to significantly improve the model. Firstly, the rudder on most 'men of war' was fabricated from several pieces. For reasons of strength and durability this involved the use of different timbers. A strip of elm for durability usually enhanced the edge of the rudder adjacent to the sternpost, and indeed the sternpost itself. This bearding would be of half-round or triangular section, to permit adequate movement of the rudder. Similarly, the bottom edge of the rudder was fitted with an elm sole of rectangular section, (**Fig.13.39**).

Hanging the rudder to the sternpost, if given some thought, can often be made to look better than by using the 'kit' formula. Let us take the hinges first and make sure that they are fitted the right way round. The pintle (pin) fits on the rudder above the gudgeon, which fits on the sternpost. The eye of the gudgeon stands proud of the sternpost but the pintle is housed in a gap cut into the bearding on the front edge of the rudder. The length of the gap should be such as to allow the gudgeon to pass under the end of the pintle before the rudder is lowered to make the hinge. A recess on the starboard side of the gap nearest to the waterline permitted the fitting of a wood-lock. Fitted after hanging the rudder, this prevented the pintles lifting out of the gudgeons, (**Fig.13.40**). Since several pintle/gudgeon units are involved, care in marking out is called for, but well worth the effort when you see the result. There certainly will not be that wide and incorrect gap between rudder and sternpost seen on so many models built from kits. The majority of kits supply pintles and gudgeons in some form or another, most being in the shape of pre-formed brass strips ready-drilled for pinning to the rudder or hull, (**Fig.13.41**). Both pieces of the hinge are identical and a separate pin is required to make up the hinge assembly. In some less sophisticated kits, the modeller has to make up everything from brass strip and heavy gauge wire.

While I appreciate that not everyone has workshop facilities to make pintles and gudgeons in a more authentic way, using what is supplied can be made to look quite reasonable.

Another enhancement to consider is the fitting of a spectacle plate or frame to the rear edge of the rudder. This is essentially a metal 'U' bracket holding a ring each side, to which the chains of an auxiliary steering system are attached, (**Fig.13.42**). The chains also prevented the rudder from being totally carried away in the event of an accident or damage in battle. When not in use,

the ends of the chains were attached to eyebolts on the transom just below the quarter galleries. However, the modeller should be wary of 'gilding the lily' and remember that spectacle plates were not fitted until the latter part of the 18th century.

Model stands

Model stands have always been the source of serious comment in my experience of kit building. Why? Mainly because too many kits still ignore the requirement and leave them out. A stand serves two significant purposes; it supports the finished model for display and provides a cradle for the hull during construction. Three basic types can be seen in **Fig.13.43** and all have provision for attaching the model, (**Fig.13.44**), always remembering to leave access to the screw heads for emergency removal. A firm favourite is the use of brass pedestals on a wooden base, although the use of the wider hull supports permits some imaginative decorative work. Another nice touch is to trim the edge of the supports with thick felt or baize strip, which protects the under-surface of the hull.

Fig. 13.43

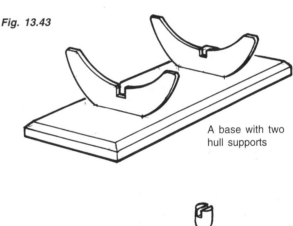

A base with two hull supports

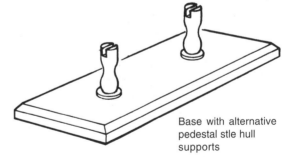

Base with alternative pedestal stle hull supports

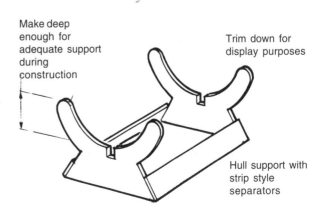

Make deep enough for adequate support during construction

Trim down for display purposes

Hull support with strip style separators

203

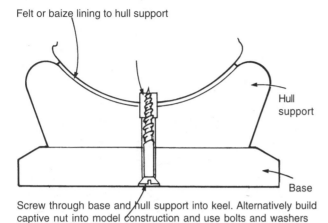

Felt or baize lining to hull support

Hull support

Base

Screw through base and hull support into keel. Alternatively build captive nut into model construction and use bolts and washers

Fig. 13.44 Fixing model to stand

Kit enhancement

I suppose that most model-makers make their first model sailing ship from a kit. There are exceptions of course, but for those with limited facilities, a kit allows something reasonable and presentable to be built. However, if the aim is to build a model that has that something extra in terms of quality, accuracy and overall presentation, there are many things that can be done to improve the kit-based model.

When it comes to accuracy, you would expect that having paid a considerable sum of money for your kit, the manufacturer would have done all the research necessary to provide drawings and documentation that were right. Unfortunately, this is not always the case and indeed, it is quite surprising the degree of error that can sometimes be found with a kit for an extremely well known and documented vessel.

So the message is, do some research of your own, not only to confirm what you are given in the kit, but also to stimulate a more personal contact with the subject. This has a knock-on effect in that you attain a deeper knowledge of aspects of the vessel other than its construction and, I believe you therefore make a better model. I would hasten to add that any research that you do should be done before the commencement of building so that the results of your findings can be built into the model rather than be the subject of later modification.

The quality of the model can be enhanced in several ways. Make sure that the overall appearance of your model is correct for the year quoted. An ideal example of this is H.M.S. "Victory". Her appearance today in the Portsmouth Dockyard is different to her appearance at Trafalgar and, again, not how she looked when launched.

However, probably most enhancement lies in the area of fittings, which, in many cases come from a proprietary range of parts and may fall into the classification of being 'near enough' rather than 'just right'. Look therefore at anchors, pumps, ships' wheels and rigging blocks. With regard to the latter, the usual problem is that the blocks supplied for rigging the top end of the ship are too large and may need replacing with a smaller size. The other 'bits and pieces' can usually

be adapted to present a more truthful representation of the equipment in question.

The real benefits of research become more apparent when you consider what can be added to the model that is not provided for in the kit. Masts are typical cases in point. Few were of round section throughout their length, having bottom ends, mastheads and hounds, of square or octagonal section, **(Fig.13.45)**. Yards too, were seldom of round section throughout their length, the mid-section being octagonal. In fact, yard construction sometimes dictated the use of battens at the centre section, these being held in place by iron hoops, **(Fig.13.46)**. For those anticipating making yards with octagonal sections from round dowel, remember that the size of the dowel should reflect the dimension

Fig. 13.45

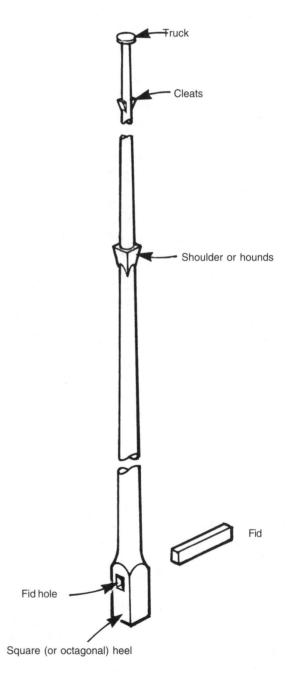

Truck

Cleats

Shoulder or hounds

Fid

Fid hole

Square (or octagonal) heel

Fig. 13.46 Two piece yard

measured across the corners of the octagon and not the size across its flats.

Check to see how the stays are attached to the masts. So many times one sees the stay lashed around the mast with no means of preventing the stay from slipping down. The masts should have hounds or cleats. It certainly wasn't a case of the biggest man in the dockyard putting his thumb more heavily on the knot! There was also quite a bit of complexity in the construction of the tops and items such as bolsters should not be overlooked, **(Fig.13.47)**. The provision of a fid in the heel of a mast, **(Fig, 13.45)** to stop it sliding down through the trestletrees, also adds a nice touch. Mast caps were often bound with an iron band, a feature that can easily be simulated with a strip of card and painted black, **(Fig.13.48)**.

Stirrups and footropes can sometimes be difficult to put on in a natural looking way, the problem being that the stirrups if made from thread, as often proposed in a kit, never hang right. Use fine wire. The same applies to the footrope, which looks much better if it has a natural sag between stirrups.

There are many occasions when you see a more than respectably built model spoilt by lack of attention to the installation of the guns. There really should be a little more finesse than four blobs of glue under the wheels to hold the carriage to the deck. For a start, blobs are unnecessary if you pass the assembled carriage across a sheet of abrasive paper to produce small flats on the wheels. An unseen smear of adhesive is then possible. Obviously, scale plays a big part in any decision as to how much detail can be put on a gun carriage in the way of rigging. Reference to **Fig.13.49** will help make that decision. Many modellers are content to rig only the breeching rope and ignore the side tackle. However, the eyebolts in the inside surfaces of the bulwarks for that side tackle should not be omitted.

Carronades, **(Fig.13.50)** were rigged in a similar manner to a carriage gun although the barrel recoil was taken within a slide rather than the whole unit moving back on wheels.

Fig. 13.47

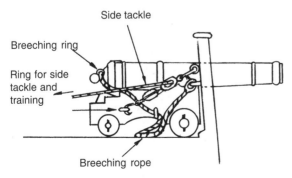

Bolsters

Trestletrees

Crosstrees

Check whether crosstrees curved back or were straight

Side tackle

Breeching ring

Ring for side tackle and training

Breeching rope

Fig. 15.49 The gun and carriage

Fig. 13.48

Iron band around cap

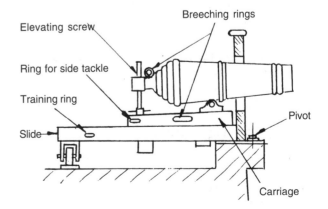

Elevating screw

Breeching rings

Ring for side tackle

Training ring

Slide

Pivot

Carriage

Fig. 13.50 The Carronade

Appendix

Emergencies

As with most model makers, there always comes a time when I unexpectedly run out of something and, again like most people, I want it yesterday. **Squires Model and Craft Tools** of Bognor Regis obviously cannot perform that particular miracle but, in many instances, an order placed reasonably early in the day by telephone will result in a delivery the following morning. Their catalogue conjures up the impression of a model maker's Aladdin's Cave coupled with a very efficient rub of the magic lamp! For virtually everything you may want to build your model, you will not do yourself a better favour than to contact **Squires Model and Craft Tools, 100 London Road, Bognor Regis, West Sussex, PO21 1DD**
Telephone 01243 842424

Magazines

The "Mailboat" page in *Model Boats* magazine will often yield comment and advice from readers and, in some cases, the Editor may pass your letter on to someone known to have specific knowledge concerning your problem.
Highbury Leisure Publishing Ltd., Berwick House, 8-10 Knoll Rise, Orpington, Kent BR6 0PS
Alternatively, there is the Model Boats website at www.modelboats.co.uk where again there is the facility to correspond and seek help.

Chapter 4 - H.M.S. "Victory"

The kit for H.M.S." Victory" is retailed and distributed by JoTiKa Ltd..
Jotika Ltd., Model Marine Warehouse, Hadzor, Droitwich, WR97DS
Telephone 01905 776073
Email – nelsonsnavy@ jotika-ltd.com

Chapter 5 – H.M. Cutter "Lady Nelson"

Victory Models by Euromodels and Amati are distributed by Euromodels.
Euromodels, Woodgreen Farm, Bulley, Churcham, Gloucester, GL2 8BJ
Telephone 01452 790800

Chapter 6 - H.M.S. "Mars"

The kit is one in the Caldercraft Nelson's Navy series manufactured and distributed by JoTiKa.
Jotika Ltd., Model Marine Warehouse, Hadzor, Droitwich, WR9 7DS
Telephone 01905 776073
Email: nelsonsnavy@jotika-ltd.com

Chapter 7 - "Endeavour" J Class

This Amati kit is distributed by Euromodels. A catalogue of all kits and associated products handled by them can be found on their website together with a list of local stockists.
Euromodels, Woodgreen Farm, Bulley, Churcham, Gloucester, GL2 8BJ
  www.euromodels.co.uk

Chapter 8 - The Armed Transport "Bounty"

This Amati kit is distributed by Euro Models.
Euromodels, Woodgreen Farm, Bulley, Churcham, Gloucester GL2 8BJ
Telephone 01452 790880

Chapter 9 - H.M.S."Agamemnon"

Manufacture, retail and trade distribution of the kit for H.M.S. "Agamemnon" and all other kits in the Caldercraft Nelson's navy series is by Joyika.
JoTiKa Ltd. Model Marine Warehouse, Hadzor, Droitwich, WR9 7DS
Telephone 01905 776073
www.jotika-ltd.com

Chapter 10 – The English Carronade

This Mantua kit is distributed by Euro Models.
Euro Models, Woodgreen Farm, Bulley, Churcham, Gloucester, GL2 8BJ
Telephone 01542 790800
Email: euromodelkit@hotmail.com
Web-site on www.euromodels.co.uk

Chapter 11 - H.M. Barque "Endeavour"

Manufacture, retail and trade distribution of the kit "Endeavour" and all other kits in the series is by JoTiKa.
Jotika Ltd. Model Marine Warehouse, Hadzor, Droitwich, WR9 7DS
Telephone 01905 776073

Chapter 12 - Victory launch

The Panart kit for Victory's Launch is distributed in the UK by Euro Models.
Euro Models, Woodgreen Farm, Bulley, Churcham, Gloucester, G12 8BJ
Telephone 01452 790880

Other sources

Cabinets

A good quality unit is well worth the expense and can be obtained from *Timbercraft Cabinet Displays, Abercorn House, York Farm Business Centre, Watling Street, Nr Towcester, Northants. NN12 8EU*

References

The Masting and Rigging of English Ships of War by James Lees ISBN 0 85177 290 0
Eighteenth Century Rigs and Rigging by Karl Heinz Marquardt ISBN 0 85177 586 1
Rigging Period Ship Models by Lennarth Petersson ISBN 1 86176 061 2
Nelson's Favourite - H.M.S. "Agamemnon" at War 1781 - 1809 by Anthony Deane ISBN 1 86176 106 6
H.M.S. Victory as in 1805 by Basil Lavis, published by David MacGregor Plans/Neptune Publications.
The Arming and Fitting of English Ships of War 1600-1815 by Brian Lavery ISBN0 85177 4512
The Anatomy of Nelson's Ships by C. Nepean Longridge ISBN 1-85486 122 0
Anatomy of the Ship. The Armed Transport "Bounty" by John McKay
Conway ISBN 0 85177 502 0

Other books by the same author

The Period Ship Handbook   ISBN 1-85486 081 X
The Period Ship Handbook Volume 2   ISBN 185486 132 8
The Period Ship Handbook Volume 3   ISBN 1 85486 200 6
Period Ship Kit Builders Manual   ISBN 1 85486 228 6

All of the above published by Special Interest Model Books
www.specialinterestmodelbooks.co.uk

Index